Becoming Ethical

A parallel, political journey with men who have abused

Alan Jenkins

Russell House Publishing

First published in 2009 by
Russell House Publishing Ltd.
4 St. George's House
Uplyme Road
Lyme Regis
Dorset DT7 3LS

Tel: 01297-443948
Fax: 01297-442722
e-mail: help@russellhouse.co.uk
www.russellhouse.co.uk

British Library Cataloguing-in-publication Data:
A catalogue record for this book is available from the British Library.

ISBN: 978-1-905541-40-9

Typeset by TW Typesetting, Plymouth, Devon

Printed and bound by CPI Group (UK) Ltd, Croydon, CR0 4YY

Russell House Publishing

Russell House Publishing aims to publish innovative and valuable materials to
help managers, practitioners, trainers, educators and students.

Our full catalogue covers: social policy, working with young people, helping
children and families, care of older people, social care, combating social
exclusion, revitalising communities and working with offenders.

Full details can be found at www.russellhouse.co.uk and we are pleased
to send out information to you by post. Our contact details are on
this page.

We are always keen to receive feedback on publications and new ideas
for future projects.

Contents

Part Five: Collaborative Evaluation on the Journey

There is no road to peace, peace is the road.

Ghandi

It is indeed my opinion now that evil is never radical, that it is only extreme, and that it possesses neither depth nor any demonic dimension. It can overgrow and lay waste to the whole world precisely because it spreads like a fungus on the surface . . . That is its banality. Only the good has depth and can be radical.

Hannah Arendt (1978)

There is a crack in everything. That's how the light gets in.

Leonard Cohen

Acknowledgements

For Maxine, your generous love and intuitive wisdon inspires, challenges and delights.

For Josh who knows to seek truth in difference.

For Rob, whose friendship, integrity and vision lights the path.

For Bert and Muriel, your striving for an ethical life points the way.

For Michael, you continue to nourish and transform in eternal return.

Preface

This book is a practical guide for anyone who works in the field of interventions with men who have engaged in violence or sexual abuse towards partners and family members.

The book argues that intervention practices must move beyond attempts to coerce, confront or educate a seemingly unwilling or unmotivated man. Instead, it offers **respectful intervention practices,** necessitating a parallel journey by the therapist, which:

- assist men in finding an **ethical** basis and means to cease abusive behaviour and develop new ways of relating
- are informed by **political**, rather than psychological, metaphors of explanation and understanding, seeing intervention in terms of power relations and practices within families and communities, and within the institutional, statutory and therapeutic settings in which men participate
- move to a **restorative** project which promotes: the cessation of violence and abuse; the restitution for harm done to individuals, community and culture; and a reclamation of a sense of integrity for the person who has abused.

Becoming Ethical builds on the invitational model, introduced by Alan Jenkins in his book *Invitations to Responsibility* (Dulwich, 1990) which has sold over 20,000 copies. This updated guide:

- documents recent developments in invitational thinking and practice
- addresses the challenges, contradictions and practical dilemmas that invitational intervention poses
- stresses the importance of an ongoing engagement with these dilemmas, to allow practitioners to develop their own ethical, respectful and just ways of relating to their clients.

The most significant development in invitational theory and practice is the emphasis on the workers' **parallel journey to becoming ethical**. The book argues that such a parallel journey:

- acknowledges the political nature of the intervention
- shifts the emphasis of the intervention away from an 'us and them' attitude
- has a far more substantial impact, in assisting their clients to challenge abusive behaviour, than any practice methods or techniques for intervention.

Introduction

Over the past 10 years, I have frequently been moved to update and rewrite *Invitations to Responsibility*. This book was first published in 1990 and my ideas and practices have continued to evolve. However, over this period of time, I have become increasingly aware of diverging possibilities and less certain about the things I know to be *true* in intervention with men who have abused. I am more and more attuned to the challenges, contradictions and practical dilemmas that intervention poses for workers in this field and increasingly convinced that ongoing engagement with these dilemmas and challenges can allow us to discover means to enable ethical, respectful and just ways of relating with our clients and members of their communities. The development of new skills and intervention strategies is beneficial. However, it is our own ethical *becomings* which inevitably promote the cessation of violence and the development of respectful ways of relating by our clients.

In this book, I will address ideas and practices which my colleagues and I have found helpful when engaging with these dilemmas. I offer this somewhat overdue attempt to document more recent developments in invitational thinking and practice with men who have abused members of their families and communities.

New developments in invitational practice

Developments in the invitational model have been increasingly concerned with intervention as a political process; one which is unavoidably concerned with power relations and practices within families and communities and within the institutional, statutory and therapeutic settings in which men participate. In *Invitations to Responsibility*, I described how these power relations and practices both reflect and contribute to broader cultural interests, political structures and hierarchies. These broader interests and structures inform and are informed by our behaviour, ways of relating, and the conclusions that we draw as individuals about our sense of identity.

Invitational practice continues to be informed by political rather than psychological metaphors of explanation and understanding; the *journey towards respect* remains an ongoing and evolving political journey rather than a quest to resolve psychological disturbance, modify specific behaviours or achieve prescribed states of psychological health and well-being.

Recent formulations in the invitational model take into account developments in gender studies and post-structuralist thinking, with more recent conceptualisations concerning the natures of desire and power relations, particularly as they relate to violence and concepts of masculinity.

Invitational theory and practice is concerned with processes of *becoming ethical*. Concepts of *becoming* place an emphasis on fluidity, transition and moving towards certain modes of existence, whereas states of *being* suggest fixed or stable forms of identity. The journey, *becoming ethical*, might be contrasted with states of *being respectful*, or alternatively, *being abusive* and the various characterlogical meanings which tend to be attributed to the individual on the basis of his violent or non-violent practices:

He is a respectful/compassionate man.

He is an angry/impulsive/abusive man.

He lacks empathy/remorse/concern for others.

He has an abusive personality.

I have long been interested in provoking movement beyond the sense of limitation and insufficiency accompanying conceptualisations of violence and abusive behaviour which are informed by notions of psychological and personality deficit or of human nature.

The apparent socio-cultural determinism of descriptions of gender, masculinity and socialisation, in considerations of ways that dominant cultural ideology might sanction violence, can be equally limiting and disabling for the development of respectful ways of relating. The everyday possibilities for men's individual and collective resistance become overlooked in exclusive preoccupation with deterministic limitations which are attributed to cultural institutions and practices.

The traditional focus upon the psychological *nature* of the *perpetrator* or *offender* assumes fixed and static ideas about identity in which a focus upon violence and what it says about the person's character generally takes primacy and overshadows possibilities for the discovery of ethics and respectful preferences with the man. The naming and interpretation of violence becomes privileged over the discovery of a sense of agency or the capacity to actualise ethical interests that might point towards respectful modes of existence. The man becomes regarded as limited or deficient; he requires correction and education; his violent or impulsive nature must be contained and his behaviour must be modified. Such concepts shape the restraining notion of the *violent man* with investments restricted to states of *being*. They often fail to open up new possibilities for *becoming*.

Invitational theory is informed by a Deleuzian conceptualisation of desire, whereby life and processes of living are regarded as inherently productive and expansive. Our lives are continually shaped by a multitude of *flows of becoming* which have infinite possibilities. We continually discover ways in which we actualise aspects of these flows and are constantly constructing a somewhat unstable sense of identity, particularly in the context of flux between our ethical strivings and the restraining influences of dominant cultural interests and power relations. These processes for actualisation lead to the restricting or limiting of possibilities for becoming, sometimes even a sense of *capture* or *restraint* by dominant cultural interests. However, we are continually faced with an infinite range of differences with unlimited possibilities for becoming and we are continually re-evaluating, discovering and re-discovering new options for how we might live our lives (Deleuze and Guattari, 1987; May, 2005).

The invitational focus on *becoming ethical* provokes the discovery of ethical ways of living and relating; of preferences which are respectful to each person's strivings and an investment in a sense of integrity. The exploration of ethics can provide a reference point for challenging restraining influences and freeing up a capacity to engage productively with life rather than constraining its possibilities. Investments in *flows of becoming* which are creative and which open out to new possibilities can inform new ways of thinking about identity. A shift away from restrained, fixed and static concepts of *self* and *being* tends to invoke vibrant and creative discoveries of possibilities which can open up ethical visions of fairness and respect of difference. The processes of *becoming ethical* can inform expansive concepts of love which move beyond notions of control and rigid suppression of difference.

The concept of *becoming ethical* does not relate to any humanistic appeal to notions of essential goodness within individuals, nor does it prescribe conformity to externally prescribed moral standards or values. This concept respects the productive concepts of life and desire, as proposed by Deleuze, which transcends notions of human character and points to ethics which are immanent to the strivings of individuals and communities to engage with life. *Becoming ethical* evokes creative processes in which we search for and clarify what is important for ourselves, our families, communities, cultures, environments, spirituality, and so on:

- *How do I want to live?*
- *How do I want to relate to others?*
- *What kind of person do I want to become?*

We become increasingly accountable to these ethics, other people and our world, as we discover ways of investment that might allow their actualisation. *Flows of becoming* are many and varied, springing from the infinite and creative potentials of life. *Becoming ethical* represents engagement with a series of such flows which are never fully actualised but which point to vital and preferred modes of existence.

Invitational practice is concerned to engage with the complexities of the journeys embarked upon in *becoming ethical*. Such journeys represent remarkable investments in the face of dominant cultural interests which can be contradictory and ambivalent. For example, a dynamic tension often exists between interests and practices which relate to acquisition and control and those which relate to fairness and equity. It is in this context that *becoming ethical* cannot be reduced to simplistic prescriptions to follow external moral codes. Invitational practice requires us to recognise and honour the extraordinary capacities of individuals and communities to choose their own ethical pathways, in the face of adversity and in the face of the challenges of restraining, dominant cultural interests and power relations.

The journeys which constitute *becoming ethical* are not defined or constrained by a pre-determined end point. These journeys are open-ended and always moving towards new possibilities and preferred modes of existence. Such journeys do concern the discovery, production and actualisation of our ethics which inevitably brings us face-to-face with our own violent and abusive practices, a sense of contradiction and consequent processes for *becoming accountable*. This necessitates us facing the shame which inevitably accompanies our realisations about dishonourable acts and their effects upon ourselves and others. In a journey of *becoming ethical*, we are required to face and appreciate the effects and consequences of our violence and abusive behaviour. Invitational practice places considerable focus upon the clarification and repositioning of the experience of shame from a context which is *disabling* and debilitating, to one which is *enabling* and which signifies integrity and promotes ethical ways forward.

Invitational practice recognises the harm done to individuals, families, communities and cultures by abusive actions and the ethical journey is located within the broader context of a *restorative project* which promotes:

- *the cessation of violence and abuse*
- *restitution for harm done to individuals, community and culture*
- *reclamation of a sense of integrity for the person who has abused*

This project is informed by a creative and expansive concept of *restoration*; to add new life or vigour, rather than a nostalgic concept which looks backwards towards reclaiming what has existed in the past (Jenkins, 2006). The *restorative project* is concerned with opening up possibilities for tolerance and respect of difference through practices which entail *reaching out towards the world of the other*. This project has a rich ethical foundation which tends to become increasingly interconnected with the man's own strivings and preferences.

Acts of violence and abuse disrupt and undermine potentials for tolerance and respect of difference and restrain new possibilities for relating, in specific relationships and at broader community and cultural levels. *Reaching out towards the world of the other* involves an active interest in understanding, respecting and appreciating the experiences of others and informs the motivations to cease violence and make restitution for harm done. It is through these kinds of realisations and practices that reclamation of integrity can be possible and new kinds of relationships can be developed. The restorative project is informed by an expansive and *generous* concept of love which promotes and values difference, whereas practices of violence tend towards the suppression, control and elimination of difference (Protevi, 2003).

Practices of *accountability*, whereby we are required to hold our practice accountable to the experiences of those who have been, or are likely to be, harmed by abusive behaviour, remain vital to the ethics and effectiveness of invitational intervention (Hall, 1996). These practices lie at the heart of *becoming ethical* and concern the necessary journeys towards appreciating the nature and effects of abusive behaviour and respecting difference.

Perhaps the most significant consolidation in invitational theory and practice is the notion of the *parallel journey* for workers. This concept refers to understandings of the political nature of intervention and the belief that our journeys as workers must mirror the journeys of our clients. The focus on the *parallel journey* is regarded as paramount in work with men who have abused; standing alongside the vital notion of *accountability* to the experiences of those who have been subjected to abuse. The maintenance of our own journeys towards *becoming ethical* has a far more substantial impact, in assisting our clients to challenge abusive behaviour, than any practice methods or techniques for intervention. *Becoming ethical* in our own *parallel journeys*, shifts us away from an *us and them* attitude and leads us towards a sense of common humanity and purpose with our clients. We embark on a parallel political journey which addresses identical politics as part of the broader *restorative project*.

About this book

This book is organised into five parts, with four case studies being revisited throughout the book, from initial engagement through to restitution and couple or family restoration.

In Part One, invitational theory concerning the nature and politics of violence, resistance and restorative practice is detailed. Principles for holding an effective political position in intervention are outlined.

Part Two outlines the paradigm for invitational practice and is illustrated by the four case studies. This paradigm includes practices which address restraints, establish an ethical foundation and address abusive practices. Separate chapters address accountability and group intervention concepts and practices.

In Part Three, a map with guidelines for an ethical journey is outlined and practices for facilitating this journey, in the context of a restorative project, are described. Applications of the invitational paradigm in ceasing abusive behaviour, making restitution for harm done and demonstrating respectful ways of relating are described and illustrated.

Part Four concerns invitational practice within a relationship and family context.

In Part Five a collaborative, invitational process is outlined for evaluation of goal attainment by men who have abused.

Please note that:
1. The focus of this work is male violence. A generic use of the term, 'the man' throughout the text, refers to men who have perpetrated abusive behaviour.
2. The theory and descriptions of invitational practice in this work are focused upon men in heterosexual relationships and family structures. Application of these concepts to work with gay men requires extra consideration of the politics of sexual preference and apart from a brief example given in Chapter 14, is outside the scope of this book.

The application of invitational practice with young people who have acted in violent or abusive ways is detailed in Jenkins (2006a,b, 2005a,b, 1999).

Part One

Violence, Abuse and the Politics of Intervention

CHAPTER 1

Violence, Resistance and Restorative Practice

To chastise violence outright, to condemn it as 'bad', is an ideological operation par excellence, a mystification which collaborates in rendering invisible the fundamental forms of social violence. It is deeply symptomatic that our Western societies which display such sensitivity to different forms of harassment are at the same time able to mobilise a multitude of mechanisms destined to render us insensitive to the most brutal forms of violence – often, paradoxically, in the very form of humanitarian sympathy with the victims.
(Zizek, 2008)

Sometimes doing nothing is the most violent thing to do
(Zizek, 2008)

The nature of violence

In invitational theory and practice, violence and abusive behaviour are conceptualised and understood in a political context as practices concerned with the use and effects of power; ubiquitous and inevitable in all kinds of relationships, including those we initiate with our clients.

Violence is defined broadly as any attempt to influence, coerce or control another person where there is potential to cause harm, violate the integrity of the other or disrespect the other's differences.

Accordingly, practices of violence are concerned with promoting conformity and sameness through imposing one's own ideas and preferences and through judgement, intolerance and the suppression of difference. Violence undermines and disrupts possibilities for respectful collaboration between individuals and communities and results in injustice and suffering. Violence serves to restrain and prevent the emergence of new, alternative and creative modes of existence.

Becoming vigilant towards violence

Invitational practice is concerned with all forms of violence, in the context of its *restorative project*. Distinctions and clarifications about forms of coercion, violence and abusive behaviour must continually be drawn in determining accountable and effective practice.

Whilst all coercion has the potential to cause harm, not all forms do produce harmful violation or lead to disrespect of individuals, particularly when enacted within an accountable context where this potential is considered and the nature and effects of coercive action are carefully monitored. For example, police action to prevent a person causing harm to others and many forms of parental discipline of children, can be respectful to all individuals concerned and to the broader community. Justice processes which mandate therapeutic intervention when men act abusively, can promote safety, respect and accountability within families and communities and do not necessarily disrespect or violate the integrity of those men. The notification to authorities of acts of abuse and the potential for future risk requires forms of coercion but fulfils community responsibilities for safety of its members, without necessarily violating any individual's well-being. These actions can be taken within an accountable context where they are sanctioned by communities through their statutory authorities, laws and codes of conduct. It is unhelpful to label these coercive actions as violence, when they are carried out by persons with appropriate statutory authority and in a context of accountability which places priority on ensuring fairness and respect for all people concerned.

However, it remains helpful to regard all forms of coercion as potentially violent. These acts have the potential to harm, violate and disrespect, even when necessary and when performed with honourable intent. To recognise this potential can assist in ensuring maximum accountability and minimum harm. There is a fine line between responsible and accountable forms of coercion and acts of violence which do cause harm; a distinction which can easily be lost sight of in the process of attempting to act in the service of a just cause. A review of the practices and justifications used when nation states initiate war or an examination of police practices used to interrogate suspects of crime, will effectively highlight this dilemma.

Invitational practice recognises the role of community institutions and authorities in establishing codes of conduct and sanctions with respect to violence and abusive behaviour and the need for these statutory authorities to be informed by and reflect the interests of the community and to promote respect and justice for all members. We are required to respect and complement these interests. However, there is little place for the use of coercion within Invitational practice itself. We act within a broader community and statutory context where coercion is at times necessary and practices of violence are inevitable. We must strive to remain vigilant and accountable regarding the inevitability of violence in our own practices:

- *How might we develop ways to consider and monitor the potential for harm, violation and disrespect in our practices?*
- *How might we minimise the use of coercion in our practices?*
- *How might we recognise violence when it inevitably enters our practices?*
- *How might we ensure that we remain accountable for any violence in our practices?*

Misguided blueprints for living

These dilemmas become intensified when we consider the ubiquitous nature of violence that does cause harm, violation and disrespect and the apparently noble and honourable justifications for its everyday use. Harm, violation and disrespect may not be the primary objectives or intent of this violence, even when they appear to be the main consequence.

Violence is clearly not the preserve of a select psychologically disturbed or deviant group of individuals. We all can and at times do enact violence which does cause harm and offence to others. Much of this violence is enacted with a sense of entitlement and justification and follows a common formula:

- Sense of affront or outrage; *How dare you . . .!*
- Desire to correct; *I'll show you!*
- Corrective or punitive action; *Take that!*
- Attribution of responsibility; *You deserved it!*
- Entitled sense of justification; *Now don't do it again!*

We frequently justify violence in the name of justice or education when it is enacted in the service of a supposedly noble aim which concerns righting of perceived wrongs, correcting a supposed injustice or conferring an 'earned' punishment and deterring any future 'wrongdoing'.

Male violence, both individual and collective, is commonly enacted as a form of 'legitimate' self-defence against perceived disrespect or threat from others. In this context, violence is regarded as a means for reclamation of a sense of lost honour and respect and is justified in the name of personal or even national security. Violence is frequently enacted and justified in the name of love; *'I'm just a jealous guy'*, or in the name of human nature and limitation; *'She pushed me to my limit; I just lost it'*.

If we examine the stated intent and justifications of the person who enacts violence together with the actual consequences of acts of violence, these acts clearly offer misguided and ineffective means for enabling justice, education, love, security and other honourable aims. This notion of a *misguided blueprint or recipe* for living and relating to others is developed as a key Invitational concept for establishing a productive and enabling understanding of violence which can assist men to face and address their abusive behaviour.

When does violence constitute abuse?

Violence is clearly ubiquitous in virtually all relationships and communities. However, it is unhelpful to regard *all* acts of violence, even when they entail physical violence, as constituting abuse.

Violence does have the potential to be abusive when the person who enacts it:

- possesses a significant advantage or privilege, in relation to the other, by virtue of factors which confer power, such as age, strength, ability or conferred status.
- experiences an exaggerated (and generally ongoing) sense of entitlement in relation to the other, thereby justifying its use.
- abdicates responsibility for the well-being of the other (generally on an ongoing basis) and thereby justifies or excuses its harmful consequences.

A context for abuse requires a differential of power or privilege and frequently results in the abused person feeling fearful and intimidated with a sense of entrapment or enforced accommodation to the needs and demands of the abusing person.

This distinction might be developed further in the following examples:

Andrew is highly critical, overbearing and domineering with his partner Anne and their three daughters. He tends to impose extremely unrealistic expectations and is judgemental, critical and unforgiving when a *'mistake'* is made. When members of Andrew's family do not meet his expectations, he speaks to them in deprecating ways and expects them to act on his advice. He lectures and shouts at family members, calling them *'stupid'* and other offensive names, if they question his opinions or directives. He has grabbed and shaken Anne on occasions. All family members feel intimidated and frightened of Andrew and are often afraid to speak their points of view in his presence.

Andrew is employed as a team leader in a manufacturing organisation and frequently feels frustrated and *'stressed out'* in his relations with management and members of his team. Andrew's workplace is characterised by somewhat rigid hierarchies of authority and a culture of vigilance, mistrust and criticism.

Evan, aged 28, is struggling in his efforts to *'get* (his 11-year-old son) *Steven to stop running amok and behave himself'*, at home and at school. Evan's efforts include giving frequent *'good hidings'* with a wooden cane. At these times he shouts at Steven calling him a *'loser'* and other offensive names. Steven is frightened to come home when he has been in trouble at school and is finding it increasingly difficult to manage daily responsibilities. Evan is critical of his partner, Barbara, whom he regards as, *'too soft on the boy'*. Evan defends his use of violence; *'It's the way my dad brought me up and it didn't do me any harm.'* *'My dad was strict as anything; I'm not as bad as him.'*

Evan has been unemployed for two years after a workplace accident resulting from employer negligence. He has received little support over the two years and feels *'kicked in the arse and forgotten'*.

Corey, aged 13, has been charged with assault after shaking his single mother, Judy, and throwing her across a room. Judy required medical attention following this assault. Corey was angry with his mother because, *'she*

wouldn't give me my pocket money, so I could go out with my mates'; *'She keeps on at me that my mates are druggies'*; *'She said I was turning out like my dad; she's got no right to say that'*.

Corey's father had physically and verbally abused all family members for as long as Corey could remember. He eventually abandoned the family when Corey was eight years old. Throughout his childhood, Corey has worried about his mother. He often tried in vain to stop her from being hurt and to protect her. The family have struggled financially since Corey's father left.

Andrew, Evan and Corey have all enacted violence which has frightened, hurt and intimidated family members. Aspects of their experiences appear to be quite similar. All three have felt affronted by the actions and reactions of family members and each has been preoccupied with an ongoing sense of personal injustice concerning experiences of unfair treatment by others. They have all acted coercively with an ongoing sense of exaggerated entitlement, have felt justified in their use of violence and have continued to abdicate responsibility for the harmful effects of their actions.

The violent actions of Andrew and Evan clearly fit the criteria for abuse. Clear differentials in power and privilege exist between themselves and those they have hurt by virtue of factors such as physical size, age, position in family, access to resources and gendered interests. Family members are experiencing intimidation and entrapment. However, the context for Corey's violence is more complex. Corey is physically stronger than his mother and has a clear physical advantage. However, Judy is an adult with status and privileges that Corey does not enjoy. In this case, power hierarchies are contradictory and inconsistent:

- *Does Corey's violence constitute abuse?*
- *What would it mean if we focused upon the parameters of gender and physical strength, but ignored the adult-child dimension of power relations?*

Sexual violence and abuse are constituted by the same parameters as any other forms of violence and abuse. Sexual assault requires an exaggerated sense of entitlement along with an abdication of responsibility for the feelings and well-being of the abused person who is in effect treated as an object to be conquered, possessed and used by the abusing person. A differential in power makes this abuse possible. These common factors are reflected in David's actions and statements:

> David, aged 37 years, sexually abused his 11-year-old niece on numerous occasions over a period of 12 months. When initially interviewed, he asserted, *'We have a special relationship; we love each other'*; *'Perhaps it's wrong but she wanted it too'*; *'I would have stopped if she didn't want to go on'*.

Sexual assault is frequently perpetrated and justified as 'legitimate' conquest or in the name of love. David has justified his abusive initiatives as if they were reciprocal actions of equal partners and has attributed responsibility to an 11-year-old girl.

Sexually abusive behaviour is often justified as a response to provocation and in the name of human nature and limitations; *'She asked for it'*; *'She turned me on'*; *'I couldn't help myself'*.

When differentials of power and privilege are consistent and unambiguous, violence most often constitutes abusive behaviour and tends to be ongoing with high levels of fear and intimidation, coerced compliance and a sense of entrapment.

It is no surprise that the most common sites of abusive behaviour are aligned with dominant and institutionalised cultural hierarchies of power. Abuse and neglect of children, harassment on the basis of ethnicity, sexual preference or employment status and abuse of women by male partners, all reflect dominant cultural interests which entail institutionalised differentials of power and privilege.

However, despite the effects of a history of men's physical and sexual violence towards women, incidents of relationship violence by men towards women are not always best understood as abuses, in that hierarchies of power and privilege in relationships can be complex and are not always experienced solely along traditional gender lines.

The distinction between violence and abuse informs significant differences in Invitational practice. Intervention paradigms for situations of abuse require recognition of differentials in power and privilege and practices which address abusive behaviour in a context of safety and accountability. These practices are distinctly different in circumstances of inequity when

addressing abuse as opposed to situations of violence. Most of the practice described in this book is directed towards addressing abusive practices. However, practices which address distinctions between violence and abuse will be detailed in the chapter concerning couple and family intervention (see Part Four).

- *How might we draw distinctions between violence and abuse when power hierarchies are inconsistent or ambiguous?*
- *How might we develop practices which take account of differentials in power and privilege within relationships and communities?*
- *How do we reconcile these distinctions and their implications for practice with our client's lived experiences and their views about what constitutes abuse?*
- *How might our well-intended intervention practices inadvertently constitute forms of abuse?*

Politics of violence – capture of desire

Invitational practice is informed by a political analysis of violence and abusive behaviour whereby these everyday and ubiquitous acts are regarded as integral to the interplay of power relations that shapes all aspects of our lives and relationships.

I have previously described how practices of violence and abuse are ever-present in shaping the everyday transactions of cultural institutions in government, business practice, sport, international relations etc. The criteria for abusive behaviour (power differential, exaggerated entitlement, justified coercion, abdicated responsibility) in fact constitute prescriptions or recipes for competence, adequacy and success in dominant masculine culture. These prescriptions reflect values that promote conquest, acquisition, competition, ownership and entitlement to power and resources, without a requirement of responsibility for one's actions and their consequences upon the welfare of others. Similarly, hegemonic ideas about male sexuality prescribe sexual entitlement and conquest without responsibility for the well-being of others (Jenkins, 1990). The concept of violence as ubiquitous in the political, social and cultural structures and practices of everyday life is explored and critiqued in detail by Zizek (2008) and Chomsky (2002) and in relation to masculinity, by Edwards (2006) and Messerschmidt (1993).

The Invitational model is informed by considerations about desire and power developed by post-structural philosophers, particularly Gilles Deleuze and Michel Foucault. Violence and abusive behaviour are understood within a political context which concerns a plethora of intersecting and interconnected power relations and practices which are often hidden or invisible to participants. Our concepts of self or identity, including notions of masculinity, are in fact produced through these power relations and practices. Both Deleuze and Foucault have described the historical composition of such concepts, through differentiation and connection of characteristics which have political intensity, such as social class, gender, age, race, occupation and sexual preference. (Deleuze and Guattari, 1983, 1987; Foucault, 1971, 1972). We continually position ourselves and are positioned within hierarchies of power which relate to these characteristics and which come to constitute dominant forms of masculinity. Ideas and practices which serve to exaggerate entitlement, justify the use of coercion and abdicate responsibility for the welfare of others, inform power negotiations in the establishment and re-establishment of hierarchies amongst men. Such positioning and negotiating produces a fluid process of identity construction with a range of identity conclusions for individual men. These power relations and identity conclusions are produced by desire, or striving to become, but they also serve to capture or enslave desire within certain limited investments. Certain aspects of desire, or human striving, become coded into cultural interests which eventually appear as prescriptive rules, universal investments or human essences. In this way, notions of aggression, competitiveness, emotional inhibition, limited control in the face of provocation and a range of gendered experiences become regarded as *human nature* or 'the way that men are' and resistant to challenge.

In accordance with Foucault's understandings of power relations, these dominant cultural interests both provoke and are determined by ongoing practices of *complicity* and *resistance*. Ransom (1997) provides an accessible introduction to Foucault's concepts regarding power relations. Notions of entitlement, ownership and possession are indeed produced and privileged in forms of dominant masculinity. However, desire can be coded in ways that produce an infinite range of possibilities and

preferences, some of which constitute other ways of becoming and relating, and alternative forms of masculinity. Concepts and practices such as cooperation, equity, fairness, compassion and hospitality may also be culturally and individually valued and serve to resist the dominance of individuality, competitiveness and acquisitiveness. This complexity informs an infinite range of possibilities for becoming and opens up a vast potential for a broad range of identity conclusions. We are continually engaged in formulating and re-formulating a sense of identity within the flux of practices of *complicity* and *resistance* with ongoing power relations.

In this context, the use of violence may be seen to constitute political strategy, complicit with dominant cultural interests, rather than behaviour which is deviant or pathological. Indeed, many forms of violence which constitute abuse are often regarded as necessary, even admirable and noble, in the arenas of government adversarial politics, aggressive business practice, warfare and sport. Consequently, the Invitational model regards abusive behaviour as *over-conforming* to dominant cultural interests and practices and not as deviant behaviour or as symptomatic of emotional or psychological disorder. The use of the term *over-conforming* is consistent with the concept of capture of desire and highlights the fact that abusive behaviour, within an intimate relationship or family context, reflects misguided political strategy if the man's preferred striving is for a sense of connection, belonging and respect.

An effect of over-conforming to dominant masculine practice, especially when it involves abusive treatment of others in valued relationships, is frequently a sense of becoming insufficient, even becoming monstrous. Investments in life and relationships become increasingly closed, limited and static, often with a sense of detachment from ethics, especially those related to experiences of respect and love in relationships. In the world of dominant masculinity where hierarchies amongst men serve to distinguish the *winners* from the *losers*, a sense of identity may be developed which is characterised by insufficiency and blame; a *loser* identity which provides little support for initiative, agency and respect. Efforts to *become somebody*, to gain respect, to make it, through dominant practices of power meet with an increasing sense of failure and shame. Popular explanations for abusive behaviour then focus on insufficiency and blame and become increasingly influential in judgmental identity conclusions which exacerbate the sense of *being a loser*. This sense of identity is characterised by conclusions like the following:

I'm useless

I can't get anything right

I can't help it

I lost it again

What's the point

It's not fair

It's not my fault

They pushed me to my limit

The practices of power which inform and produce dominant masculinity and abusive behaviour have a cultural history. They are not invented by those individual men who have abused and who may be unaware of the nature of the power relations in which they are participating. Individual men cannot be held responsible for the origins of these practices.

However, the ongoing capacity for both *complicity* and *resistance* in all power relations, enables possibilities for these men to examine and challenge the nature of their participation. In Invitational practice, the nature and context of power relations and dominant forms of masculinity is made more visible and transparent so that patterns of *complicity* and *resistance* can be identified and named. In this context, concepts of individual responsibility and choice can become more accessible and meaningful.

- *How might we promote a focus on individual responsibility for ceasing abusive acts, whilst recognising that such behaviour is culturally constructed and informed by power relations and practices that are ubiquitous in the experience of all men?*

Politics of disadvantage

The nature of and propensity for capture of desire and consequent complicity with dominant cultural interests becomes even more complex when the effects of disadvantage or subjection to forms of oppression and abuse are considered. Early feminist analyses of domestic abuse obviously focused on women's experiences in patriarchal cultures and tended to regard men who have abused as a somewhat homogeneous group concerned with the maintenance of power and control over women. However, contemporary analyses highlight the heterogeneity of men who abuse and a much broader range of disrespectful, violent and abusive practices perpetrated in the service of patriarchal hierarchies which may be based on factors such as race, social class, sexual preference, age etc. (Connell, 1995, 2000; Edley and Wetherell. 1995, 1997; Edwards, 2008; Hooks, 2004). Men who have abused come from a variety of social classes, ethnic and family backgrounds, and can have widely different experiences in relation to levels of privilege and advantage, family and community support and experiences of subjection to abuse and harassment. They constitute a far from homogeneous group.

I see many men with histories of having been subjected to disadvantage and marginalising practices by other men within their communities. These practices, of course, reflect and reinforce dominant cultural interests. They occur in contexts such as child abuse, economic disadvantage and racial harassment. Such ongoing practices of subjugation produce a sense of *being done to* and exacerbate identity conclusions of *being a loser*, characterised by inevitable feelings of worthlessness, insufficiency and a profound and pervasive sense of injustice. Members of marginalised communities frequently experience ongoing injustice and discrimination in their daily lives. Whilst much of their experience of disadvantage is rendered invisible to others, they are more likely to be held accountable for their abusive actions and are more likely to experience criminal justice sanctions than members of privileged communities.

Attempts to protest such injustice are generally ignored or overlooked by those with greater privilege. A sense of injustice often becomes increasingly reflected in forms of impotent protest which can be accompanied by violence or abusive behaviour. Such behaviour may reflect a sense of desperation and protest in the face of extreme and ongoing inequity and injustice. However, whilst the violence tends to be noticed and addressed, the protest or resistance is often overlooked or ignored. When the interests of the privileged are safeguarded and such protest is overlooked or ignored, violence frequently becomes directed towards family members or others in more disadvantaged or vulnerable circumstances rather than towards those who are oppressing or subjugating (Campbell, 1993; Morton, 1997; Zizek, 2008). Opportunities for the capture of desire are extended as misguided forms of protest inevitably serve to reproduce the power practices and interests of dominant forms of masculinity. Through futile forms of resistance and desperate attempts to *become somebody*, these men become further marginalised and increasingly detached from their own sense of ethics and their own communities (Wexler, 1992). It is in this context that some activist groups gain support by regarding marginalised minorities as the cause of their difficulties; pitting men's rights against women's rights or 'white' against Aboriginal or Asian, and fail to address the significant injustices which actually disadvantage them and which support dominant cultural interests.

The politics of disadvantage have particular implications for intervention practice. Disadvantaged men seldom feel powerful or in control and may not experience their abusive behaviour as concerned with maintaining power and control over their partners. Appeals by intervention workers to these men to face up to and take responsibility for abusive actions or understand the impact of these actions upon others, are likely to be experienced as another chapter in a history of *being done to*. Subsequent resistance to these appeals and expectations can lead to confrontation and further marginalisation in intervention programmes. This is especially the case when these expectations are maintained without any attempt to understand the nature and impact of the man's experiences of victimisation and marginalisation by other men. We can easily overlook or discount the man's experience in over-zealous efforts to hold him accountable for his own actions or through our own misguided attempts to prevent him from using his own life experiences as justifications or excuses for his actions.

As a child, Evan (see page 5) and his siblings lived under the tyranny of his father who hurt and terrified them on a daily basis. He continually worried about his mother's safety and came to resent his father who appeared to regard him as 'useless' and 'a failure'. Evan's life became increasingly dominated by feelings of anxiety, resentment and injustice.

As an adult, Evan's sense of injustice grew steadily in the workplace where, 'I was always the shitkicker; I was never given a go'. He experienced considerable resentment after the workplace accident when his employers took little responsibility and offered little support. A compensation matter has been held up for reasons unknown to Evan who continues to feel, 'kicked in the arse and forgotten'.

Evan's experiences of abuse and injustice throughout his childhood and in the workplace provide stark expressions of the hierarchical politics of dominant masculine practice. A sense of *being done to* and ongoing preoccupations with personal injustice afford opportunities for capture of desire and *complicity* with dominant cultural interests. Interestingly, these experiences also afford opportunities for *resistance*. However, Evan's preoccupations are likely to be restraining in terms of his readiness to address his own abusive behaviour.

- *What might it mean if we expect a man to face up to abusive behaviour, take responsibility for his actions and understand what he has put others through, when no-one else (including ourselves) has attempted to understand his experiences of injustice and what he has been put through?*
- *What does it mean if we expect something of the man that we are not prepared to provide for him?*
- *How can we acknowledge and address a man's experience of disadvantage, marginalisation or victimisation, without sacrificing a focus on responsibility for his own abusive actions and without promoting stories of blame and justification?*

A common focus with abusive practices

Abusive practices have tended to be examined and addressed in discrete categories, such as sexual abuse, domestic violence, child abuse, racial harassment, etc., which supposedly require different kinds of specialist expertise provided by different services and agencies. The common nature and effects of all forms of violence and abuse tend to be obscured by these differentiations, even to the extent where abuse of children can go unnoticed in programmes that maintain a primary focus on partner abuse. Categorisation of types of abuse can be helpful in that it tends to ensure that the needs of specific individuals or communities are attended to. However, it can create a blindness or even complacency towards the responsibilities and needs in other groups, even with regard to our own unwitting violence and abusive behaviour.

I am increasingly convinced that it is helpful to hold a broad focus which takes into account common aspects of the nature and politics of all forms of violence and abuse. Our work with individual men is likely to reveal a variety of different sites where abusive behaviour is practiced and requires constant vigilance and monitoring of the potential for abuse in our own practices. Invitational practice invites ongoing reflection upon the ubiquitousness of violence and abusive practices in all aspects of all relationships, communities and cultures.

We may, for example, justify warfare and the invasion of another culture or country in the same ways that we justify violence in the form of coercion and confrontation in statutory or therapeutic intervention; in the service of honourable and noble goals where the ends are seen to justify the means. These justifications may be no different in nature to those used by a man who has assaulted his partner and belittled his children because he perceives that they have acted in ways which he thinks are dishonourable or disloyal and therefore require 'correction'.

The Invitational model is concerned with all forms of violence and abusive practice. We have a responsibility to be vigilant for and to critique violent practices whether they are enacted by our clients, statutory and community institutions or (especially) by ourselves.

In contrast to the 1990 publication, this book will attempt to recognise and highlight important differences in the nature of abusive practices, without compartmentalising different sites of abuse and violence into discrete or specialist categories.

Politics of resistance – ethics and protest

The restorative project which concerns the cessation of abusive behaviour, restitution for harm done and reclamation of integrity, is an ethical project which respects the complex interplay of *complicity* and *resistance* in all power relations. We have already considered how the capture of desire by dominant cultural interests might only be partial, and identity conclusions drawn by men who have abused might be unstable and fluid in nature. In fact, every tendency towards capture and limitation also

offers an infinite set of possibilities for *resistance* and new ways for becoming. The discovery and clarification of a man's ethical preferences and strivings for respectful ways of becoming and relating lies at the heart of Invitational practice.

Traditional intervention practices have tended to maintain a focus on confronting and challenging abusive behaviour, often assuming that the man is solely or primarily motivated by an intent to harm, and to control and diminish those he has subjected to abuse. In this context, attempts by the man to represent himself as ethical might then be regarded as inauthentic, devious and manipulative strategies to avoid facing responsibility for his actions; they require immediate confrontation and correction.

The Invitational model acknowledges the existence of these motivations but recognises that the man may be unaware of the nature of his participation or *complicity* in power relations and hierarchies and in the ongoing production of dominant forms of masculinity. He may at times feel vengeful or contemptuous towards family members. He may want to degrade, diminish or hurt them at these times. However, he may also be motivated by desires or strivings to give and receive love, respect and nurture, but unwittingly be committed to investing in misguided and destructive prescriptions or recipes for achieving these desires; recipes and prescriptions for *becoming somebody*, building relationships and establishing love and respect through power practices of dominant masculinity. Yet this man is likely to have also engaged in non-violent and respectful ways to try to fulfil these desires, involving practices more consistent with his strivings, but lost sight of these investments which have become overshadowed in the reproduction of dominant masculine practice.

A man might perpetrate abuse, in the name of love, when he acts in controlling, hurtful and diminishing ways at times when his partner attempts to engage in separate activities, friendships or expresses ideas or preferences that are different to his. Exploration of his thinking and actions may reveal a desire for a loving relationship with a strong sense of connection and belonging. However, alongside these strivings lies a concern that his partner's different preferences challenge this vision and her commitment to the relationship. This man's investments appear to be complicit with culturally dominant and popular conceptualisations of *domestic love* which promote and value sameness whilst suppressing difference. I first heard this term used by a colleague, David Jones, in 2003. According to this recipe, love requires that each partner share the same thoughts, interests and feelings. Such a blueprint prescribes a form of ownership with a sense of entitlement to coerce and 'correct' the other in order to enforce sameness and thereby preserve love in the relationship. In this misguided quest for love, the man will desperately reproduce more of the same dominant masculine power practice, as he perceives an inevitable and increasing loss of love and respect from his partner. These practices pose important dilemmas for Invitational practice about the nature of the man's intent:

- *Is this man wanting to control and diminish his partner or is he wanting to develop a connected and loving relationship?*

When we meet this man, he will most likely be steeped in a sense of injustice and failure, characterised by experiences and attributions of blame and insufficiency. These experiences will be reflected in identity conclusions of *being a loser*. He will most likely anticipate that our judgements will also be deprecating and denigrating, perhaps anticipating another experience of being judged as insufficient.

- *How might we attend to this man's abusive behaviour **and** remain open and alert to possibilities of an ethical intent or preferences for respectful ways of relating?*
- *How might we listen to this man without judging his intent and preferences **and** without diminishing the nature and seriousness of his abusive behaviour?*

Invitational practice has become increasingly concerned with the discovery, naming and clarification of ethics, which include strivings for fairness, respect, compassion and accountability, and the practice of ethical behaviour. Despite the seemingly rigid and restrained patterns of experience of men who have abused and long-standing histories of violence and disrespectful behaviour, it is generally possible to discover ethical preferences and strivings which can open up new and alternative possibilities.

The productive and creative understandings of desire and becoming, proposed by Gilles Deleuze, enable somewhat revolutionary and expansive ways to open up considerations of new possibilities and alternatives to rigid and fixed notions of identity and restrained patterns of behaviour. Our lives are not restricted or constrained to certain states of being. We are continually invested in a multitude of flows of becoming which involve experiences and activities, some of which are complicit with and reproduce dominant cultural interests and some of which are resistant and produce creative and alternative interests. Specific identity conclusions are continually reached in the course of these ongoing investments. However, these are only brief stable moments within ongoing flows of becoming; they are fluid and changeable and are constantly negotiated and revised. We are not restricted to or fixed in any particular state of identity or being.

Becoming ethical refers to an enabling of ethical possibilities which arise in the states of flux between practices of *complicity* and *resistance* in all power relations. Whilst individuals tend to reproduce and conform to dominant cultural interests, they also demonstrate resistance to such interests. Invitational theory and practice respects and aims to attend to and highlight this complexity. When experiences of capture by dominant interests are examined alongside knowledge and practices which resist these interests, alternative and often preferred ethics can become clearer and more apparent. A man's strivings might relate to cooperation *as well as* competition, protection *as well as* exploitation and fairness, respect and *sharing as well as* personal acquisition for individual gain. As this complexity is made explicit, alternative and ethical ways of relating can become increasingly apparent. A fluid and expansive range of options which promote new identity conclusions becomes possible. As ethical strivings are contrasted with abusive actions and their effects, a growing sense of contradiction results which demands resolution. The process of *becoming ethical* allows for opening up of visions and strivings for fairness and respect and investment in options which might produce a greater sense of integrity.

Deleuze's ethical project proposes that we do not judge flows of becoming and the modes of existence that they imply according to external or supposedly universal moral standards. A flow of becoming, and its associated activities and interests, may imply or point to new modes of existence with a capacity to affirm the power of life, to open up and enable new possibilities for life which are vital, creative and which value life.

Such flows of becoming and possibilities might be regarded as healthy or ethical, by reference to criteria similar to those considered by Nietzsche in his examination of ethics in *Beyond Good and Evil*. Flows of becoming and interests which point to modes of existence which restrict diversity, shut down possibilities, disable and devalue life, often in the name of 'higher' moral values, reflect ethical dis-ease and promote a 'sickly' life (Nietzsche, 1990; Smith, 1997, 2003; Marks, 2005).

The restorative project is developed in relation to ethical flows of becoming and the actualisation of ethical positions which support fairness and respect of difference through *reaching towards the world of the other*. The capacity to move beyond what we know and experience and to extend ourselves through creative and novel connections which point to new possibilities, constitutes an ethical flow of becoming which informs all aspects of the restorative project and of Invitational practice. *Becoming ethical* implies openness to and respect of diversity with a creative desire to reach out and embrace difference and to imagine new modes of existence. Ethical flows of becoming are likely to support non-violative and respectful relationships which privilege fairness and a sense of accountability.

Becoming ethical enables us to personally examine and evaluate our own experiences and actions, in terms of the modes of existence they point towards or imply, rather than via external standards of morality. In this context, we may examine our intentions alongside our actions and evaluate congruence and integrity:

- How effective are my efforts and actions towards actualising my ethical strivings and visions?
- To what extent are my efforts opening up possibilities which enhance my life and the lives of others?

When a man ceases abusive behaviour and embraces more respectful ways of relating, it will be on the basis of consideration of his own ethics, not by the imposition of someone else's ethics or some external moral code. However, ethical ideals and preferences of men who have abused can be easily overlooked, ignored or taken for granted, in the face of their shocking and destructive actions. Such *under-estimation* is especially likely when the man presents with stories of minimisation and blame and appears to take little responsibility for his actions,

demonstrating an apparent disregard of the harmful impact of his actions upon others.

Intervention practices which are based on models of psychological deficit, can compound this *under-estimation* of men's capacities for respectful and ethical behaviour, by focusing on descriptions of personality disorder and character deficits in empathy, anger-management, impulse control or social skills. Deficit models tend to promote intervention practices which focus on the correction of bad habits and attempts to teach new ethics and skills. These corrective practices often inadvertently *under-estimate* the man's own ethics, preferences and ability to determine and initiate his own respectful directions.

In Invitational practice, our *parallel journey* towards *becoming ethical*, requires that we remain open to possibilities and the likelihood that the man who has abused may:

- experience a sense of ethical intent or striving, despite his abusive actions.
- hold preferences and some desire for just, equitable and respectful ways of becoming and relating.
- be capable of discovering and recognising his own ethics and preferences for respectful ways of relating.
- be able to recognise and address contradiction between his ethics and his abusive actions.
- be able to make respectful choices which are congruent with his own preferences and ethics.
- be prepared to decide for himself to embark on a journey towards *becoming ethical*; a journey towards integrity and respect which might accord with his own values and preferences.

Evan (see pages 5 and 9) was initially reluctant to participate in an intervention programme and was experiencing an extreme sense of injustice as a result of the statutory child protection authorities, *'sticking their noses into my business'* and *'wanting to tear my family apart'*. He protested, *'Steven needs to be put in line or he'll go down the tube'*.

Evan had walked out angrily and prematurely from two previous psychological assessments and declared, *'They are wankers; they just put you down; they haven't got a clue'*. The ensuing psychological reports referred to Evan as having a *'personality disorder'* with *'poor impulse control'* and with a *'poor prognosis for change'*. These reports reflected earlier assessments, when as a juvenile, Evan was described as *'conduct disordered'*. Evan's mother had also described him as, *'just like his father'* with a *'short fuse'*. Evan himself had secretly come to fear that he may be a *'useless'* person who *'manages to stuff everything up'*.

Conversations with Evan, about his concerns and hopes, soon revealed an ethic of protest; a belief in *'standing up for yourself'* in the face of perceived injustice. Evan asserted that he also believed in *'standing up for others'*, particularly when they were disadvantaged and not able to stand up for themselves. In the context of tacit legitimisation of a right to protest, Evan related stories of having tried in vain, as a young child, to stand up for his mother and protect her from his father's violence. He related times when he had *'stuck up for'* others by acting protectively towards friends and gradually was able to name and define preferred ethical qualities which included, *'loyalty'*, *'sticking together'* and *'standing up for your beliefs'*.

When asked about the qualities he thought were important in being a Dad, Evan spoke of *'protection'*, *'teaching right from wrong'* and *'standing by your kids'*. He felt that these were ethics that his father may never have considered. At this point, he lowered his head and appeared anxious and ashamed. He had begun to reflect on his abusive actions and on further inquiry, Evan acknowledged that he had not always acted according to these ethics. These realisations and acknowledgements in fact provided evidence for the authenticity of his belief in the importance of honesty, *'standing up for your beliefs'* and *'standing by your kids'*. From this ethical reference point, Evan was able to begin to face up to and address his abusive behaviour towards his son.

Appeals to ethics

Our parallel ethical journey, in Invitational practice, requires that we privilege fairness and respect of difference in all interactions with the man who has abused, as we listen for, attend to and enquire about evidence of respectful and ethical preferences. In this way, we can promote the discovery, development and expression of his ethics. This may at times involve *appeals to an ethical sense of self*, when we respond to our client's experiences. Ethics of fairness and respect are highlighted and emphasised through appeals to concepts of self which might appear somewhat essentialist in the relativist world embraced by

post-structuralist traditions. Such appeals involve forms of inquiry which imply personal ethical reference points and provoke recognition of a distinction between the *person* and the *acts* he may have perpetrated:

How does this (ethical step/action) fit with the person you really are becoming?

How much are you beginning to show your true colours?

Ethical concepts and practices are of course co-constructed in therapeutic intervention where the man's development is thought of in terms of flows of becoming towards preferred ways of living and relating which are considered and clarified within a collaborative project. However, these preferences and strivings are also regarded as being grounded in an ethical commitment or underpinning which affirms life and which can be thought of as having certain absolute qualities. This accords with a Deleuzian notion of desire and becoming which is creative and productive and which constitutes a positive flow of strivings which constitute life. For an accessible description of Deleuze's concepts regarding desire and becoming, see Buchanan (2000); Colebrook (2002a, 2002b, 2006); Due (2007); May (2005). In this sense, respectful ethics are already there to be discovered and also needing to be constructed, throughout the course of intervention.

Appeals to an ethical sense of self are made in the service of understandings concerning the nature of desire and faith in the productive and revolutionary potentials of flows of becoming. Such appeals privilege the ethics of fairness and respect of difference as cornerstones of the journey, *becoming ethical*; which might inform a sense of becoming which is vital, life-enhancing and which honours the potentials of life. Whilst there are many ethical interests, fairness and respect of difference are regarded as having some primacy in determining faith in oneself and others and a sense of integrity. These ethics do tend to survive in the face of adversity. They are perhaps never totally destroyed or lost, even in circumstances of invasion and extreme violation. They lie at the heart of survival and constitute the soul of integrity. Ethical appeals implicitly honour and support these qualities.

Fairness and respect of difference involve strivings which also accurately and honestly reflect the ethics that inform intervention practice. Such appeals reflect the necessary ethical declarations by workers in their parallel journeys and serve to promote transparency and openness in intervention.

Invitational practice concerns the identification and examination of respectful ethics which reflect the man's own preferences and strivings in order to enable the development of ideas and practices which are fair and respectful to others. As workers, our *parallel journeys* similarly must engage with openness, fairness and respect and requires an ongoing critique of our own thinking and practices of power. We cannot facilitate a journey towards respect if we position ourselves in an *us-and-them*, judgmental stance or imagine that we stand apart from dominant cultural interests, power relations and practices. We have a responsibility to act ethically and with transparency regarding the concepts which inform our practices. We are never entitled to impose our ethics upon others.

- *How might we maintain a fair and respectful position which remains open to possibilities regarding a man's respectful ethics and preferences, in the face of his shocking and disrespectful actions or his apparent insensitivity or disregard for the hurt and distress experienced by those he has abused?*
- *How might we hold a generous form of love which enables the realisation of difference and opens up ethical possibilities?*
- *How do we monitor and prevent the unwitting reproduction of dominant cultural power practices and interests in our intervention practices?*

Politics of intervention

Be careful when you fight the monsters, lest you become one.

(Nietzsche, 1990)

As intervention workers, we inevitably become part of the network of power relations in the man's life. We operate within community agencies and institutions and within a broader social context which reflects dominant cultural interests and practices of power. We occupy positions of privilege and power relative to our clients and we will inevitably reproduce inequalities of power and privilege in our work. Our practice has both the potential to respect and

to disrespect the man's differences, ethics and integrity. Our interventions can enable and help to open up possibilities for ethical flows of becoming with respectful identity conclusions and they can (inadvertently) support a disabling status quo which confirms identity conclusions characterised by insufficiency, desperation and blame.

Traditional intervention theory and practice, with men who have abused, has tended to rely upon processes of confrontation, correction and education. These processes invoke the metaphor of *colonisation*; a kind of psychological invasion which readily justifies the use of coercion and violence, in the service of the noble cause of stopping abusive behaviour. The use of the term *colonisation* does not imply that the consequences of intervention are akin to the devastation wrought upon indigenous communities by the invasions of western colonising powers, although it must be noted that indigenous people are over-represented in prisons and 'correctional' facilities in Australia and in other colonised nations. The use of the term points to the ubiquitous nature of colonising tendencies in the power practices of the privileged within communities. Those with membership of privileged groups often feel entitled to impose their interests and cultural practices upon those who are less privileged and less advantaged. The privileged often act from a position of assumed expert knowledge and authority and a sense of moral and cultural superiority. They attempt to subdue, subjugate, conquer, take over and convert members of less privileged sections of the community. When attempts to 'educate' with the use of 'reason' fail, the use of coercion and force is seen as justified. Colonising practices are often carried out with 'noble' aims and the conviction of good intention, with a sense of 'right' and higher moral ground, but often with blindness, disregard and even contempt towards the effects of these actions upon the less privileged members of the community and their experiences.

Colonisation involves processes of determining and labelling deficiencies in others, followed by correction, coercion and control. These practices are accompanied by sets of justifications and rationalisations, whereby the ends are seen to justify the means. Such practices can be seen to involve the same kinds of rationale and action which constitute all forms of abuse. Individual men are pathologised and confronted through a kind of 'benevolent' bullying. This creates an adversarial context that either produces passive accommodation or perhaps protest, but with little ethical realisation and behaviour change. We replicate the power dynamics of abuse, serving to provide yet another chapter in the man's story of disadvantage, by replicating the very behaviour we are attempting to stop. In this context, those who have already encountered disadvantage are further marginalised and confirmed with the status of *being a loser*.

Following a period of imprisonment for assaulting his uncle, Rob was mandated to attend a violence intervention programme. He has a history of violence-related offences for which he had served previous time in prison. He had attended a men's group in prison in which he was regarded as *'disruptive'* and a malcontent. Not surprisingly, he had found this men's group unhelpful.

When I met Rob, his sense of injustice was palpable, particularly at having been sent to see yet *'another headshrink'*. At first, Rob was reluctant to speak about his experience and what was important to him. However, it gradually became apparent that he had experienced a long history of disadvantage and injustice. He and his younger sister were abandoned by their father and sent to live with an uncle, when their mother was hospitalised with a severe psychiatric illness. Both children were regularly physically abused and humiliated by the uncle. Rob discovered that his uncle had begun to sexually abuse his sister. Rob tried to protect his sister by speaking out on her behalf but was not believed, and he tried to deflect his uncle's physical and emotional abuse away from his sister and towards himself. He tried to be *'like a father'* to his sister. In fact, Rob was also sexually abused by his uncle but did not feel ready to disclose his own victimisation until much later on.

Rob had never felt taken seriously or listened to by others. In the men's group he was confronted about his violence and his vengeful patterns of thinking. He was encouraged to consider alternative ways to 'manage his anger', which might not involve violence or retaliation. However, he was not permitted to speak about his hurt and outrage regarding his uncle's abusive behaviour. Attempts to do this were regarded as attempts to excuse or justify and thereby avoid responsibility for his actions.

His past protective concern for his sister was apparently regarded as patronising and an attempt to avoid responsibility for his current actions. Rob's attempts to voice protest were quickly disqualified and he experienced a familiar sense of not being listened to and not taken seriously. He learned to keep quiet and simmer in a silent protest which was punctuated by occasional outbursts in the group. Other group members were encouraged to confront Rob's 'minimisations' and lack of engagement with group processes and he was pushed to the margins of the group as someone who 'doesn't get it'. Attempts to confront Rob in order to 'get through to' him, led to him taking steps to defend himself with responses which appeared increasingly irresponsible. When encouraged to consider non-violent means to address his 'anger' at his uncle, he would respond, *'The bastard deserved every bit of what he got; I should have killed him.'* Any evidence which might support the possibility of preferred ethics such as loyalty, protectiveness or resistance to injustice; evidence which might suggest that there is more to Rob than his violence and which might inform an ethical position, seemed to be completely discounted or overlooked.

Rob was subsequently 'diagnosed' as *'borderline personality disordered'* with *'severe impulse control and empathy deficits'*. His experience in the men's group appeared to confirm yet another chapter in a life of 'being done to' and needing to fight for his survival. He was once again regarded and made to feel like a 'loser', as his own ethics were underestimated and ignored and his protest against genuine injustice disqualified. Rob was expected to take steps to address his violence that the group leaders were not prepared to take on his behalf.

Invitational practice is concerned with the discovery, naming and actualisation of the man's own ethics and preferences and the legitimisation of protest or resistance to injustice. When ethics are ignored and attempts are made to suppress protest, the ensuing adversarial context is likely to produce self-defence and exacerbate attributions of blame. This, of course, promotes a diminishment of any sense of responsibility for violence or abusive behaviour. The man might rightly resist our oppressive and unjust behaviour but within this context of *colonisation,* protest is often *reactive* rather than *creative* and can frequently become misguided and misdirected towards individuals and communities in more disadvantaged and vulnerable circumstances. Our efforts to stop violence and abuse may in fact serve to exacerbate it.

I became increasingly curious about Rob's capacity for survival as a young person, without the support of others; his ability to *'keep moving'* and continue to try to protect his sister. I enquired about the origins of these qualities and invited him to name them. He declared that he believed in *'sticking up for what is right'*, *'speaking your mind'*, *'standing by'* the people you care about and *'sticking up for the underdog'*. I wondered and enquired about how these ethics had survived in the face of such adversity. Rob strongly affirmed the importance of protest; of not *'taking (injustice) lying down'*.

At one of our subsequent meetings he looked forlorn and apologetic as he stated, *'I think I blew it'*. Rob told me that he had again been reported by the police and warned to stay away from his uncle. He explained that the uncle had approached him and taunted him, knowing that he was on parole and at risk of being returned to prison. When I enquired about the effects of his uncle's taunts, he replied, *'I saw red; I wanted to kill him'*. I asked about what he then did. Rob replied that he punched his hand into his own fist and said, *'I'll kill you if I see you again'*. He then walked away despite his uncle's continued derisive comments.

I became curious about what might have led him to walk away when he felt like killing his uncle. Rob responded, *'I don't want to go back to prison'*. I continued to enquire about why this is important. Rob looked perplexed at my need to ask such a question but stopped and reflected for a while before responding, *'Gemma (his four year old daughter) needs a Dad'*. I continued my enquiry about why this was important to Rob. He appeared resigned to my seemingly obvious questions and replied, *'She needs love'*; *'I don't want her to go through what I went through'*. Together we acknowledged and honoured the necessity and the challenge in putting Gemma's needs first, despite and in the face of Rob having felt so much hurt and injustice in his own life.

It seemed apparent that Rob had never before engaged in such a conversation about his ethics of care and concern for his daughter or attempted to define what was important to him as a father. He began to clarify what he was standing up for and some of the things that were important in his life and to place these ethics in a historical context. From this ethical perspective, Rob could begin to engage in a process in which he was open to consider more effective and enabling ways of standing up for himself and his family.

Ethics of restorative practice

The restorative project constitutes the broad context for Invitational practice and concerns creative renewal with the opening up of ethical possibilities for the man who has abused and for us as workers, in our *parallel journeys*. The goals of restorative practice are the cessation of abusive behaviour, restitution for harm done to individuals and communities, and reclamation of integrity.

Restorative practice is informed by three concepts which are regarded as vital ethical positions or strivings in our journeys and our clients' journeys towards *becoming ethical*:

1. Fairness – the ethic of protest
2. Restitution – the ethic of remorse
3. Respect of difference – the ethic of generous love

1. Fairness – the ethic of protest

Justice is always 'to come', deferred, and can never finally arrive. Instead, justice is the radical future that haunts the time of the present, or the law of the same, and is 'impossible' in an important sense. You cannot claim that this or that social organization is just, as justice is not a present thing. It is an openness towards difference (the future) that is always both betrothed to the law, whilst simultaneously interrupting the calculations of the law.
(Derrida, 2002, paraphrased by Reynolds and Roffe, 2004)

All violence is an attempt to achieve justice.
(Gilligan, 2000)

The concept of *fairness* in Invitational practice reflects an aspiration which is regarded as vital in any intervention that seeks to promote respectful relationships which are free of abuse. *Fairness* is not sought by appealing to a universal code of 'human rights' which might be seen to exist in the form of an external truth and then applied in various sites of injustice. Concepts of 'equal opportunity' similarly construct striving in life as a competition in acquisition, albeit from an equal start, in which there will inevitably be winners and losers. Deleuze points to an ethics which is based upon the recognition and appreciation of differences rather than the application of judgemental standards. Accordingly, *fairness* is regarded not as an outcome, but as an ongoing ethical responsibility and commitment to critique and reflection on practice.

Considerations of *fairness*, within the Invitational model, draw upon Foucault's understandings of power and Derrida's conceptualisations of justice (Foucault, 1971, 1972; Derrida, 1992, 1994). These ideas are understood in the context of Deleuze's ethical project which considers notions of desire and striving in terms of flows of becoming which point towards modes of existence that seek and embrace difference in ways that enhance, enrich and enable life (Deleuze and Guattari, 1983, 1987).

The concept of *fairness* is an ethical position which aspires to the establishment of a 'non-violative relationship to the other' which respects and 'sustains the other's difference and singularity' (Larner, 1999: 46).

Such a relationship entails an openness to difference which:

- respects the other's capacity for thought and action, which is at times *complicit* with and at times *resistant* to, dominant cultural interests and power relations.
- appreciates the creative tension in the contradictions between *complicity* and *resistance* in power relations and the opportunities it provides for inspiration and the imagination of new possibilities.
- allows for the hidden interplays of power relations, in all forms of interaction, to become visible, articulated and open to critique.
- embraces the paradox in holding a position of power in order to subvert dominant power relations.
- fosters ongoing critique of power relations in the relationship with the other.

The ethical challenges posed by the concept of *fairness* are considerable. Fairness requires that we hold an ethical position on justice, which requires our investment in a specific set of power relations with the inevitable construction of power hierarchies. Our intervention programmes are specifically aimed at stopping abusive behaviour. We also act from positions of institutional power, invested in us by virtue of our roles, training and expertise. Our ethical responsibility requires that we engage in ongoing critique and scrutiny of our actions and this context, if we are to act ethically and minimise violence towards our clients. If we embrace this paradox, we must aspire to enact 'a power that is non-hegemonic'; one that does not align itself with dominant power relations; one 'that allows the other to *say everything* . . . to think their own thoughts, to have their own feelings . . . to write their own narrative'. This might be regarded as a 'political *position taking* towards discourses of power which aligns itself with the voices of the marginalised and the many' (Larner, 1999: 44–6). In a similar vein, Deleuze stresses the potential for ethical flows of becoming, in the concept, *becoming minoritarian* which requires subversion of dominant and hegemonic power relations and structures, resisting ownership and control and opening up to what might be possible (Deleuze and Guattari, 1987; Conley, 2005).

The ethics that inform the Invitational concept of *fairness* are based on reaching out towards and consideration of the experiences, feelings and needs of others; recognition and respect of individual differences, particularly in a context of an imbalance in invested power and privilege in the relationship. To responsibly hold a position of power, we must endeavour to ensure that we do not impose or promote unjust expectations, particularly those that might require the man to demonstrate forms of consideration that we are not prepared to afford him.

Invitational practice endeavours to make place for, legitimise and promote protest against injustice. The concept of *fairness* entails an ongoing commitment to protest hegemonic structures and forms of power. Traditional intervention models have tended at best to be ambivalent about protest, frequently regarding it as a strategy for distraction, justification or avoidance of responsibility for abusive behaviour. In that context protest is confronted and suppressed in the name of promoting responsibility. However, the revolutionary and creative potentials in *resistance* to dominant cultural interests and power relations are likely to be ignored or overlooked. To attempt to suppress or pathologise the ethic and practice of protest against injustice is unfair and unhelpful and constitutes a form of colonisation or oppression in intervention practice.

Fairness requires an ongoing critique of power relations in which the personal and political are intimately connected. The practice of *fairness* in our parallel journeys requires that we:

– strive for non-violative relationships that respect singularity and difference in the other.
– never expect anything of the other that we have not provided to them.
– make place for protest in our relationships with the other.

- *How might we challenge violence and abusive behaviour without reproducing abuse?*
- *How might we ensure that we never expect our client to take steps towards consideration of others that we are not prepared to take on his behalf?*
- *How might we make place for protest without diminishing responsibility for abusive behaviour?*

2. Restitution – the ethic of remorse

When it is lucid, remorse . . . is an astonished encounter with the reality of the ethical.
                                            (Gaita, 1991)

The restorative project is concerned with opening up new possibilities through *reaching towards the world of the other* and aims towards restitution for harm done to individuals, communities and culture. The Invitational concept of *restitution* moves beyond ideas about *apology*, as described in *Invitations to Responsibility* and the practices which have become increasingly popular in restorative justice and cultural reconciliation projects. My colleagues and I have described the problems which arise in restorative practice as apology often becomes regarded as an externally prescribed moral obligation which places a requirement or obligation upon the offended person or community to forgive. Practices of apology frequently become captured by Judeo-Christian traditions which link atonement and forgiveness and offer only nostalgic forms of restoration which provide little opportunity for anyone to realise the nature of abusive acts or their potential impact upon others. Such apologies tend to be made in the service of appeasing others or seeking to be released from responsibility for one's actions through a 'quick

fix' of forgiveness and forgetting (Jenkins, Hall and Joy, 2002).

Such expectations are apparent in the demands by a man who had physically, verbally and sexually abused his marriage partner over a period of ten years:

> *I have owned up to it. I am coming to counselling. I have said I am sorry. She should forgive me. What more is she expecting? Why can't we get back together?*

Rather than *apology*, which has become corrupted by misunderstandings, I have found the concept of *restitution* to be more helpful in restorative practice. Restitution involves a process of expanding one's understanding through acknowledging the abuse of power inherent in the original harmful actions, and consideration of the feelings and experiences of the others whom one has harmed. Restitution is informed by remorse, which is centred on the experience of those who have been hurt by the abuse, rather than the sense of personal distress and loss felt by the person who has abused. Restitution points towards renewal, whereas apology frequently invokes nostalgia.

David had abused his partner, Amy, and terrified his children, who witnessed some of this abuse, over a period of several years. David wrote the following passage in an attempt to apologise for his actions:

> *I am really sorry. I will never treat any of you like this again. I think we can make it work if you just give me another chance. We can put this behind us and have the family we have always dreamed of.*

David genuinely felt sorry, and was committed to ceasing abusive behaviour. However, his statement reflects a self-centred preoccupation with a desire for Amy to relinquish her angry and hurt feelings, pardon him, and reconcile with him.

Only when David was invited to consider closely the profound effects of his abusive actions upon family members, alongside recollections of his father's hollow apologies to his mother in similar circumstances, did he begin to recognise the offensive and reactionary nature of his apology. This led him to embark on a patient journey towards a restorative understanding of his family's experiences and needs.

Acts of restitution require acceptance of the abused person's entitlement to make their own judgments about whether or not to relinquish feelings, pardon or reconcile. There can be no strings attached. The person who has abused is prepared to accept whatever decision is taken by the other. There can be no expectation or requirement for forgiveness.

The concept of restitution severs any link or expectation between acts of atonement and expectations of forgiveness and reconciliation. Derrida in his essay *On Cosmopolitanism and Forgiveness* invites us to examine and elevate the concept of forgiveness beyond the popular and banal. He examines the concept of reparation in the context of attempts by nation states to address crimes against humanity, and notes that forgiveness is often sought or offered 'in the service of a finality' where it 'aims to re-establish a normality' (Derrida, 2001: 31). He goes on: 'Forgiveness is not, it *should not be*, normal, normative, normalising. It *should* remain exceptional, extraordinary, in the face of the impossible: as if it interrupted the ordinary course of historical temporality' (ibid: 32).

Derrida highlights a paradox; 'There is the unforgivable. Is this not in truth, the only thing to forgive?' (ibid: 32). He continues, 'If one is only prepared to forgive what appears forgivable, what the church calls "venial sin", then the very idea of forgiveness would disappear'. When we consider that 'forgiveness forgives only the unforgivable', we face an aporia or paradox which opens up remarkable possibilities in forgiveness but which highlights the consideration that forgiveness cannot be conditional and 'should never amount to a therapy of reconciliation'.

Restitution requires a journey of atonement which involves a shift from a self-centred to an other-centred focus, through:

– political realisation about the nature and effects of abuse.
– recognition and reparation for the harm caused.
– resolution, through acceptance of the preferred outcomes of those that have been hurt.

This is clearly a political journey towards *becoming ethical* through *reaching towards the world of the other*. Its reference point is the man's own ethics; his preferences for his own ways of living and relating with others. To facilitate this journey, we are required to be open to the possibility that there may be more to this man than violence, minimisation of responsibility and self-centred demands for forgiveness and forgetting. Our parallel journey requires openness to the possibility that this man might value qualities such as partnership, caring, compassion, mutual respect and equity, yet be pursuing them in extremely misguided and destructive ways. He may be attempting to pursue ethical goals, using cultural blueprints that inadvertently promote controlling behaviour, disrespect and violence.

When a man acts from a sense of exaggerated entitlement and abdicates responsibility for his actions, he will be used to relying upon others to take action on his behalf, in regard to his abusive behaviours. He may not be wilfully cruel or nasty, but he may never have taken the time or trouble to think about his partner's experience. He may be used to relying upon her to tolerate his abusive behaviour, worry about it, try to prevent it, walk on eggshells around it, and take responsibility for coping with its consequences (Jenkins, 1990).

A journey which promotes restitution involves becoming accountable to the experiences and needs of those who have been subjected to abuse:

- *Who is doing the work to address the effects of abusive behaviour?*
- *Who thinks most about the impact of abuse?*
- *Whose job should it be to think about it?*

The ethic of remorse – windows to shame

I have found Raimond Gaita's work to be extremely helpful in clarifying ethics in restorative action. Gaita regards the experiences of *love* and *remorse* as fundamental in understanding ethical practice. Through these experiences, we come to appreciate 'the full humanity', 'inalienable dignity' and the 'unique and irreplaceable nature' of others (Gaita, 1991: xxii).

Gaita highlights the experience of remorse as 'a pained, bewildered realisation of what it (really) means to wrong someone' (ibid: xiv). We ask ourselves:

My God what have I done?

How could I have done it?

The experience of remorse is 'an awakened sense of the reality of another . . . through the shock of wrongdoing the other' (ibid: 52) and is clearly vital in meaningful restorative action.

Used by permission of Michael Leunig

It is not possible to embark upon a restorative journey without facing shame. The experience of shame is a sense of disgrace which unavoidably accompanies deeper realisation about the nature and impact of dishonourable and destructive actions. Invitational thinking and practice is therefore concerned to address the experience of shame and what it means to face shame.

However, this experience of shame initially seems highly restraining and disabling for men who have abused family members – the shame often feeling toxic to the point of annihilation. Shame and disgrace tend to motivate desperate attempts to run and hide from their presence. Many men invest much of their time and energy in desperate strategies to avoid recognition of the nature and effects of their abusive actions. This toxic experience of shame informs much of the initial and ubiquitous minimising and justifying of abusive behaviour.

Here we must recognise a distinction between *shaming* and *facing shame*. When a man faces shame, he comes to his own realisations through recognising a contradiction between his ethics and his actions. By contrast, shaming others is a political act, an attempt to coerce or compel through the attribution of shame and, not surprisingly, tends to further exacerbate avoidance of responsibility. Our work cannot be ethical if it employs shaming practices. Our job is to provide *safe passage* to assist the man to discover and face the inevitable sense of shame which will accompany his own realisations about the nature and effects of his abusive practices (Jenkins, 2005).

Like any set of experiences and practices which relate to power, shame has both repressive and creative aspects. However, shame has tended to receive bad press in popular literature, where ideologies concerning enlightenment through individual growth, self-expression and self-actualisation, have emphasised the repressive potential at the expense of the creative. Shame has tended to be regarded as restrictive; something to be overcome or overthrown along with all oppressive structures; an obstacle to enlightenment and liberation of the self (Schneider, 1992).

However, Schneider invites us to consider the creative potential of shame and to situate self-development in the context of community. He asserts, 'Shame is not a disease . . . it is a mark of our humanity.' Shame can be valued as, 'a pointer of value awareness', whose 'very occurrence arises from the fact that we are valuing animals' (ibid: xviii-iv). Schneider regards shame as vital in social relations because it is 'aroused by phenomena that would violate the organism and its integrity' (ibid: xxii). Shame offers us a warning regarding potential violation and can help protect privacy. 'To avoid the witness of shame' is regarded by Schneider as akin to removing the brakes on a motor vehicle because they might slow it down.

The experience of remorse which opens a *window to shame*, is vital in all restorative projects. In the context of Indigenous–White reconciliation, Gaita stresses that 'national pride and national shame . . . are two sides of the same coin'. 'They are two ways of acknowledging that we are sometimes collectively responsible for the deeds of others' (Gaita, 2004: 8).

Gaita points out such a a dilemma in an address by an Australian Prime Minister who asserted, 'We settled the land, fought the fires and withstood the droughts. We fought at Gallipoli and later stood against murderous tyranny in Europe'; but refused to acknowledge that, 'We took the traditional lands and smashed the traditional way of life. We brought the disasters, the alcohol. We committed the murders. We took the children from their mothers' (ibid: 7).

Gaita highlights the interconnectedness of the ethics, *remorse* and *love* when he contends:

> The wish to be proud without sometimes acknowledging the need to be ashamed is that corrupt attachment to country – I will not call it love – that we call jingoism. The sense of national shame is really nothing other than the plain, humbled acknowledgment of the wrongs in which we have become implicated because of the deeds of our political ancestors and which a faithful love of country requires of us.
>
> (ibid: 8)

Such an experience of shame and remorse does not require debasement or wallowing in self-loathing. This would constitute a *corrupt* or self-indulgent expression of shame. The ethical experience of remorse involves *reaching towards the world of the other* and motivates restorative action through processes of restitution and reparation.

A further distinction can helpfully be made between *discretion-shame*, which enables the anticipation and prevention of a potential shameful act and *disgrace-shame*, which may follow its enactment. Both forms have an adaptive and creative potential in the maintenance of respectful relationships (Schneider, 1992). Effective intervention can allow for a man to appreciate and develop a sense of *discretion-shame* in future interactions with others, through facing *disgrace-shame* regarding his past abusive acts.

However, communities face complex dilemmas regarding their responses to abusive behaviour and attributions of shame. Facing shame can only be meaningful and adaptive when acts of violence or abuse are regarded as shameful within a community and there are effective and accessible means to determine and evaluate both discretion and disgrace whilst maintaining a sense of belonging in the community. Herein lies the paradox of shame. Despite some ambivalence, physical and sexual abuse of family members is generally regarded as a shameful conduct in most communities. However, many communities, particularly in the United States, have sanctioned shaming practices which tend to be excluding and marginalising of those who abuse and which serve to exacerbate shame avoidance (Braithwaite, 1989, 2002).

A further complexity in facing shame concerns the necessary distinction between *disgrace-shame* and *mistaken shame*. A sense of shame can be wrongly attributed or mistaken by men who have abused, particularly when they have also been subjected to injustice and disadvantage. These men are likely to face an additional challenge, which can result in extreme confusion, through ongoing and pervasive subjection to shaming discourses by others. It is one thing to experience shame as the result of realisations about one's own dishonourable or unethical actions. In this context, shame might be regarded as appropriately attributed. However, the politics of disadvantage frequently promotes the attribution of shame to disadvantaged men, when unjust or dishonourable acts are not perpetrated by these men but by others with greater privilege or power.

A disadvantaged man might, for example, experience a sense of failure in relation to not achieving 'success' in the form of certain culturally sanctioned life goals, despite having unequal access to opportunities and resources. A sense of shame may be mistakenly attributed with these experiences of disadvantage or 'failure'. Such attributions can be the result of dominant cultural expectations and interests (e.g. *not being man enough*) or the sense of culpability and worthlessness which often accompanies experiences of subjugation to abuse, marginalisation and disadvantage. These experiences might be regarded as *mistaken shame*, in that shame is experienced when there is no discernible, dishonourable act, which has been carried out by the man. The shame might be more appropriately attributed to others who support or benefit from injustice or oppression.

Mistaken shame is perhaps similar to Nietzsche's concept of *false shame* which Schneider (1992: xxi) describes as 'shame without strength – empty . . . a product of fear and embarrassment, not love and respect', which results from 'having mistaken oneself . . . having underestimated oneself . . . a lack of reverence for oneself', often as a result of 'wrongful humiliation' (Nietzsche, 1967).

Gilligan (2000) highlights the relationships between violence and shame avoidance, particularly in the context of mistaken shame, in his research with disadvantaged men who have committed violent crimes. He regards violence as 'an (misguided) attempt to replace shame with pride'.

> The secret is that they feel ashamed – deeply ashamed, chronically ashamed, acutely ashamed, over matters that are so trivial that their very triviality makes it even more shameful to feel ashamed about them, so that they are ashamed even to reveal what shames them . . . Because nothing is more shameful than to feel ashamed.
>
> (ibid: 111)

The ethic of remorse – recontextualising shame

The ethic of remorse is pivotal in enabling the restorative project. This ethic informs meaningful and accountable restitution practices which can offer reparation to those harmed by abuse and which provide a means for ethical reclamation where a sense of integrity might feel authentic and warranted. Our ethical responsibility is to provide *safe passage* or an environment which is conducive for the man to face and consider several distinctions so that shame can be recontextualised or repositioned from an experience that is restraining to one which is enabling. These include:

- The capacity to identify and name dishonourable acts and the power relations which determine them, in order to appropriately attribute responsibility and shame. The man might then address the dilemma, *Whose shame is it?* He might then be assisted to face shame associated with dishonourable acts he has carried out and define and reattribute the shame he may have mistakenly carried on behalf of others or in the service of unhelpful cultural and gendered expectations.
- The distinction between a dishonourable *act* and the *person* who has carried out the act. The man can be assisted to discover new possibilities and means of evaluating his integrity, through consideration of the realisations, positions and actions he takes in relation to the abusive act. This generally involves a gradual transition from an initial state of dishonour and disgrace in judgements of self, towards judgements that the abusive actions are dishonourable and disgraceful.
- The *person-act distinction* can enable new understandings about the ethical possibilities for reclamation in facing appropriately attributed shame. The painful journey in facing shame can seem meaningful and warranted in the context of the restorative goals of taking responsibility, restitution and reclamation of integrity. How else might the man consider any kind of meaningful restitution or develop any authentic sense of honour, integrity and inner strength; how might he move beyond abusive practices, without facing the shameful realities of his abusive actions and their potential effects upon others? The painful effects of facing shame demonstrate the man's developing ethical integrity and can create possibilities for new and alternative judgements of self as honourable which are earned through willingly taking courageous steps to face the *disgrace-shame* which inevitably accompanies ethical acknowledgement and realisation. What becomes possible is the recognition; *I committed a terrible act*, alongside the understanding, earned through such processes of reclamation; *I am not a terrible person.*
- The vital distinction concerning the man's own initiative or motivation, to address his abusive behaviour, in the face of external expectations and pressures. He may decline or accept our invitations to face responsibility and shame in relation to his abusive actions. Restorative

possibilities are clearly enabled when a man makes his own ethical choice to face shame, rather than accommodates to coercion or shaming by others.

An adaptive sense of shame is of course informed by cultural attributions of shame towards the perpetration of abusive acts. However, justice or therapeutic interventions which are *shaming* may serve only to further confuse the distinctions between the *person* and the *act* and foster accommodation or avoidance strategies. The choice to face shame, in a safe and supportive environment, can enable respectful action, which is likely to be owned by the man and incorporated into a sense of ethical becoming with respectful identity conclusions.

The processes involved in a meaningful and accountable journey towards addressing and taking responsibility for abusive behaviour require facing shame. It is not possible to understand the political nature of abuse, to develop empathy and compassion for others or to engage in any meaningful form of restoration or reclamation of self without facing shame.

Attempts to bypass the issue of shame serve only to promote avoidance or a sense of accommodation, or going through the motions of restorative action. The man's sense of identity remains based on avoidance strategies and on the edge of the disrespectful identity conclusions of *being a loser*. It is in this context that popular formulations which draw distinctions between *shame* and *guilt*, have been rejected as unhelpful in the Invitational model. Such conceptualisations tend to regard *guilt* as a developmentally 'mature' feeling of regret which focuses upon the abusive actions. The action is judged to be bad or wrong. Thus *guilt* is privileged and regarded as a more desirable focus than *shame*, which entails a judgement of the identity of the person who has carried out the action; the person is judged to be bad. Greater possibilities for restoration and growth are seen to ensue, in the supposedly more self-enhancing context of *guilt* (Fossum and Mason, 1986).

I can appreciate the spirit of such formulations in attempting to draw the *person-act* distinction. However, they serve to privilege *guilt* and can promote bypassing or hastening the significant developmental journey of transition from a shameful judgement of *self* to a shameful judgement of the *act*, and the social role that this gradual transition can serve for all concerned. It

might be regarded as 'mature' for a person who has abused to experience shameful judgements of himself; indications that he perhaps is experiencing some understanding of the seriousness and gravity of the act of abuse, along with the potential impact upon the abused person. This level of judgement may be helpful in the context of the principle of *accountability* and in restitution to the abused person, who could feel justifiably affronted by the abuser too readily embracing *guilt* and bypassing *shame*. A sense of reclamation and restoration of integrity is earned through the painful journey of facing shame and committing to restitution. *Guilt* is a concept which has meaning in a legal context, but little relevance as a reference point in therapeutic intervention, where it can obscure the importance of facing shame in the journey.

If a man decides to face and address abusive behaviour and wants to make significant efforts towards atonement, restitution and restoration, he cannot do this without facing shame. To address abuse requires embarking on a journey in which he is assisted to position himself in relation to shame, so that he can *look shame squarely in the eye*. This is an inevitable and necessary part of this journey. Our role is to remain highly attuned to windows of opportunity throughout intervention; to provide *safe passage* with enabling means to assist the man to address shame and to decline means which are likely to be disabling to self and others.

- *How might we assist men who have abused to face shame without shaming them?*
- *How might we facilitate a sense of social inclusion and belonging when we assist men to face shame?*
- *How might we find enabling ways to address our experiences of shame when we recognise our own unwitting violence and abusive actions in our parallel journeys?*

3. Respect of difference – the ethic of generous love

Love is freeing bodies from the organism and subject, allowing their triggers and patterns to interact and form new maps that allow new types of flows and hence new affects . . . Love is complexity producing novelty, the very process of life.

(Protevi on Deleuze, 2003)

When the power of love overcomes the love of power, the world will know peace.

(Jimi Hendrix)

All you need is love.

(John Lennon)

The restorative project is primarily concerned with opening up possibilities for tolerance and respect of difference through practices which entail *reaching out towards the world of the other*. This is an active process which promotes seeking out, understanding and appreciation of the experiences of others, their singularity and their differences.

Violence and abusive behaviour restrain possibilities for tolerance and respectful collaboration in relationships and communities. The ethics and practices of *reaching out towards the world of the other* are closely interconnected with the ethics and practices of fairness, remorse and non-violence. An active interest in understanding and appreciating the experiences of others informs the motivation to cease abuse and make restitution for harm caused to others. New and respectful relationship possibilities are likely to arise in this context.

The restorative project is informed by an expansive concept of *generous love* which promotes and values difference, whereas practices of violence tend to be informed by notions of *domestic love* which support the suppression, control and elimination of difference. Deleuze regarded this expansive concept of love as pivotal in understanding ethics. According to Deleuze, who elaborated concepts originally proposed by Nietzsche and Spinoza, ethics that are in the process of emerging can either affirm or detract from desire and life. They can be productive, creative, expansive, opening up possibilities and embracing difference, or alternatively, restrictive, repressive and reductive of options (Deleuze, 1981; Nietzsche, 1990; Smith, 1997; Colebrook, 2002a, 2002b; Protevi, 2003).

A Deleuzian notion of love departs from common domestic understandings by regarding love as an 'encounter with another that opens up to a possible new world' (Colebrook, 2002b: 17). Such a notion of love refers to a power to move beyond what we know and experience directly; to reach into and imagine the world of the other. Love requires extending oneself through creative and novel connections, which point to new possibilities that may be expansive, and creative. Love entails reaching out and embracing differences. This generous form of love stands in stark contrast to domestic forms of love, which

reflect a kind of capture by dominant cultural interests. These concepts of *domestic love* prescribe requirements for commonality and sameness, along with the suppression of difference. ('*If you love me you will think the same as I do and I can feel entitled to challenge and suppress any differences you express, in the name of love.*') *Domestic love* is not always repressive but can prescribe ownership and a sense of entitlement to correct the other and enforce sameness. The concept of *generous love* fits with an expansive concept of restorative action and supports non-violative and respectful relationships, which privilege fairness and accountability.

Our own parallel journeys as therapists require us to act with a generous sense of love when working with men who have abused. We are required to reach out and become open to understanding ethical possibilities in the man's preferences. Ethically, we can only enable the man to express his own preferences, we cannot impose our own concepts of what is right or wrong.

Gaita highlights the importance of extraordinary acts of love along with the experience of remorse in the development and understanding of ethics. He describes an 'ethic of renunciation' which requires that we keep fully amongst us:

> those who suffer severe, ineradicable and degrading afflictions
>
> (and) those who have committed the most terrible deeds and whose character seems to fully match them
>
> (Gaita, 1991: xxxii)

In a similar vein, Iris Murdoch highlights an ethical task whereby expressions of love enable us 'to see the world as it is' (Murdoch, 1970: 40). Through expressions of love, compassion and justice, we can come to appreciate the reality and humanity of another person. This task has utmost ethical priority in consideration of how we might live.

Gaita's concept of ethics stands in stark contrast to currently popular ethical theories such as those of Peter Singer, whose 'practical ethics' appears to concern the weighing up of relative consequences, in a utilitarian consideration of the 'greater good' (Singer, 1993). Relative, utilitarian considerations can be used to justify any number of injustices in the name of the greater good, including the indefinite detention of refugees, marginalisation of indigenous communities and lying by politicians.

Restorative practice has also been influenced by concepts such as *hospitality* (Derrida and Dufourmantelle, 2000), which concerns the offering of place and welcome to the outsider or stranger. The practice of *hospitality* requires that we recognise our privilege and attend to the needs and feelings of those who may be experiencing disadvantage or marginalisation. Irigaray appears to extend the concept of *reaching towards the world of the other* by inviting us to renounce aspects of privilege by 'unsheltering' the self and becoming 'a stranger in (our) own house' in consideration of 'opening up to encounter' with another (Irigaray, 2002: 45, 70–1).

The term *generous love* was influenced by Rosalyn Diprose's concept of *corporeal generosity*. Diprose regards generosity as not simply an individual virtue but an 'openness to otherness', which is fundamental to social existence and the ethical constitution of self. For Diprose, this concept is intimately linked with social justice whereby generosity 'grounds a passionate politics that aims for a justice that is not here yet' (Diprose, 2002: 2, 9, 14). In a similar way, *generous love* is regarded as a fundamental condition for fair and respectful relationships which is opened up and expressed through the journey towards becoming ethical.

Invitational theory and practice has long been concerned with the principle of *accountability* of practice to the experiences, needs and feelings of those who have been subjected to abuse (Hall, 1996). Our parallel journeys require that we endeavour to hold our practices accountable and open to critique and scrutiny by those who have been abused and their advocates, in order to effectively invite men who have abused to imagine and appreciate the potential harm caused by their abuse. Our work must at all times be informed by and accountable to the experiences of those who have been abused or are at risk of abuse.

Processes of accountability require the active pursuit of opportunities to critique theory and practice in partnership with those who have been subjected to abuse and their advocates, with openness to the obligation to appreciate and incorporate feedback into practice (see Chapter 6).

Over many years, I have struggled to hold my practice accountable to these concepts which inform the ethic of generous love. When a man attempts to justify shockingly abusive behaviour and appears to show indifference, even contempt, for those he has harassed and terrified, I find it difficult to be respectful and open to possibilities. I must make it my business to try to understand what family members have experienced as a result of being subjected to his abuse. If I fail to experience outrage and grief, I become part of the problem. Yet I must find ways to act from love rather than from states of judgmental tyranny when working with such a man. I rely upon my community of colleagues, and their love, for critique and support in this challenging endeavour.

- *How might we ensure that we maintain respect of difference and act from a generous sense of love in the face of adversity and challenge to our ethics and principles?*
- *How might we develop effective practice which is both accountable to the man's experiences and needs* **and** *to the experiences and needs of those who have been harmed by the abuse?*

Summary – pathways for resistance

The schematic diagram below summarises pathways which produce complicity with, and resistance to, dominant power relations and interests. The captive influence of cultural interests and experiences of disadvantage produce a profound sense of mistaken shame and loss of agency. A sense of insufficiency and resignation may be compounded with the shaming attributions of others and the man's attempts to avoid the experience of disgrace associated with his abusive actions. In this context, the man's identity conclusions are those of *being a loser*. Acts of complicity are reflected in behaviour and experience which reproduce exaggerated entitlement and the abdication of responsibility.

Acts of resistance can be reactive or creative. When reactive, they constitute reductive and misguided forms of protest and action which become complicit with and support the sense of *being a loser*. When creative, they open up new possibilities for ethical realisation.

Creative forms of resistance tend to be discovered and actualised in relationships characterised by fairness and respect of difference in which the ethics of remorse and generous love are privileged.

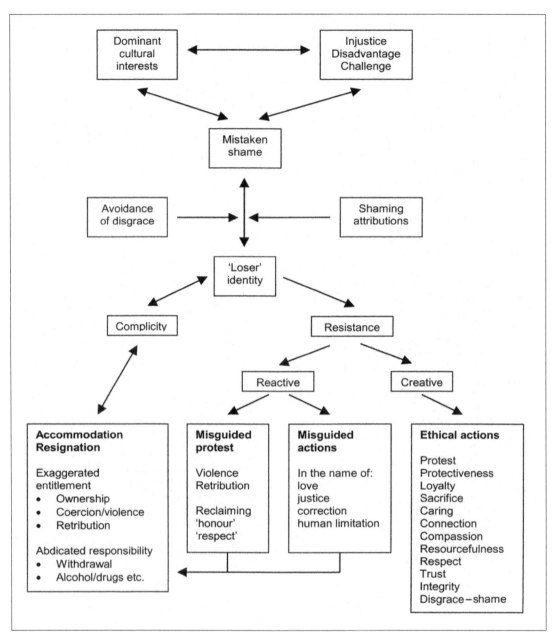

Figure 1.1 Pathways for resistance

CHAPTER 2

The Politics of Intervention

Informing principles of practice

The invitational model is informed by the following principles of practice; *safety, responsibility, accountability, respect* and *fairness*. These principles derive from practical consideration of the ethics of restorative practice. Our parallel journeys must remain centred around the restorative ethical foundations of *fairness, remorse* and *generous love* as we strive to realise each principle of practice. Whilst these principles have remained constant over the past decade, there have been some shifts in emphasis over this time. The principles were initially developed as guidelines for addressing the behaviour of men who have abused. They are now regarded as principles which must inform our own actions in intervention; our own parallel journeys towards becoming ethical.

- The *safety* and well-being of those at risk of abuse and harm remains paramount in intervention. Intervention practices must strive never to compromise the safety and well-being of family and community members.

- Intervention practice promotes the acceptance of *responsibility* by individuals for facing and addressing their own abusive actions and their effects upon others. However, the concept of *taking responsibility* entails an ongoing journey or investment based upon our own ethical strivings, rather than external moral codes or standards.

  No individual can take responsibility for the origins of violence and abusive behaviour which arise from dominant cultural interests that support patriarchal power relations and structures. However, each of us can hold a position regarding our complicity with or resistance to these cultural interests; we can hold a position, in our ethical journeys, which subverts these interests.

  The *parallel journey* entails a political responsibility to invest in a journey of *becoming ethical* which is identical in nature to the journeys we invite our clients to take and requires an ongoing critique and reflection on

our ethics, power practices and the effects of our actions upon others.

Given the cultural and institutional construction of violence and abusive practices, we have an additional responsibility to become activist; to create and support community environments which can support and enable the acceptance of responsibility by individual men. We have a responsibility to resist and challenge practices in community and statutory institutions for intervention when they fail to hold men accountable for their actions. We must resist institutional practices which are organised in ways which are overly adversarial, coercive or shaming and thereby inadvertently promote avoidance rather than acceptance of responsibility by individuals who have abused (Jenkins, 1991, 1994, 1996).

- All intervention practices must strive for *accountability* to the experiences and needs of those who have been or who are at risk of being subjected to abuse.

  The principle of accountability requires that we enact ongoing collaborative processes which strive to ensure that our intervention practices access and are informed by the experiences, feelings and needs of those who have been abused. Intervention practices must be transparent and open to scrutiny and critique by individuals who have been subjected to abuse and community advocacy groups.

  We cannot ethically and effectively assist men to try to understand and appreciate the impact of their abuse upon others, if our intervention programmes are isolated or disconnected from the experiences of people who have been abused. This requires ongoing liaison and collaboration with services and community groups who address all aspects of abusive practice and its effects.

- Intervention practice must be *respectful* to the man who has enacted abusive behaviour and should promote integrity with respect of self and of others.

  Our work should promote ethical realisation and expression through respect of the singularity of others and their differences. The practices for *reaching towards the world of the other* inform our *parallel journeys* and provide a vital catalyst that can enable our clients to invest in developing respect for self and others.

- Intervention practices should foster equity and a sense of *fairness* for men who have abused and for members of their families and communities. Intervention practices should be experienced as fair and just by all whose lives have been affected by the abuse.

  The principle of *fairness* legitimises and promotes protest against injustice and subversion of dominant cultural interests which tend to colonise, restrict and marginalise. *Fairness* is pivotal in informing practice which is non-violative, collaborative and which enables the discovery and expression of respectful ethics. Practices based on fairness provide the key to a sense of motivation and agency to invest in a journey towards respect; one which is not restrained or derailed by passive accommodation or impotent adversarial protest, in the face of perceived invasion or occupation. This principle and associated practices have assumed greater emphasis and significance in recent Invitational practice, particularly when working with men who have experienced considerable disadvantage in their lives.

Statutory context

These practice principles can be best maintained when intervention programmes are situated in a collaborative and complementary relationship with statutory agencies. Much abusive practice violates statutory criminal codes and requirements for safe families and communities, and we are obliged to be accountable to them. It is statutory authorities, such as police, courts and child protection agencies, who have the mandates to ensure safety within our communities and the authority to take coercive action to:

- ensure the protection of those at risk of being harmed.
- clearly and unequivocally label abusive behaviour as unacceptable.
- apply appropriate sanctions following criminal action.
- establish mandates for individuals to address and cease abusive behaviour.

It is useful to draw distinctions between the role of statutory authorities who are empowered in our communities to use coercive processes to stop abusive behaviour and to protect individuals, *and* non-statutory intervention programmes which are designed to effect the cessation of abusive behaviour and the development of respectful ways of relating.

Close collaboration with statutory authorities enables the possibility of a safe context to engage with men in intervention programmes and to make these programmes accountable to the community. This requires the use of specific structures and processes which can ensure ongoing liaison and feedback between intervention workers and statutory authorities. Some of these structures include *limited confidentiality agreements*, reporting requirements and methods for providing feedback on *goal attainment* (see Part 5) to statutory authorities and agencies.

Liaison with these systems can also assist statutory agencies by enabling reform of statutory processes to better promote community safety and accountability by removing restraints in these systems to the acceptance of responsibility for abusive acts. Invitational practices fit well with Restorative Justice processes which can together promote effective and accountable paradigms for the cessation of abuse (Daly, 2005, 2006).

Holding a political position

All practice concerns a variety of power relations and is political in nature. Invitational practice requires holding a political position which is ethical in relation to the five informing principles. The parallel journey for counsellors, becoming ethical, is developed and realised by holding all practice accountable to these principles through ongoing reflection and critique which is situated within a political rather than a psychological context. When safety, responsibility, accountability, fairness and respect are privileged in an ongoing manner, intervention with men who have abused and members of their families is likely to be helpful in stopping violence and abusive behaviour and promoting respectful behaviour.

Invitational practice requires ongoing political consideration, reflection and collaboration to develop:

- Ethical practices to ensure accountability.
- Ethical practices for assessment.
- Ethical practices for engagement.

Politics of accountability

Invitational practice with men who have abused requires that we develop and maintain ongoing practices which hold our work accountable to the experiences, needs and feelings of partners, family members and members of the community who have been affected by, or who might be affected by, abusive behaviour. This entails an active commitment to seeking understanding of the impact and effects of the man's abusive behaviour and the needs of those who have been harmed or who are at risk of harm. We must actively initiate and maintain an ongoing connection with those who have suffered or are at risk of abuse, in order to ensure that our work is sensitive to and informed by their experiences and needs. This connection may involve direct contact with family members or liaison with advocates who can reflect the experiences of those who have been abused.

Traditionally, much intervention with men who have abused has been conducted in isolation from the efforts to assist, and the experiences of, those who have been subjected to abuse. Such disconnection and isolation can frequently inadvertently lead to disrespectful and insensitive intervention practices being developed in the service of stopping abuse.

The principle of accountability raises a series of political dilemmas, especially the challenge of how we might respectfully access the experience of people who have been subjected to abuse without adding further to their trauma. Many women who have been subjected to abuse have felt judged and criticised in their contacts with authorities such as police and clergy, and have become used to often conflicting opinions about what action they should take.

How might we ensure that we hold our work accountable to the experience of those who have been subjected to abuse without contributing to abused persons:
- *Feeling further disadvantaged, traumatised or sub-jugated?*
- *Feeling responsible or obligated to assist in intervention with the person who has abused?*
- *Feeling obligated to minimise or downplay the effects of abusive behaviour, reconcile with or forgive the person who has abused?*

Accountability practices are described and discussed in greater detail in Chapter 6.

Accountability practices are complemented by the concept of *limited confidentiality* which aims to respect the man's entitlement to privacy but not at the expense of the safety and well-being of any person who has been subjected to or is at risk of abuse.

Limited confidentiality agreements are established with men early in intervention practice. These agreements support accountability meetings with family and community members and serve to privilege their safety and well-being. The nature and purpose of accountability meetings is explained along with their vital role in developing the man's ethical journey. Confidentiality is limited in order to:

- provide feedback to family and community members about the nature and goals of intervention and the man's attendance and participation.
- notify family and community members of any concerns the counsellor may have about the safety or well-being of family and community members, as a result of comments or actions by the man.
- notify statutory authorities of any acts of violence or abusive behaviour which are criminal or which breach statutory requirements.

The concept of *limited confidentiality* is presented as a helpful and enabling set of practices. Limited confidentiality offers far more than a means of monitoring and surveillance of the man's behaviour and potential risks to others. Whilst it places priority on the safety of others, this concept enables the realisation of the man's ethical goals in ways which would not be possible without deep understanding of the experiences and needs of family and community members. Possibilities for restitution and restoration would be limited without such practices.

The explanation and discussion of *limited confidentiality* is best initiated at a time when the man is ready to listen and consider the possibilities it may offer. This may not be the case early in the initial counselling meeting, if he is preoccupied with feelings of injustice or highly minimising his own abusive behaviour and responsibility for it. Such a conversation will most likely be perceived as judgmental and restrictive and may lead to the escalation of an adversarial interaction. Once the man has begun to acknowledge an ethical intent for respectful relationships and demonstrated some degree of concern about his abusive actions, this conversation can take place. Until this time it may be necessary to prevent or interrupt conversations which could lead to notifiable disclosures of abuse and a potential experience of deception for the man which could then follow the counsellor's statutory obligations.

At a broader level, the principle of accountability requires that we develop and maintain ongoing connections with community groups, agencies and organisations which provide advocacy and support for people who have been subjected to abuse. These connections can help ensure that we continue to strive to hold our concepts and practices accountable to the experiences of people who have been abused.

The establishment of such connections involves a parallel journey, and requires ongoing feedback and reflection to effectively negotiate potentially adversarial politics in order to build collaborative relationships:

- *What kinds of concerns might advocates have about counselling intervention with men who have abused?*
- *What kinds of experiences might have fuelled these concerns?*
- *How might we listen and research in order to understand advocates' concerns better?*
- *What personal/organisational experiences might we need to attend to in order to listen to advocates' concerns and needs?*
- *How might we take account of these concerns and needs in our practices?*
- *How might we subvert cultural and organisational practices which tend to be adversarial and competitive (eg funding submissions etc)?*
- *How might these concerns and dilemmas reflect the politics in relationships and families affected by abusive behaviour?*
- *What might it mean for our work with abuse to find collaborative and respectful means of addressing these concerns?*

Collaborative relationships between agencies can result in recognition of common goals concerned with stopping violence and building respectful relationships. Theory and practice can be mutually informing and can open up creative possibilities for programme development. Counsellors working with men can listen deeply and take account of the experiences and needs of those who have been abused. Advocates can offer helpful consultation and critique in a context which is collaborative and respectful, rather than adversarial; a political context which mirrors the processes in effective intervention.

Other practices for accountable collaboration are detailed in Chapter 6.

Politics of assessment

Models and programmes designed to address male violence have traditionally commenced with elaborate and detailed psychological assessment. Structured interviews and psychometric tests are frequently employed to categorise the man in terms of supposed psychological deficits and strengths and any apparent risk of causing harm. These methods of diagnosis and prognosis first categorise the man and are then used to guide programme selection. Conroy and Murrie (2007) and McMaster and Bakker (2006) provide a detailed review and critique of risk assessment measures and methodology.

Assessment practices are political in nature and impact greatly upon the man's commitment to address his abusive behaviour. Many men, particularly those who have experienced disadvantage in their lives, will anticipate our scrutiny and (unfavourable) judgement of their defects, failings and flaws. Assessment practices are often conducted in a colonising context, with little consideration of the man's experience of the assessment process or its relation to other events in his life when he may have felt disrespected, ignored, underestimated or 'done to'. A man may well experience a sense of objectification when he is subjected to psychological invasion, in the form of a battery of tests, with the results evaluated by external experts. Whilst these kinds of assessments can be conducted more respectfully, in a collaborative context which is respectful of the man's ethics and agency, it is difficult to establish a respectful context for becoming ethical when this is the man's introduction to therapeutic intervention. The man who has treated others as objects becomes objectified himself. A politic is established where intervention rapidly becomes a context for the reproduction of violence and abusive behaviour.

Ethical assessment practices foster a sense of collaboration which promotes the man's self-assessment and provokes ethical action. The parallel journey requires ongoing feedback and reflection:

- *How might we ensure that our assessment practices are collaborative and non-invasive?*
- *How might we avoid privileging external judgement and promote a context for self-assessment?*
- *How might we prevent the reproduction of violence in the name of assessment?*

Invitational assessment practices

Invitational practice concerns four kinds of ongoing, collaborative assessment where the man and other family or community members participate in the discovery, naming, documentation and at times quantification of concepts which are vital in both the planning and evaluation of intervention. Assessment is not conducted prior to or separate from intervention but is an integral and ongoing aspect of Invitational practice.

These collaborative assessment projects concern the following concepts:

- ethics
- restraining ideas and practices
- responsibility
- readiness

Assessment of ethics

The counsellor remains focused upon evidence of ethical preferences for ways of living and relating which are respectful of self and others. These reflect flows of becoming which open up possibilities and respect of both singularities and differences. They may be expressed in ways which contrast with dominant ways of living that are reductive, limiting and restrictive of difference. The man is invited to notice and reflect upon evidence of thinking and behaviour which might accord with respectful ethics and preferences. He is encouraged to name the ethics and preferences that this thinking and behaviour reflects, to explore their historical development and their significance in terms of the person he wants to become.

Invitational practice is based on the assumption that a man will not meaningfully invest in respectful directions that do not accord with his own ethics and preferences. Consequently, an initial responsibility of the counsellor is to collaborate with the man in collating an ethical inventory which will become a reference point to assist him to consider, develop and evaluate the significance of new steps and possibilities. There

can be no meaningful intervention without ongoing and collaborative ethical assessment:

- *What does this man believe in?*
- *What kind of person does he want to become?*
- *What kinds of relationships does he want to develop with others?*
- *How does he want to be in these relationships?*

Practices for assessment and clarification of ethics are described in Chapters 3 and 4.

Such ethical consideration requires us to engage in a parallel process of ethical reflection and clarification. Without ethical investments in hospitality, fairness, consideration and generous love, we are unlikely to be able to assist the man in his journey towards respect. The counsellor's ongoing journey towards becoming ethical is pivotal in effective intervention practice.

- *How might I create place for this man to explore and express who he wants to become?*
- *How might I listen to and hear what is important to him?*
- *How might I remain vigilant for evidence of thinking or actions which reflect his ethical preferences?*
- *How might these engagement practices fit with the person I am becoming and the ways I am wanting to be in relation to others?*

Assessment of restraints

A focus upon ethics calls for an ongoing, collaborative assessment of *restraints* to realisation of ethical preferences.

- *What is preventing this man from realising his ethical preferences?*
- *What is stopping him from becoming the person he wants to be?*
- *What is stopping him from relating in the ways he prefers?*

Collaborative assessment of restraints is not concerned with assessment of limitations or deficits concerning factors intrinsic to the man's nature or personality. This form of assessment is attuned to the possibility that there may be contradictions between the man's stated intent and his actions and is focused towards recognising and naming misguided ideas and practices which thwart the realisation of ethical preferences. These ideas and practices are not intrinsic to the man's nature or psychological makeup. They reflect the influence of popular and dominant cultural blueprints or recipes which prescribe misguided means for establishing a sense of competence and adequacy and for developing intimate relationships. The man's desire may be regarded as captured or restrained by unhelpful and 'dangerous' cultural interests which are reflected in the misguided ideas and practices that inform violence and abusive behaviour.

- *What blueprints or recipes seem to have guided this man's attempts to realise his desired ways of living and relating?*
- *How might these blueprints be undermining his hopes and visions?*
- *What popular ideas and dominant cultural interests might be reflected in these attempts?*

A developmental history of the man's unwitting investment in such misguided ideas and practices over time and his inadvertent complicity with dominant cultural interests can be mapped. These restraints are represented in patterns of behaviour which reflect:

- exaggerated entitlement and self-centred preoccupation.
- abdication or avoidance of responsibility for his actions.
- over-reliance upon others.

Patterns of over-reliance characterise a common form of interactional restraint; a pattern of interaction which prevents the realisation of ethics. In many situations of abuse, as the man becomes increasingly self-preoccupied and abdicates responsibility for his actions, he grows to be increasingly reliant upon family members to anticipate his moods, to tolerate or excuse his behaviour, to accommodate and defer, all in order to prevent conflict and cope with the consequences of his abusive behaviour.

A parallel ethical journey requires that we engage in ongoing reflection and critique regarding our relationship with the man and his family members and the inevitable potential for interactional restraints in this context which may inhibit the man's journey towards respect.

Common interactional restraints which influence therapeutic relationships include:

- *responsibility overload*
- *responsibility under-estimate*

A context for *responsibility overload* exists when we expect something of the man which we (and most likely, others) have not attempted to provide him with. Such a context for unrealistic and unfair expectations exists when we:

- expect the man to take responsibility for his actions which have hurt others, without acknowledging and appreciating that no-one may have taken responsibility for past abuses or injustices which he may have suffered.
- expect the man to show consideration for others or demonstrate remorse, in the absence of us attempting to understand or consider his experiences of disadvantage or abuse.
- overlook current or past injustices that the man may have experienced, whilst encouraging him to face responsibility for his actions.
- take for granted any of the man's ethical ideas and practices, whilst encouraging him to take responsibility for his own abusive behaviour.
- overlook or disrespect his cultural values.

For example, Rob's (see page 15) 'disruptive' and uncooperative behaviour in the prison men's group is understandable in the context of responsibility overload. Group facilitators expected Rob to take responsibility for his violence and consider its effects, but were not prepared to consider his experiences of injustice and the effects of this. His own ethics and protest were disqualified. Group facilitators inadvertently were expecting Rob to take steps that they were not prepared to afford him. This constitutes a set of unfair expectations which not surprisingly restrained Rob from addressing his own violence.

A context for *responsibility under-estimate* exists whenever we over-privilege our own ethical ideals and fail to explore or consider the man's own ethics and capabilities. In this context we are likely to assume a position of moral superiority and judgemental arrogance. A context for under-estimation may exist when we:

- engage in judgemental, coercive and confronting practices to further our agendas.
- fail to collaborate with the man by imposing our theories and labels for ethics or problems.
- draw on deficit explanations of behaviour.

– employ labels which denote identity (e.g. sex offender, perpetrator etc.).
– proffer unsolicited and gratuitous advice.

Evan's (see page 12) initial reluctance to participate in psychological assessment and intervention is understandable in the context of responsibility under-estimation. Evan had previously experienced assessment and investigation as intrusive and invasive. He was used to 'being done to' and having his own ideas and concerns overlooked or ignored by authorities. His subsequent diagnoses of 'personality disorder' and 'poor impulse control' served to confirm a fear that he really was 'useless'.

In both contexts, we contribute to patterns of interactional restraint which are complicit with dominant cultural interests and serve to inhibit the man's journey towards realising ethical preferences. Through practices of supervision, critique and reflection, we can challenge and prevent such restraining practices and enable our own parallel ethical journeys.

Assessment of responsibility

Invitational practice requires an ongoing, collaborative assessment and documentation of evidence which indicates efforts that the man (and family members) have taken to stand apart from restraining ideas and engage in respectful practices which accord with their preferred ethics. Two structured forms of assessment are commonly used:

• Responsibility assessment
• Goal attainment rating

Responsibility assessment provides a helpful alternative to traditional concepts of risk assessment. Ongoing focus on risk of causing harm tends to provoke a context for hyper-vigilance, suspicion and scrutiny, which in turn can foster mistrust, defensiveness and secrecy and a heightened likelihood of harmful behaviour. The monitoring of risk can further promote tendencies to minimise responsibility and divert attention away from abusive behaviour. Responsibility assessment protocols assist evidence-based judgements concerning safe contact between the man and family/community members and other statutory decisions. However, they involve processes which are attuned to

ethics, individual agency and investments in new and alternative actions. Responsibility assessments are well suited to principles and practices of restorative justice (see Part 5).

Goal attainment rating is a collaborative form of responsibility assessment which forms the basis of evaluation methodology in invitational practice. Structured interviews allow the man, along with relevant witnesses to his actions, to collaboratively canvas a range of ethical indicators in his behaviour and conduct. These include, indices of responsibility for abusive behaviour, signs of facing and negotiating developmental challenges, patterns of self-reliance, indicators of equity, respect of difference, shared responsibility and interdependence in relationships. Evidence of goal attainment is sought and offered for reflection, critique and quantification by all concerned. The collaborative nature of goal attainment ratings allows for a rich interview process which constructively highlights and quantifies levels of the man's achievements and gaps in ethical realisation (see Part 5).

Assessment of readiness

Readiness is a key concept in invitational practice which subverts traditional and deficit-based ideas concerning the man's capacity or ability to take new steps or change his behaviour. Invitational practice aims to address restraints which might inhibit ethical becoming and thereby support a sense of readiness to take ethical steps. The concept of *readiness* concerns the man's motivation and a sense of agency to open up new possibilities and take new steps towards realising aspects of his ethical journey.

A man's *readiness* to take new steps will be enhanced by:

– understanding how these steps fit with his own ethics and preferences.
– feeling that the steps are achievable and the pathway is safe.
– believing that taking the steps may help him achieve his preferred personal and relationship goals.

In invitational practice, readiness to take new ethical steps often hinges on consideration and reflection about the extent to which these steps might promote three vital outcomes in the restorative project.

- *How might these steps help the man to:*
  - *Cease abusive behaviour.*
  - *Make restitution to those who have been hurt.*
  - *Reclaim of a sense of self-respect and integrity.*

It is absolutely vital that a man is able to consider and articulate the significance and meaning of any step he is contemplating, in relation to these three broad outcomes.

Readiness is specifically assessed and addressed in relation to preparedness, appropriateness and timeliness for journey steps which involve:

- Facing up to abusive behaviour
- Facing shame
- Restitution
- Reconnection with family members

As counsellors, we are required to engage in ongoing reflection, critique and supervision concerning our own readiness to participate ethically in intervention, particularly as we attempt to negotiate apparently conflicting priorities established through interplay between the five informing principles. Invitational practice provides an ongoing challenge in attempting to maintain priorities upon safety and accountability to those subjected to abuse, concurrently with respect and fairness with regard to the man who has abused. These challenges are particularly highlighted in situations where the man initially minimises the nature and impact of his actions or appears to regard trauma and harm caused by his abusive behaviour with indifference or contempt.

They went to sea in a sieve, they did;
In a sieve they went to sea:
In spite of all their friends could say,
On a winter's morn, on a stormy day,
In a sieve they went to sea.
And when the sieve turned round and round,
And everyone cried, 'You'll all be drowned!'
They called aloud, 'Our sieve ain't big;
But we don't care a button, we don't care a fig:
In a sieve we'll go to sea!'

They sailed away in a sieve, they did,
In a sieve they sailed so fast,
With only beautiful pea green veil
Tied with a ribbon by way of a sail,
To a small tobacco-pipe mast.
And everyone said who saw them go,
'Oh, won't they be soon upset, you know?
For the sky is dark, and the voyage is long;
And, happen what may, it's extremely wrong
In a sieve to sail so fast.'

The water it soon came in, it did;
The water it soon came in:
So, to keep them dry, they wrapped their feet
In a pinky paper all folded neat;
And they fastened it down with a pin.
And they passed the night in a crockery-jar;
And each of them said, 'How wise we are!
Though the sky be dark, and the voyage be long,
Yet we never can think we were rash or wrong,
While round in our sieve we spin.'

And in twenty years they all came back, –
In twenty years or more;
And everyone said, 'How tall they've grown!
For they've been to the lakes , and the Torrible zone,
And the hills of the Chankly Bore.'
And they drank their health, and gave them a feast
Of dumplings made of beautiful yeast;
And everyone said, 'If only we live,
We, too, will go to sea in a sieve,
To the hills of the Chankly Bore.'

Far and few, far and few,
Are the lands where the Jumblies live:
Their heads are green, and their hands are blue;
And they went to sea in a sieve.

(Excerpt 'The Jumblies' – Edward Lear)

Part Two

Becoming Ready for the Journey – An Invitational Paradigm

Introduction

Respectful practice requires our readiness to embark on a parallel journey throughout which we hold a political position that is ethical in relation to the five informing principles. In Invitational practice, this parallel focus is regarded as the key factor which can enable us to assist our clients to in turn become ready to embark upon their ethical journeys.

The concepts developed and illustrated in Part Two constitute a paradigm for Invitational practice that is continually applied right throughout intervention from initial engagement until completion. The Invitational paradigm describes practices which help shape ethical strivings in our parallel journeys, keeping us attuned to the man's readiness to embrace an ethical position of his own. Through careful reflection and enabling practice, we can prevent unhelpful and restraining interaction and assist the man to open out ethical preferences, face his abusive actions and commit to an ethical journey. These processes, which involve readiness and establishing commitment, are pivotal in the restorative project. An itinerary of steps or stages for the journey can only be meaningful once such readiness and commitment has been established.

Pivotal Invitational concepts and practices which constitute this paradigm will be described and illustrated, in relation to several case examples, in the following chapters.

In Chapter 3, four case studies concerning men who have abused are introduced. These case studies are revisited throughout the book in order to illustrate Invitational theory and practice. The initial presentations by men who have abused can be challenging. Practices of anticipation and reflection are detailed which can prevent our engaging in unhelpful and restraining patterns of interaction, in relation to these challenges. Invitational concepts such as *curiosity about restraint* and *listening for intent* are outlined as practices which can help us to remain open to ethical possibilities for ourselves and our clients.

Chapter 4 concerns practices which open space and make place for the discovery and exploration of men's ethical preferences and strivings. An ethical conversation becomes possible in which there is place for clarification of the man's desires along with protest against injustice. The discovery of *ethics in the face of adversity* and the subversion of limiting ideas about cycles of abuse are central in this conversation.

In Chapter 5, practices are detailed which bring a focus to the man's realisations about contradictions between his ethical strivings and his abusive actions. In the context of recognised ethical preferences, a sober conversation about abusive behaviour can highlight its destructive impact and provoke a sense of shame or remorse. Invitational practices which reposition shame from a disabling to an enabling experience, are pivotal in assisting the man to develop motivation and a commitment to face his abusive behaviour and its affects upon others.

Chapter 6 details practices for ensuring that intervention processes remain accountable to the experiences, feelings and needs of those who have been affected by abusive actions.

In Chapter 7, the Invitational paradigm is applied to a group setting with a focus on ethical realisation and establishing readiness and commitment to face abusive behaviour in a therapeutic group.

Chapter 8 gives an overview of a restorative project

CHAPTER 3

Enabling Ethical Practice

Reflecting on challenge

The initial presentations of men who have abused (and family members) can provide huge political challenges for counsellors to maintain an effective balance between priorities of safety, responsibility and accountability to those who have been hurt, and priorities of fairness and respect in relation to those who have abused. When we attend to the experiences of those who have been subjected to abuse and then hear the abusing person's accounts with minimised responsibility and external blame, it can become difficult to maintain a respectful stance. It can be extremely challenging to maintain faith in ethical possibilities, in the face of ongoing accounts of hurt, trauma and betrayal and the man's seeming disregard for the well-being of others.

These dilemmas are exacerbated when there appears to be little we can do to stop others from being hurt or to create a safe environment for family members, especially children. Such challenges place extraordinary demands upon us to take action to try to stop violence and abusive behaviour and to make it safe for others. In the cultural and agency contexts of economic and time efficiency, where brief intervention is expected to produce sparkling results, pressures for fast and efficient performance can rapidly lead to feelings of disillusionment where we question our own competence and abilities with increasing anxiety, frustration, exhaustion and disillusionment.

It is vital that we maintain ethical integrity in our parallel journeys when facing these dilemmas and challenges. This requires patience, perseverance, preparedness for ongoing reflection and an enduring sense of curiosity; qualities which enable a spirit of generous love. These are difficult qualities to hold onto when our clients present in ways which can seem ethically bankrupt.

Such initial presentations may reflect a profound sense of injustice with feelings of hostility and contempt:

> The little shit deserved what he got.
>
> You bastards always take the woman's side.

> She needed to be pulled down off her high horse.
>
> She shows what she's got, then thinks she doesn't have to put out.

or with indignant minimisation of the nature and effects of abusive behaviour:

> It was an accident.
>
> I'm not a violent man; I didn't hurt her.
>
> I only touched her; I didn't have sex with her.
>
> It has been blown out of all proportion.

Responsibility for violence may be attributed to those who have been harmed:

> She doesn't know when to stop.
>
> She pushed me to my limit.
>
> I wouldn't have touched her if she didn't want me to do it.

and problems of abusive behaviour can be redefined as unreasonable, unfair and conspiratorial allegations:

> You are not even allowed to discipline your children these days.
>
> A man can't even cuddle his kids without being accused of something.
>
> It is not violence that is the problem; it is her stupid ideas.
>
> Surely I'm allowed to get angry now and then.

The man's initial presentation may appear completely self-concerned:

> You've gotta talk to her and get her to see some sense.
>
> She can't do this to me.
>
> I've said I'm sorry; why can't she just forgive and forget?
>
> I'll never hit her again; why can't we just put this behind us?
>
> Doesn't she realise I could go to gaol?

Alternatively the man's presentation may reflect a sense of helplessness and insufficiency:

> *I just snapped; I lost it.*
>
> *I can't help it; I guess I am just like my old man.*
>
> *What can I do? You're the expert; you tell me.*
>
> *I think maybe I loved her too much.*
>
> *If only I knew why I do it.*
>
> *There is something wrong with my head.*

sometimes saturated with feelings of impotent self-deprecation:

> *I am useless; I'm stuffed.*
>
> *I never get anything right.*
>
> *I am just full of shit.*

The nature and effects of challenge

If we take these destructive, self-centred and impotent presentations at face value, we might assume that there is little more to the man than ill-intent, disrespect, an inability to consider others and a general sense of deficiency and incompetence. Any ethical qualities will be overlooked and will remain invisible to us and perhaps to the man himself. However, Invitational practice requires a 'both-and' as opposed to an 'either-or' way of thinking (Goldner, 1998). Despite their disrespectful and self-centred attributions about violence, many of these men will also feel concern about, want to cease and be capable of ceasing their abusive actions.

These self-centred preoccupations reflect exaggerated and reactive forms of culturally dominant, restraining ideas and interests. They are not unique constructions or inventions by these individual men. However, minimisations and unhelpful attributions of violence are usually more apparent on initial contact, when a man may feel wary and guarded about the nature of intervention, particularly when he is struggling to avoid feelings of anxiety, worry, shame or grief about the consequences of his violence. This tendency may be even greater when men present as a result of external pressures such as ultimatums by family members threatening to leave the relationship or as a result of police, justice system or child welfare initiatives and mandates.

The man may feel vengeful and blaming but also want to cease abusive behaviour and long for respectful relationships. He will be well-practised at avoiding responsibility for his actions by attributing his responsibility to external events or factors over which he feels he has little influence. Attempts to address violence tend to be based upon restraining explanations and ideas which inevitably require others to take responsibility on his behalf. He may directly blame others and demand that they change their ways or tolerate his behaviour. More often, his inactivity, avoidance and failure to take responsible action has implicitly required others to take action on his behalf. Family members become relied upon to:

– show concern and worry about the man but excuse or tolerate his actions.
– take initiative to advise, confront or to try to set limits on his behaviour.
– monitor his moods to prevent outbursts of violence.
– try to remove pressures and challenges from his life.
– try to placate or calm him down.
– maintain secrecy about his violence.
– deal with the consequences of his violence in isolation and silence.

This pattern of reliance constitutes a significant form of interactional restraint whereby others are required to work harder than he does to address his abusive behaviour. As family members feel compelled to become practiced in accommodation, deference and in trying to set limits, the man becomes increasingly reliant upon and gradually loses a sense of influence and agency in his own life.

Practices for anticipating and reflecting on challenge

A history and propensity towards such patterns of interactional restraint provokes inevitable challenge for us as intervention workers to enable respectful possibilities without unwittingly reproducing restraining patterns of reliance when counselling men who have abused.

Invitational practice is informed by ongoing reflection in an environment which can provide support for counsellors with ongoing debriefing and supervision. Intervention is most effective when it is conducted with the support of a team whose members can offer ongoing critique and support for workers to find ethical means to address challenges.

Invitational practice requires that we reflect on personal challenges and provocations which arise when we experience self-centred and disrespectful attributions:

- *How is this challenge affecting me?*
- *What am I thinking I should be able to do?*
- *What are my expectations of this man?*
- *What are my expectations of myself?*
- *What are the expectations of my agency or management?*
- *How do these expectations leave me feeling?*

In these initial reflections, we may become aware of experiences and feelings such as:

– impatience and frustration regarding the man's seeming inability to acknowledge and understand the nature and effects of his violence.
– anxiety, urgency and pressure to find means to effectively engage with the man within a limited window of opportunity and time.
– outrage concerning the man's cavalier disregard for the feelings of others whom he has hurt.
– worry and concern for the safety and well-being of others at risk of further harm.
– grief concerning the extent of harm done to others, including the man himself.
– a sense of vicarious shame in the face of the ubiquitous nature of male violence and abusive behaviour.
– anxiety and grief when reminded of our own experiences of violence.

These reflections are not intended to remove or expel any of these feelings. It is not regarded as helpful for us to become desensitised in the face of abusive behaviour and the harm it causes. If we stop feeling outraged, saddened, anxious or concerned about abusive behaviour, we are likely to become part of the problem. These experiences are linked with our own ethics and sense of integrity.

Through reflection and team support, we can become more aware of the nature of these feelings and reactions and better manage their influence in our work with men. There are times when it can be appropriate and helpful to share these feelings and reactions with our clients. However, it is vital that we afford opportunities to our clients to discover their own ethics and to

experience their own reactions, before we offer to share and lest we attempt to impose our own. Reflection can assist us to understand and monitor an inevitable political tendency to allow our own feelings and reactions to be used, whether wittingly or unwittingly, in ways which lead men to feel that we are attempting to coerce or intimidate them to feel and react as we do.

Having identified expectations, reactions and feelings, we can reflect upon and discuss with team members the political tendencies which these experiences might provoke:

- *How might my expectations, reactions and feelings stop me from being open to recognising evidence of ethics and respectful preferences with this man?*

This consideration invites us to identify unhelpful potentials and possibilities which might reproduce or establish patterns of interactional restraint in our relationship with the man. We can then consider how to prevent patterns of *responsibility overload*:

- *How might these reactions and feelings lead me to establish unrealistic and unfair expectations which require him to think, feel and act in ways which have not been afforded to him?*
- *How might these expectations lead to practices which unwittingly foster an escalating sense of injustice?*
- *How might these practices lead me towards becoming insensitive and disrespectful to the man's experience whilst expecting him to become sensitive and respectful to the experiences of others?*
- *What implication might these have for the man's ethical journey?*
- *What implications might this have for my sense of integrity?*

and how we might prevent patterns of *under estimation of responsibility*:

- *How might these expectations, reactions and feelings lead me to establish expectations which underestimate his ethics, preferences and capabilities?*
- *How might these expectations lead to practices which inhibit or prevent him discovering his own ethics and respectful preferences?*
- *What possibilities could these lead me to overlook?*
- *What implications might this have for the man's ethical journey?*

- *What implications might this have for my sense of integrity?*

When we reflect upon, discuss and monitor these inevitable tendencies, we are likely to subvert the establishment of patterns of interactional restraint which tend to disrupt and derail therapeutic intervention. Simply by avoiding and preventing interactional restraint, we open up possibilities for the man's ethical journey and reduce the likelihood of reproduction of further violence and abusive behaviour. We create a vital foundation for respectful practice.

We will now consider practical means of examining our potential experiences and reactions and preventing restraining patterns of relating, in the light of several characteristic case presentations. These considerations will then lead on to practices which enable an opening up of ethical possibilities when working with men who have abused.

Introduction to case examples

Invitational practice will be highlighted and illustrated with reference to the following case examples which represent typical clients who are referred or present for therapeutic intervention. The initial presentations of four men are detailed below. Invitational practice will be described and illustrated in relation to each of the case examples throughout the remainder of the book.

Jack

Jack, aged 28, was referred for counselling in the form of a police ultimatum, following an incident where he shook and slapped his partner, Sue, aged 25, whilst she was holding their four-year-old son, Paul. Sue left with Paul following this incident.

Jack's initial presentation is characterised by feelings of injustice and desperation to reunite with Sue and Paul:

> *She can't do this.*
>
> *She is not thinking about the family and Paul.*
>
> *She should come back where she belongs.*
>
> *You people are always on the woman's side.*

Jack has demanded that the counsellor do something to restore his relationship with Sue.

Tom

Tom, aged 38, did not attend an initial family meeting following a Youth Court mandate that his 14-year-old son, Peter, receive counselling. Peter was convicted of the indecent assault of his 5-year-old cousin, Leanne.

Peter attended this initial meeting with his mother, Judith, aged 32 years. Peter was easily distracted and appeared to take little responsibility for his actions, responding to most inquiries with 'I dunno'. Judith explained that Tom had not wanted to attend the meeting, stating:

> *I don't see what it has to do with me.*
>
> *He's made his bed; he can lie in it.*

Judith explained how Tom, 'tries to be a good father' but he is 'strict' and 'has a short fuse'.

The counsellors learned that Peter received 'regular hidings' with a belt from his father. He was subjected to humiliating punishments where he felt frightened and hurt. Peter had been assaulted by his father in a public place when he was ten years old and this had resulted in brief but ineffective intervention by child protection authorities which appeared to have been terminated as a result of Tom's uncooperative attitude.

The context for responsibility overload for Peter soon became apparent. He was being expected to take responsible actions to address abusive behaviour that others might not be taking on his behalf. The counsellor decided to make further attempts to make contact with Tom and to notify child protection authorities. In a telephone conversation with Tom, he stated that he was extremely busy and was dismissive of the concept of counselling;

> *You people just give him a slap on the wrist.*

Tom also asserted:

> *I believe in discipline.*
>
> *I've tried to put him on the right path.*
>
> *Peter is going down the tube.*
>
> *He just doesn't give a stuff.*
>
> *(What he's done) is the last straw.*
>
> *There is nothing more I can do for him.*
>
> *He is on his own now.*

I have got nothing to say to him.

He doesn't give a shit; well neither do I.

Kevin

Kevin, aged 57 years, was referred on the initiative of his partner, May, when his 9-year-old granddaughter, Susie, disclosed that he had been touching her genitals. May was distraught and confused. She felt deeply betrayed by Kevin and blamed by Susie's parents who no longer wanted to have contact with her unless she separated from Kevin. May was extremely worried that Kevin was 'depressed' and had talked of 'taking his own life'.

Other extended family members thought that, 'too much had been made of this'. Kevin was regarded as a favoured grandparent whom 'the children loved to death'. They thought that Kevin should be forgiven for his 'indiscretions'.

Kevin wept copiously throughout the initial meeting whilst lamenting:

I've done a terrible thing to an innocent little girl.

I've let the whole family down.

How can I ever look Susie's family in the face again?

May has been a rock. I don't deserve someone like her.

I can't go to prison. May needs me. It would eat Susie up with guilt.

I don't know what to do.

Kevin revealed that he had been talking and praying regularly with his parish priest and that he had found solace in God's forgiveness.

Barry

Barry, aged 32 years, lives with his partner, Eve, and their 9-year-old son, Colin. Eve has urged that he attend counselling to 'learn to control his temper'. Eve has felt increasingly fearful of expressing her own points of view and worried about the effects of violence upon their son. Barry's physical and verbal violence has increased in frequency and intensity over the 10 years they have been together. Barry is very remorseful and apologetic after incidents where he has physically abused Eve and promises, 'I wont do it again'.

Eve states:

I walk on eggshells around him.

He goes off at any little thing.

I can't stand the way he is always criticising Colin.

We can't seem to get anything right in his eyes.

At his first counselling meeting, Barry asserts:

I've got a short fuse.

I just snap.

I don't know what happens; I lose control.

Enabling possibilities

In invitational practice we are striving to subvert the development of interactional restraints which are conceptualised in terms of responsibility overload and underestimation. This is achieved through ongoing political reflection and the maintenance of high levels of curiosity about ethical possibilities:

- *What else might there be to this man besides violence, abusive and disrespectful behaviour?*
- *How might I open myself to other possibilities in the face of such challenging and restraining presentations?*
- *What evidence of potentially respectful qualities might I recognise that makes me wonder and leaves me feeling curious to make further inquiries?*

Two enabling themes constitute the initial focus of invitational practice:

– curiosity about initial restraint.
– listening for intent.

Curiosity about restraint

Our initial curiosity may be directed towards the nature of restraining ideas and practices which could be preventing the emergence of ethical possibilities at the initial contact. Rather than wonder about the causes of his seemingly antagonistic and disrespectful comments, we might wonder about restraints:

- *What is preventing this man from addressing and challenging disrespectful ideas and practices?*
- *What is preventing this man from recognising and expressing any respectful preferences?*
- *What might be rendering any respectful preferences invisible?*

In wondering about possible restraints, we might consider:

- *How has this man been used to being treated by others?*
- *How might he be regarding me and my intervention?*
- *How might he expect me to think and act towards him?*
- *What kinds of beliefs might he have about himself?*

A sense of injustice in the context of impending judgement can be highly restraining in initial contacts with men who have abused, particularly those who have experienced considerable and enduring disadvantage in their own lives. Jack and Tom both present in manners which convey a palpable sense of personal injustice. Their assertions of blame and self-justification reflect righteous indignation with the judgements of others and self-centred demands.

Police have recently threatened to charge Jack with an offence and have supported Sue's entitlement to leave him. He has experienced some coercion to attend counselling.

Tom has previously been challenged by Child Protection authorities who regarded him as 'abusive' and 'uncooperative'. He refers to them as 'dickheads' who 'should mind their own business'.

We might wonder about the extent to which Jack or Tom have felt criticised, judged and censured by others, particularly by others in more privileged positions, throughout their lives. To what extent have they felt others have been interested in their views and feelings, listened to them or taken them seriously?

Few men actually expect that we will support or endorse their abusive actions, despite their explicit justifications and expressions of blame. Most expect that we will judge, perhaps even shame or humiliate them. A likely expectation is that we will point out the error of their ways, confront them about their dishonourable actions and chastise them for their inadequacy. The greater the disadvantage experienced by the man and the more marginalised his community, the more likely is this perceived threat of judgement, shame and humiliation. Therapeutic intervention may be anticipated as yet another experience of injustice, of *being done to* by someone in a position of privilege and authority.

When a man anticipates such judgement and humiliation, he is likely to be guarded, mistrusting of us and ready to defend himself against being disrespected and put down.

An initially hostile and uncooperative presentation may reflect concerns which transcend contempt for others and selfish interest, such as:

– concern about invasion and occupation.
– fears of defeat and further loss, including loss of face.
– feeling overwhelmed by shame.

We should not lose sight of the significance of the man's concern about being shamed. This concern frequently reflects an underlying preoccupation or sense of being haunted by shame in relation to his abusive actions. We should remain open to the possibility that a hostile presentation, whilst appearing 'shameless', may reflect the devastating consequences of having judged his own behaviour as shameful and a desperate need to shore up a sense of self-respect, albeit through misguided practices of avoidance and blame.

Patterns of initial restraint can also be reflected in self-centred presentations in which the man appears helpless, insufficient and highly reliant upon others to take action on his behalf. These presentations may be experienced as somewhat pathetic rather than directly hostile but frequently reflect the same underlying fears and concerns.

Kevin expresses remorse at his abusive actions but his remorse appears to be corrupted by self-centred fears of the consequences of his actions; criminal justice outcomes and the potential loss of family connection and support; perhaps where favoured grandparent status is supplanted by the monstrous image of *paedophile*.

Kevin appears as worried about the possibility of judgement, shaming and consequences of his abusive actions as the man who totally denies abuse. I experienced his presentation as a helpless and pathetic plea:

I am not a monster; I am terrified; Please protect me.

The sense of helplessness carries an implicit invitation for others to take initiative and responsibility on this man's behalf, perhaps to reassure, pardon or affirm some essential goodness.

We might wonder about a possible history of this pattern of reliance upon others, including family members and his parish priest. What are the effects of Susie's family challenging this pattern? How might others be taking initiative to address the extended family schism?

- *How might expectations associated with Kevin's pattern of reliance restrain his initial presentation in therapeutic intervention?*

In a similar manner, Barry acknowledges a range of abusive actions, expresses a degree of remorse and a desire never to abuse again. His remorse appears corrupted by a sense of insufficiency or seeming inability to have influence over his abusive actions. I experienced his presentation as a resigned and impotent end point:

I can't help it; It's the way I am.

arry appears to invite us to take initiative on his behalf, either to acknowledge and accept his *limitations* or to work hard to find a solution to an *impossible* dilemma.

As with Kevin, we might wonder about a possible history of Barry relying on others to take initiative on his behalf to prevent and deal with the consequences of his abusive actions and events associated with them.

It would be easy to under-estimate ethical possibilities with all four of these men. Self-centred preoccupations along with apparent absence or corrupt and impotent expressions of shame constitute shocking presentations which might provoke a sense of limitation and incapacity. The maintenance of curiosity about initial restraint promotes patient listening and enables our readiness to avoid participation in restraining patterns of interaction which might overload or under-estimate our clients. We become open to wonder about the nature of expressions of entitlement, patterns of avoidance of responsibility and patterns of reliance in the context of the man's history of life experiences and his misguided attempts to relate and to manage the consequences of his abusive actions.

Listening for intent

This invitational concept is informed by the idea that men who have abused may also embrace preferences for ethical and respectful ways of relating which are not consistent with their disrespectful actions. The concept requires our careful consideration of ideas, practices and cultural interests which may be restraining possibilities in the man's experience and an openness to the likelihood that there might be more to this man than blame, minimisation and disrespectful attitudes.

Listening for intent requires that we observe and listen carefully to the man's words and attend to his actions with curiosity and vigilance for evidence that suggests possibilities of an ethical intent which might transcend minimisation and justification of violence. In this way we can assist the man to draw distinctions between his ethical intent and his disrespectful actions:

- *What is this man passionate or desperate for me to understand about him?*
- *What else might I hear in his passionate or desperate statements, apart from minimisation and justification?*
- *How might I listen, acknowledge and attend to what is important to him, without promoting an irresponsible story?*
- *How might I better understand his intent?*
- *What does this man believe in?*
- *What kind of person does he want to become?*
- *What kinds of influences has he tried to stand apart from?*

When we relate to our clients with a mindset of curiosity in listening for intent, our enquiries are informed by preoccupations which include:

- *What is important for Jack?*
- *What more is there to the person Jack is becoming, apart from self-centred desires to restore his relationship, minimise violence, and claims to entitlement and ownership with demands for others to change their ways?*
- *What ethical preferences might easily be overlooked in this context?*

- *What is important for Tom?*
- *What more is there to the person Tom is becoming, apart from self-righteous blame, judgement of others, vengeance and minimisation of his abusive behaviour?*
- *What ethical preferences might easily be overlooked in this context?*

- *What is important for Kevin?*
- *What more is there to the person Kevin is becoming, apart from self-centred reliance upon others and desperate needs to escape consequences for his actions?*

- *What ethical preferences might easily be overlooked in this context?*
- *What is important for Barry?*
- *What more is there to the person Barry is becoming, apart from a sense of insufficiency, avoidance of responsibility for his actions and reliance upon others to take initiative on his behalf?*
- *What ethical preferences might easily be overlooked in this context?*

How might we approach these men in a spirit of openness to ethical preferences and avoid judgements and practices which stand to under-estimate their capabilities and possibilities for fair and respectful behaviour?

CHAPTER 4

Attending to Ethical Possibilities

Opening space for ethical conversation

On initial contact, there is likely to be little space open for ethical conversation. Jack's sense of injustice and desperation will quickly fill any space, whilst Tom's self-righteous, judgemental, vengeful and blaming attributions rapidly become intense and pervasive. Both men are likely to be sensitive and vigilant for any indication that we are attempting to judge or invade their space. Kevin and Barry both exude a sense of helplessness, impotence and paralysis that displaces agency and integrity. All will be guarding against the potentially toxic implications of facing disgrace and shame.

Our opening comments and reactions generally create a precedent which sets the tenor for the remainder of our contact with each man. We can act in ways which open up space or close it down. When we unwittingly overload or under-estimate, we provoke reactions that are characterised either by protest or accommodation with feigned compliance. Most men, especially those who have experienced disadvantage or injustice in their lives, will be used to dealing with attempts by others to establish influence over their lives. Our intervention will become yet another circumstance where the need for defence will be seen as necessary. In these circumstances, even protest becomes reactive and impotent and opportunities for ethical reclamation tend to be lost.

If our initial enquiries and responses are informed by ongoing curiosity about restraint and readiness to listen for possible intent, we may prevent significant overloading and under-estimating and help to open up ethical space.

The following practices can assist this process to become open, creative and expansive:

- Declaring a just purpose
- Attending to immediate restraints
- Declining attributions of blame
- Legitimising protest

Declaring a just purpose

The purposes of meeting with the man, along with ethical goals, are continually clarified in an ongoing manner, right throughout intervention. These purposes and goals are not imposed, but gradually established in a collaborative manner, in accordance with the man's ethical preferences. This involves an ongoing interactional process with a continual interplay between programme ethics and the man's ethics (Fig. 4.1).

I find it helpful to commence this process with a declaration of *not knowing*, where it is acknowledged that neither of us knows what is important for the other or what the other expects and the suggestion that checking this out might be a good starting point. It is in this context that I attempt to declare a *just purpose* for the meeting; one that is fair and respectful to all people

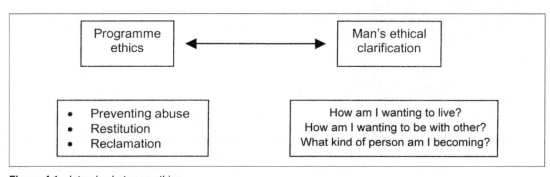

Figure 4.1 Interplay between ethics

concerned. It is vital that this *just purpose* respects fairness and promotes openness for the man to consider his own ethics.

Such declarations with Jack included:

> *I know virtually nothing about you. I only know that Sue was hurt, the police were called to your house and the police told you to come here.*
>
> *I don't know anything about:*
> *– what is important for you*
> *– what you think is important.*
> *– what you think needs to happen.*
> *– what you think about being here.*
>
> *My job is about helping people who have hurt others in their family or people they care about and who want to do something about it.*
>
> *I believe whatever happens has got to be fair and has got to respect Sue, your kids and yourself.*
>
> *This starts with looking at what is important for you?*

These statements and enquiries begin to privilege several important ethical themes:

– accountability – the purpose of our meeting concerns Jack hurting Sue.
– agency and responsibility – Jack may wish to 'do something about it'.
– fairness and respect – all persons affected should be treated fairly and respectfully in this process, including Jack.
– consideration of Jack's experience – Jack's ideas are of value and should be listened to and understood.

In this way, an interplay and balance between programme ethics and space for Jack to consider his ethical preferences could begin to be negotiated. In contrast to dominant intervention approaches, Jack's violence was not spelled out or named in detail, nor was a 'requirement' that he accept responsibility for his actions. Initial references to Jack's recent abuse mentioned only *'the incident when Sue was hurt'*, without specific attribution of responsibility. These enquiries were carefully made to name a purpose that acknowledged that we were meeting because Sue had been hurt but without under-estimating Jack's capacity to consider his own ethical position or come to his own realisations about the stand he might take in relation to his abusive behaviour.

We should carefully monitor the man's readiness to listen to and tolerate such declarations, thereby ensuring that the enquiry does not provoke an adversarial reaction. In this way we can promote openness to mutual ethical consideration and declaration.

This *just purpose*, with references to Jack hurting Sue and the need for fairness, was restated clearly on different occasions throughout the initial interviews. It could then become a reference point for intervention which is never lost sight of and which could later be clarified in increasing detail, in accordance with the nature of Jack's stated ethics and preferences and his readiness to face up to his abusive actions.

My initial contacts with Tom were by telephone, followed by a face-to-face meeting. I acknowledged that both of us had busy schedules and thanked him for making the time available to speak with me. I declared a *just purpose* in wanting to talk with Tom.

> *My job is to help Peter to take responsibility for what he has done and ensure that it never ever happens again.*

I further explained my need to meet with Tom:

> *I always try to work together with parents because I take this responsibility seriously.*
>
> *I believe it would be disrespectful to you not to consult with you about what I do.*
>
> *I believe in the important job that parents have and I need to be sure that what I do doesn't cut across or disrespect what is important to you and Judith.*
>
> *To do this job properly, I need to be sure that I understand what is important for you and what you think needs to happen.*
>
> *I can't do it on my own, I need your help – I need to work together with you.*

This *just purpose* privileges:

– a valid reason to meet – to help Peter stop abusive behaviour.
– respect for the role of parents in addressing problems with children – parents as part of the solution rather than part of the problem.
– collaboration – an appeal for Tom's assistance.
– interest in Tom's parenting ethics.

Kevin and Barry had begun to acknowledge abusive actions and to regard them as destructive to others but presented as helpless, insufficient and reliant upon others to take action on their behalf. A *just purpose*, in these circumstances, might acknowledge beginning steps taken whilst highlighting the need for action and reparation:

> *You seem to have begun to take some difficult and important steps towards facing actions which have hurt family members you really care about.*
>
> *My job involves working with people who want to take action to do something about it – they may be struggling with it but want to take steps forward that don't leave the burden on the people who are hurting.*
>
> *Perhaps this starts with understanding what is important for you and steps you are already taking:*
> *– What have you been trying to do about your actions and their effects on others?*
> *– When or how did you begin to face up to what you have been doing to . . .?*
> *– When or how did you begin to recognise how this was affecting them?*

A *just purpose* is unlikely to provoke an adversarial reaction. These declarations recognise and respect restraining preoccupations such as feelings of injustice, desperation, failure and fear of disgrace. They do not confront or shame but appeal to ethical possibilities and point towards space for their consideration. However, they also recognise that the man's actions have caused harm and that this is the reason we are meeting. This fact should be kept in the foreground as a reference point throughout intervention which can open up beginnings for the establishment of ethical preferences which might later be matched with accountable actions.

Attending to immediate restraints

When men, in circumstances like those of Jack and Tom, are invited to speak about what is important to them, their protest is likely to become apparent with actions and comments that reflect profound and intense feelings of:

– personal injustice and righteous indignation associated with judgemental, blaming and vengeful thinking.
– fear and worry abut losing family or perceived consequences of their actions.

– hurt and grief, often associated with desperate thinking and action or patterns of withdrawal.
– helplessness and failure with a sense of being lost and alone.

They are likely to be regarded by others as 'angry men'. Indeed, they may behave in ways which appear hostile, aggressive and contemptuous of others. They appear to invite confrontation and challenge from others. However, much of this hostility and aggression is an artefact of escalations of these feelings of fear, worry, hurt, etc. in adversarial situations where the man experiences or anticipates being judged, shamed or coerced. He may express surprise that others regard him as an 'angry man', when his affective experiences are along the dimensions of fear, hurt, sadness and shame rather than anger and contempt. He may protest; *I'm not an angry man; I'm not a violent man; It's other people that stuff you around.*

Men, in circumstances like those of Kevin and Barry, may experience similar fears, hurts and concerns. However, their presentations involve much less overt protest and indignation as they convey a sense of insufficiency, helplessness and resignation. They are likely to be regarded by others as 'pathetic' rather than 'angry'. They tend to invite either pity or scorn from others. Patterns of reliance have often become established whereby family members work hard to encourage, bolster or support these men whilst struggling to avoid the consequences of abusive behaviour.

Responsibility overload is best prevented in initial meetings, when we attend to the man's immediate experience and feelings by listening, acknowledging and legitimising their presence. We can endeavour to understand the history and significance of these experiences in the man's life. In this way, we privilege the principle of fairness by ensuring that we do expect the man to consider the experience of people he has hurt, without significant effort on our part to consider and try to understand his feelings and experience.

Jack rapidly began to complain about Sue's actions in leaving and her commitment to the family. He spoke quickly with righteousness indignation and appeared to be working himself up into a self-intoxicated state of personal injustice and blame.

I interrupted his flow and enquired:

Can I slow you down a bit?

I understand that Sue left with Paul last week. You had the police call and you were told to come here.
– Has anyone stopped and asked about where this has left you?
– Has anyone taken the time to find out what is important for you?
– Has anyone taken the trouble to listen to what you think and how you see it?

Jack stopped talking and looked sad and reflective. I continued:

I have a hunch you have had enough of people trying to tell you what to think, what to do and not listening to you – not taking the time to find out what you think.

Maybe coming here feels like just another time where somewhere else is going to point the finger at you and not listen to you?

Have you had a fair bit of this?

Has anyone been interested in where this has left you?

In invitational practice, self-intoxicating escalations of blame and indignation are regarded as contextual rather than characterlogical. These patterns of behaviour are not regarded as part of the man's nature, but as reactions to anticipating that he will not be listened to or taken seriously. When he anticipates that we might judge him or impose our agenda upon him, especially if we attempt to confront or 'correct' his attributions of blame, his inevitable protest reaction will be escalated.

I wondered about possible historical precedents for Jack's sense of injustice and expectations of judgement or coercion. As it turned out, later on, Jack did relate a history of betrayal, abuse, dislocation and disadvantage throughout his life, whereby he felt constantly 'done to' by others, mistrustful and needing to be vigilant about the intentions of others. At this point, without any specific knowledge of Jack's history or life experience, I needed to be mindful and open to this possibility and vigilant in anticipating and preventing any responsibility overload.

Declining attributions of blame

In attending to immediate restraints to an ethical conversation, I interrupted Jack's story of blame and invited him to focus on his immediate

experience; a sense of injustice and concern about being judged, under-estimated and taken advantage of by others and the effects of this experience in his own life. This enabled a shift in focus from well rehearsed preoccupations with blame to his immediate experience; what Jack might be feeling here and now in the context of intervention. A focus upon Jack's immediate experience could gradually become established in a forum whereby this experience would be listened to and taken seriously.

When attending to the man's immediate experience, this Invitational practice of *declination* helps to maintain a focus on his feelings and concerns without promoting irresponsible and disrespectful narratives which attribute blame and judgement towards those that he has hurt. The disrespectful narratives are obviously informed by immediate experiences of worry, injustice etc. However, they serve to distract from the authentic experience which might be closely connected to ethical strivings and concerns of utmost importance to the man. They tend to hijack the man's ethical agency and integrity.

The concept of *declination* was first detailed in *Invitations to Responsibility* and has sometimes been misunderstood as an attempt to suppress disrespectful stories of attribution. These patterns of attribution must be attended to and eventually deconstructed. It is not helpful to suppress them. However, in the early stages of intervention, these narratives of attribution can easily dominate the conversational space and lead to runaway escalations of blame or helplessness. The process of *declination* simply shifts attention from a familiar and repetitive irresponsible story by interrupting it and inviting the man to attend to his own feelings and his own experiences and how they are impacting on his life, as opposed to concern about what others may be doing.

The practice of *declination* is closely linked with the concept of *listening for intent*. If we wonder about what more there may be to a man than his irresponsible minimisations and justifications; if we wonder what else he may be passionate or desperate to get across, we will help create space for any possible ethical stories to be told.

Legitimising protest

As I began to attend to Jack's immediate experience, with concerns about intrusion and judgement, an ethic of *protest against injustice* could be named and legitimised:

There is no way I have any right to judge you as a person or try to tell you what you should do or think.

Do you believe that you are entitled to speak out for yourself if something is unfair?

Will you speak out for yourself here if you think I am trying to criticise you or treat you unfairly?

Have you needed to find ways to stand up for yourself in the past?

How would you know it was safe to speak your mind here?

Why would you trust what I say?

It is in this context that fairness can be discussed and potential injustice through responsibility overload can be named and addressed:

Jack, there is no way I would ask you to talk about what happened when you hurt Sue, when I have no idea about what is important to you and what you think should happen.

It is important to note that steps taken to legitimise protest and encourage speaking out about injustice do not generally lead to escalations of irresponsible stories with attribution of blame or contempt towards others. Such escalations tend to be provoked by attempts to suppress protest or persuade a man to address priorities that he feels unready or unsafe to consider. Legitimisation of protest generally promotes speaking out about genuine injustices where the man has been subjected to disadvantage or where he has been judged, discounted and under-estimated, rather than unfair attribution of blame or justification of his own abusive actions.

As Jack began to consider what was important to him, his *desperation* to restore his relationship and family became palpable. Jack's agitated assertions; 'Sue can't do this; She should come back where she belongs; She's not thinking about the family; She can't do it to Paul; She doesn't care', reflected a sense of anxiety and concern heading towards desperation and panic, which needed to be attended to.

When we *listen for intent*, we might see possibilities which go beyond self-centred desires to restore a relationship which are based solely on a sense of ownership and dependency. Jack was indeed frantically worried and anxious about Sue's actions. How had recent events affected

him? How was he reacting? What was actually distressing him? Were there preferred relationship and family qualities that he felt were slipping away from him? What had he hoped for and desired in this family? Might he really prefer something different from a relationship based on possessiveness and control?

I interrupted Jack's self-intoxicating assertions and contentions in relation to Sue:

Jack, you are making it clear that your relationships with Sue and with Paul are what is important to you.

You seem extremely worried about Paul.

How important are these relationships to you?

Jack declared that he was indeed worried about Paul; 'My family is everything to me.' He then reverted to criticising Sue and demanded that 'someone speak to her about her attitude' in order to 'get through to her what she is doing to Paul'. I interrupted his criticisms and demands and directed a focus back towards his own experiences and feelings:

Would anyone have any idea just how important your family is to you?

Has anyone been interested or concerned about where this has left you?

Jack's affect shifted from indignation towards sadness and I began to enquire about his experience of Sue's departure with Paul:

Were you shocked when Sue called the police?

How shocked were you when she left?

How did this affect you?

What have you been doing since then?

Jack responded that he was 'beside myself', driving aimlessly looking for Sue, telephoning friends and family and drinking excessively. He recognised that these desperate actions led to him alienating himself from his family and were making things worse, but with resignation exclaimed, 'What else can I do?'

We can help prevent escalations of desperate thinking and behaviour by interrupting desperate flows of *self-intoxication* and returning to a focus with *sober* consideration of the man's immediate experience:

Would anyone have any idea how worried you are?

Who would understand how much this has turned your life upside down?

I wondered how Jack might describe his state of mind and suggested some possible descriptors which might assist him to examine his immediate experience more closely:

How much have you felt like you are:
– running around in circles?
– totally lost?
– just not knowing what to do?
– acting in more and more desperate ways?

Gradually the affective focus shifted from indignation and blame towards worry and grief, as Jack was invited to examine and speak out about his immediate experience and as this experience was attended to, taken seriously and legitimised:

Would anyone realise how much you are missing Sue and Paul?

Who would understand how important your family is to you?

Have you spoken out about this before?

Opening ethical space with Tom

A similar process involving attending to immediate restraints, declination of disrespectful stories and legitimising protest was helpful in assisting Tom to become open to actively and respectfully support Peter.

Tom became agitated early in his first face-to-face meeting, following my proposal about possibilities of working collaboratively to help Peter address his abusive behaviour towards Leanne. Tom appeared both exasperated and resigned in asserting that Peter's sexual offence was *'the last straw'*. He declared, *'There is nothing more I can do for him'*; *'he is on his own now'*. He became increasingly agitated as he contended that counselling was *'a waste of time'*; *'You people just give him a slap on the wrist'*; *'You sit back and let kids run riot and then you put shit on the parents'*.

Tom appeared to anticipate challenge about his parenting, perhaps that he might even be blamed for Peter's behaviour. He was beginning to intoxicate himself with righteous indignation about the inadequacy and unjust nature of responses by welfare or counselling professionals.

I interrupted this flow and enquired:

Has anyone ever recognised that Peter has some serious problems?

Has anyone ever taken your worries and disappointments about Peter seriously?

This declination interrupted an escalating story of blame whilst attending to Tom's sense of injustice and concerns about being judged or not being listened to by others. The enquiry attempted to legitimise and explore Tom's concerns about Peter's behaviour.

I informed Tom that I knew he had had contact with 'the welfare' some time back and enquired about whether this had been at all helpful. Tom retorted, *'You've gotta be joking.'* I continued to enquire:

Did you think that they were interested in helping solve the problems or did it seem like they were just pointing the finger at you?

When immediate restraints, concerning a sense of injustice and wariness about intrusion and judgement, are acknowledged, it becomes possible to open up a conversation with ethical and collaborative possibilities. With Tom, I could make my position and *just purpose* clear that:

– Peter was responsible for his abusive behaviour, not his parents.
– Peter's problems were serious and required all of us to work together.
– Tom had clearly been extremely concerned about Peter's actions.
– Tom should never be held responsible for Peter's behaviour. However, it was his responsibility as a parent to help Peter take responsibility for his actions.

Opening ethical space with Kevin

Kevin's expressions of shame tended towards self-centred escalations of hollow sentiment with a shallow appreciation of the potential impact of his actions upon others, punctuated by fear tending towards panic about the potential consequences he might incur. Such escalations are best interrupted with the painful experiences of shame and named and legitimised, before enquiries are made which might open up ethical space and a sense of agency in the face of feelings of helplessness and self-centred preoccupations:

> *What would it mean if you didn't feel more ashamed than you might ever imagine?*
>
> *What would it mean if you weren't terrified about what might happen to you?*
>
> *When did you begin to realise the effects of your actions upon others?*
>
> *When did you begin to see it as a 'terrible thing' to do to an 'innocent child'?*
>
> *How have you been able to see these things and hold these images in your mind, when you are feeling so panicked about what is going to happen to you?*
>
> *What steps have you been able to take to face this, despite feeling so terrified and ashamed?*

Opening ethical space with Barry

Barry's experience of insufficiency and helplessness tended to invite increasing effort by others to address and deal with the consequences of his violence. Barry would then feel incompetent, in this context, as he made increasingly hollow promises.

We might best interrupt or prevent such a restraining pattern of interaction by refraining from offering reassurance, advice and direction. Such a declination may be complemented with enquiries that highlight ethical possibilities and agency:

> *What has opened your eyes to the serious effects of your violence upon Eve and Colin?*
>
> *What are you beginning to realise about your behaviour?*
>
> *What are you beginning to take a closer look at, that you may have ignored in the past?*
>
> *Have you taken a close look at your thinking and actions before?*
>
> *What difference is this making?*

Appealing to ethical preferences

As we *listen for intent*, with curiosity about the man's strivings as well as restraining experiences and feelings, this process is likely to subvert irresponsible and disrespectful attributions. We may rapidly discover that there is more to this man than violence, minimisation and blame. We can open up space for respectful conversation and create opportunities for the discovery and clarification of ethics and respectful preferences.

This process proceeds as a natural progression from attending to the man's feelings and reactions to an initial crisis, towards the recognition and naming of preferred ethics and principles.

It begins with enquiries like the following:

> *Where has this (crisis) left you?*
>
> *What is important for you?*
>
> *Who understands this about you?*

and progresses by asking:

> *What has been important for you to achieve in your relationship, family and life?*
>
> *What kind of relationship, family and life have you wanted to create?*
>
> *What have you been striving to achieve?*
>
> *What kind of person have you wanted to be in that relationship etc?*
>
> *What have been your hopes and visions for your relationship etc?*
>
> *How have you tried to achieve your hopes, dreams and visions?*
>
> *How have you wanted your relationship and family to be different to what you experienced as a child?*
>
> *What have you wanted your children to gain in this family?*

Invitational practices which appeal to the man's ethical sense of becoming require our vigilance and passionate curiosity which are centred in a generous form of love. Men who have become used to and anticipate critical judgement, with a sense of disillusionment and insufficiency, find it difficult to recognise and entertain ethical possibilities. Consequently, our ethical appeals must be sustained and prolonged, at times even relentless, in the face of restraining patterns of self-deprecation and resignation. In this way, we refuse to under-estimate ethical possibilities for the man.

Invitational practices which can facilitate ethical consideration include:

- Listening for intent.
- Ethical clarification.
- Connections through difference.
- Ethics in the face of adversity.

Ethical appeals with Jack

Jack was desperate to restore the relationship and family. His frantic demands and contentions; '*Sue can't do this to Paul*'; '*She's not thinking of the family*'; '*She doesn't care*', clearly reflect a sense of ownership and dependency. However, as I attended to his immediate worry and grief it seemed likely that his desire for restoration might be informed by a broader range of concerns which included but also went beyond the obvious self-centred motivations. Jack's family was '*everything*' to him. He appeared to be missing his son immensely.

Listening for intent

Invitational practice requires a spirit of curiosity about ethical possibilities and an openness to *listen for intent*:

- What else might there be to Jack's desire for connection with his family?
- Might he have hopes or desires for something different in these relationships?

As Jack acknowledged his worry and grief, I cautioned against desperate or hasty actions which inevitably lead to ill-considered judgements and might make things worse, but declared my interest in understanding better Jack's experience and hopes for his family:

> You are making it clear that your family means everything to you. It is all that matters right now but I am completely in the dark about two things:
> – I have no idea about what kind of relationship and family you have been wanting.
> – I have no idea about what led up to Sue leaving and I am concerned about where this has left you.

My *curiosity about restraint* led me to acknowledge and attend to Jack's worry and panic, his desperation and sense of isolation, and tendency towards disruptive cycles of self-intoxicating thinking and desperate action. Jack would not need to continue to complain with self-righteous indignation if the feelings underlying his sense of injustice were attended to and acknowledged. It is in this context of opening space that *curiosity about ethics* could support possibilities for sober reflection upon his ethical strivings:

> You have made it clear that your whole world has been turned upside down since Sue left with Paul.

> You are worried sick. Your family is everything to you.

> Can you help me understand more about what has been important to you; what you have been striving for in your family?

> What have you been wanting?

> What have you been trying to achieve in your relationship with Sue and Paul?

Ethical clarification

This conversation led into unfamiliar territory for Jack who appeared unused to talking about his hopes and visions for his relationship with Sue and his family. His initial responses were superficial; '*I just want a normal family*'. I persisted with my enquiries which focused on clarification of Jack's hopes and visions as a partner and a father:

> How long have you and Sue been together?

> When did you realise it was serious?

> What was special about this relationship?

> Did you have big hopes and dreams about this relationship?

> What kind of hopes and visions have you held?

> What have you been striving for?

> How have you wanted it to be different to other relationships?

> Have you been through some difficult times?

> When was Paul born?

> What changes did Paul bring to your family?

> What have you wanted for your son?

> What have been your hopes and dreams about your family?

Jack gradually began to think more deeply about his preference for a family '*where people care about each other*'. He added; '*People only think of themselves*', alluding perhaps to a long-standing experience of feeling disrespected, let down and hurt by others throughout his life and perhaps also a longing for mutual care and support. He told me that he met Sue when he was 22 years old and described her as, '*the only woman I have ever cared about*'. Jack gradually spoke of relationship qualities that he valued in terms of longing for mutual caring and loyalty; '*you care for each other*'; '*stand by each other through hard times*'; '*put each other first*'. He spoke of the value of understanding and honesty; '*I could talk to her about anything – she understood'*; *'she could talk to me too'*; *'other people only looked out for themselves'*. He appeared to place great value on a sense of belonging; *'we understood each other'*; *'we kind of fitted together'* and respect; *'She was the first person to treat me like a human being'*; *'She said I was the only person that wasn't after just one thing'*; *'It's about respect'*.

When Sue became pregnant, Jack was excited and overjoyed at the prospect of having a child, *'I realised this is it – a family for the first time'*. When Paul was born, *'I kept thinking about all the things I want to give my son'*. As I made further enquiries, he spoke of the importance of Paul feeling *'cherished'* and *'like he belongs'* in the family; *'This is his family where he feels cherished and treated special'*.

Such enquiries are motivated by curiosity and wonder about preferences and possibilities as Jack is invited to consider, name and then clarify personal and relationship ethics. An ethical conversation is developed with ongoing definition and clarification of these ethical concepts within the historical context of their development. Such a conversation is likely to be novel and challenging as concepts which have been assumed to be self-evident or which have been taken for granted are explored and clarified. Ethical concepts are both discovered and developed, taking on more profound meanings through the process of *ethical clarification*:

What made this relationship special compared to others?

How did 'respect' come to be so important to you?

What kinds of 'respect' have you wanted to offer Sue?

How have you tried to show 'respect'?

Jack defined concepts of *'respect'* in ways which included, *'standing by Sue when times are hard'*; *'thinking of her feelings'*; *'listening to Sue'*; *'showing love'*.

He was invited to further clarify these concepts:

What are the circumstances when you want to 'stand by Sue'?

How has this become important for you?

How have you tried to do this?

Through these enquiries Jack was invited into a process of clarification where the focus is shifted

from 'we', 'us' and preferences about Sue's behaviour, towards consideration of ways that he has wanted to contribute in the relationship:

What kind of person have I wanted to become in this relationship?

What kind of partner have I wanted to be with Sue?

How have I wanted to show love in this relationship?

In a similar manner, Jack was invited to clarify his ethical preferences as a father to Paul, by examining his concepts of *'cherished'* and *'like he belongs'*, moving towards consideration of:

What kind of father have I wanted to become with Paul?

How have I wanted to build a sense of belonging?

How have I wanted to 'cherish' Paul?

Connections through difference

Further clarification of concepts is often gained when ethical preferences are considered within the developmental context of the man's family of origin and childhood. Reflection upon concepts such as *'respect'* or *'belonging'* can be invited as follows:

Did you grow up in this kind of family?

Did you see this kind of 'respect' in the family you grew up in?

Did your father believe in this kind of 'respect'?

How much did you feel like you 'belonged' in your family?

How much did your dad stand by you and look out for you and your mum?

How much did you have to look out for yourself?

Jack asserted that his father was a *'selfish prick'* who *'didn't give a shit about anyone but himself'*; *'I had to bring myself up'*. He appeared somewhat anxious as he briefly alluded to hardships and challenges that he had to endure. I decided against inviting Jack to detail these challenges at this time. It seemed premature to shift the focus away from clarification of ethics and expect Jack to have developed sufficient trust to begin to disclose memories of experiences that were likely to be painful and traumatic.

The Invitational practice, *connections through difference*, can be helpful in ethics clarification.

This form of inquiry subverts the popular and restraining notion that men who have abused are simply reproducing abuse they have suffered and are becoming like the people who have abused them. The influential concept, *'intergenerational cycle of abuse'*, is considered an unhelpful and dangerous idea in Invitational practice. This popular concept not only lacks empirical evidence but blocks awareness of ethical alternatives for men who have experienced disadvantage and abuse themselves. The following enquiries are informed by this concept of *connections through difference*:

> *How have you wanted your family to be different to the one you grew up in, for Sue and Paul?*
>
> *How did you come to these decisions?*
>
> *How important has it been to you that Paul grows up in a family where he feels wanted and like he 'belongs'?*
>
> *Do you think that your Dad ever considered these things?*
>
> *How do you think your ideas and hopes have been different to those of your Dad?*
>
> *You are here because you hurt Sue, but who would understand what has been important for you and what you have been trying to achieve?*

These inquiries can be gradually broadened to include violence and concepts of safety and in ways that might be gently provocative:

> *Did you and your Mum feel safe in your family?*
>
> *How much did your Dad stand by you and your Mum?*

Jack responded that his father *'beat the crap out of Mum'*; that he had been extremely abusive to the point where *'I got away from there'* at the age of 13. He moved in with an aunt and uncle but suggested that, *'it wasn't much better there'*. Rather than expect Jack to expand on experiences of abuse and disadvantage, I continued to enquire about ethics:

> *How important is it that Paul feels safe and supported in your family?*
>
> *How important is it that Sue feels safe in your relationship?*

In this way, an ethical conversation can be extended towards preferences for safety and the relative importance of contributing to a family where no-one is hurt; preferences for relationships in which children feel 'respect' and admiration rather than fear and intimidation.

Conversations about ethics require us to remain patient and curious. We must avoid the temptation to engage in processes of subtle influence which lead the man towards conclusions that we might want him to reach. This requires considerable monitoring and reflection in relation to enquiries which concern violence and safety and which are likely to be provocative in nature. An enquiry about preferences regarding safety is only appropriate if the man has himself suggested or implied that violence or safety has been of concern to him at some time in his own life. Otherwise we run the risk of privileging our own ethical preferences and establishing colonising, moral imperatives which usually serve to under estimate the man's own realisations and to invite adversarial protest or passive accommodation. It is vital that we assist the man to choose his own names for his ethical concepts; that we avoid the temptation to colonise his experience by naming his ethics in professional language which can similarly serve to under estimate or dispute his own agency.

The process of ethical clarification is an ongoing one which serves to establish and clarify the man's own ethical foundations. Appeals to ethics are continued throughout subsequent meetings. They provide unique opportunities for the man to consider and reflect upon the qualities that he values and the ways that he wants to contribute in his relationships within his family. Clear ethical preferences provide the only meaningful reference points which might motivate a desire to address behaviour which might violate his own integrity and destroy possibilities for realising the kinds of relationship with others that he has been striving for.

Ethical clarification does not constitute a process of 'positive reinforcement' or praise of the man or his ethics. Our role should not be to evaluate the man's ethical preferences according to external moral standards or whether they please us, but to assist him to clarify how he wants to become in relationships with others. In this way he can begin to establish his own ethical reference points which might help him to become more able to evaluate the effectiveness and consistency of his own actions.

Ethics in the face of adversity

In later meetings, Jack disclosed that his father had physically and verbally abused his mother. His father drank heavily and took little responsibility in the family. He felt frightened of and hurt by his father who ridiculed and humiliated him, constantly referring to him as *'pissweak'*. Jack left home at 13 and moved in with an aunt and uncle. He was sexually abused by his uncle, felt a huge sense of betrayal and felt trapped in this family until he *'ran away'* when he was 15 years old. For two years he *'lived on the streets'* where he had a *'big problem'* with alcohol and drugs. When Jack was 17 years old, he obtained work in a pizza bar. He recognised the owner was a *'paedophile'*. Jack wanted to keep the job so he worked out ways to *'steer clear of what (the owner) wanted'*. Jack worked hard in this job and felt that he, *'started to get my shit together'*. He obtained work in a garage when he was 19 years old; *'I finally got a decent job'*. Despite limited education, Jack completed a computer course and learnt to manage the garage accounts system.

The conventional and dominant wisdom, when working with men who have abused, has been to avoid enquiry about the man's experience of having been subjected to abuse, disadvantage or injustice. This might distract the man from taking responsibility for his own behaviour and encourage him to excuse his actions or justify them as effects of past adversity. This type of thinking could be regarded as an artefact of deterministic psychological theories which seek causality of behaviour in past experiences.

I have found the opposite to be true. When we ignore or overlook a man's experience of adversity, we participate in establishing a *responsibility overload*. We expect the man to act responsibly and respectfully but are not prepared to afford him the same courtesy. In this context, he is more likely to escalate irresponsible stories of blame and intoxicate himself with self-righteous indignation.

If we attend to the man's experience of adversity, a history of *ethics in the face of adversity* may become visible, and be recognised and acknowledged.

As Jack began to relate significant events and experiences in his life, I began to wonder about what appeared to be an extraordinary resilience and capacity for survival, in the face of abuse and rejection, sexual assault and harassment, lack of belonging, family dislocation, drug and alcohol abuse and homelessness. I became increasingly curious about how he had survived these challenges and hardships and how he managed to *'look out for'* himself. Jack asserted that he was *'not a quitter'*.

Jack began to explain how he had managed to *'look out for'* himself and how he had refused to *'quit'*, in achieving and succeeding at employment, despite his disadvantaged circumstances; how he had managed to maintain a job whilst dealing with his employer's sexual harassment; how he managed to learn bookkeeping despite a lack of formal education. I openly wondered about how Jack managed to organise to *'get away'* from his family and make alternative living arrangements when he was only 13 years old. I then discovered that he had even tried to *'stick up for mum'*, before deciding that he needed to *'get away'*. When Jack disclosed his uncle's sexual abuse, his courage and determination became even more apparent and that he was *'not a quitter'* in the face of adversity.

How huge was that betrayal?

What kept you going when you were so let down?

How did you get by when 'living on the streets'?

What were you up against?

Jack managed to leave behind a life of homelessness and to quit drugs. He spoke of the decision to quit drugs at the time when Sue became pregnant with Paul; *'This was it – I knew I needed to be a proper father'*. Jack continued to strive for a respectful, supportive and connected relationship with Sue and Paul in the face of adversity and challenge. Whilst he had clearly not lived up fully to his ethical hopes and visions, it became apparent that there was indeed a lot more to Jack than violence, minimisation and blame.

We could openly wonder about these strivings and thereby appeal to Jack's ethics:

What does it say about you, Jack, that you managed to . . .?

How did you pull that off in the face of . . .?

What do you call that special quality in you that you have been striving to show?

What does it say about you as a man, a partner and father?

Ethical appeals with Tom

Space for ethical conversation could be opened as Tom's concerns about his son's behaviour were acknowledged and a direction proposed whereby Tom might be regarded as part of the solution rather than part of the problem. Ethical recognition and clarification could then be informed by the following themes of enquiry:

- *What have been Tom's hopes and visions for Peter's development?*
- *What have been Tom's aspirations and visions for his family?*
- *What kind of father has Tom been striving to become?*

These themes of enquiry are closely connected to those following which concern Tom's strivings in his relationship with Judith and which became a focus, at a later stage, when it became evident that Tom had also behaved abusively towards Judith:

- *What have been Tom's hopes and aspirations for his relationship with Judith?*
- *What kind of partner has Tom been striving to become in this relationship?*

Listening for intent

I began this process by seeking Tom's opinions about the relevance of programme aims for working with Peter:

That Peter faces up to and takes responsibility for his abusive behaviour so that he:
– never, ever abuses again.
– attempts to make amends to the people he has hurt.
– learns to treat other people with respect.
– and feels respect for himself in taking these steps.

Tom agreed that Peter must never sexually abuse again. However, he reiterated that he thought counselling to be *'a waste of time'* and court response inadequate; *'just a slap on the wrist'*.

I asked Tom what he thought needed to happen. He asserted that '(*Sexual abuse of a young child*) *is the lowest you can go'*. He told me that he had given Peter *'a good hiding'* but added, with a sense of resignation, *'that doesn't seem to make much difference these days, either'*. Once again he declared, *'There is nothing more I can do for him'*;

'He is on his own now'; *'I have got nothing more to say to him'*; *'He doesn't give a shit – well neither do I'*.

Tom looked frustrated, sad and resigned as he spoke. Despite these harsh and vengeful comments, it appeared that he may have held hopes and affection for his son at some time. Could there be more to Tom than his arrogant, judgemental, and bullying manner suggested? In a spirit of curiosity and *listening for intent*, I enquired:

What other problems have you had with Peter?

Tom shrugged and replied, *'He has been stuffing up at school and home for years'*. He related a series of behaviours that had caused offence to others, several of which had led to police cautions. He concluded that Peter, *'is going down the tube'*; *'is on his way to becoming a crim'*; *'just doesn't give a stuff'*.

I enquired about how Tom had responded to these problems. He described a range of punishments which generally included, *'a good hiding'*. Tom asserted, *'I believe in discipline'*; *'I have tried to put him on the right path'*; *'Nothing seems to work with Peter'*.

Ethical clarification

Whilst concerned about the nature of Tom's punitive reactions, I became increasingly curious about the intent of these efforts to discipline Peter:

What have you been trying to teach Peter?
What have you been trying to get across to him?
What have you hoped he might learn?

Tom described himself as, *'honest'* and *'hardworking'*. He seemed proud of having *'come from nothing'* to build up a successful car repair business, *'through my own hard work'*. He had tried to *'make Peter earn his place in the world'*, by helping him to develop qualities which included:

'honesty'
'responsibility'
'knowing right from wrong'
'earning your way'
'doing the right thing'
'facing up to responsibilities in life'

I began to invite Tom to clarify these preferences that he believed would lead to a *'good and honest life'*.

I wondered about the extent to which Tom may have worried and felt disappointment, and in relation to his efforts to assist his son's development:

> *How disappointed and frustrated have you felt in trying to help Peter?*
>
> *How much have you worried about your son?*
>
> *Has this stayed the same or got worse over time?*
>
> *Have you sometimes wound up getting to the stage where you wonder 'what's the point?' where you feel like opting out?*

Ethical clarification, in this context, requires consideration of the development of Tom's ethics, perhaps in the face of challenge and adversity:

> *You have been trying hard to teach Peter to be responsible, honest and to make good decisions in his life. It sounds like you have been trying really hard but it feels like it is going nowhere.*
>
> *What is it that has kept you trying so hard in the past?*
>
> *How have you managed to hang in there when you have been so disappointed?*
>
> *Have there been times when you have felt that you have been able to help Peter?*

These experiences point to deeper ethical possibilities in the context of Tom's strivings in his relationship with Peter:

> *What have you wanted most as a Dad?*
>
> *How have you hoped it would be with Peter?*
>
> *Have there been times when you felt that you and Peter were getting it together?*

Tom initially declared that he had had 'high hopes' for Peter and gradually spoke about hopes for their relationship; that he had 'wanted a son I could be proud of'. He looked back to a time when he had held a desire for he and Peter 'to be mates' and visions that they might, 'ride motorbikes together'. Tom then expressed regret; 'He wants none of that'.

Connections through difference

I wondered about the development of these hopes and visions and began to enquire about Tom's developmental history:

Did you have that kind of relationship with your Dad?

Tom scoffed and responded, 'He wasn't interested in me'. Then he suddenly objected, 'What's all this got to do with Peter's problems?' 'Are you saying I am like my old man?'

I reflected briefly upon Tom's objections before responding. On one hand, Tom appeared to be protesting my intrusion into his private experience, in particular a perceived judgement about his character where he felt he had been regarded as being like his father. I wanted to respect this kind of protest. On the other hand, I wondered whether Tom might be struggling himself with his own judgements of his own actions and making his own comparisons with his father; whether he might be struggling to avoid feelings of shame which often come close to the surface in these conversations.

I apologised and acknowledged that my question might have been intrusive or nosy and affirmed Tom's entitlement to protest. I then clarified my observation that Tom appeared to have been trying to make a relationship with Peter that was *very* different to the one he had had with his Dad. Not only had he tried to help Peter to make responsible judgements, he tried to make a close father and son relationship; something he hadn't experienced from his father.

I explained that I ask these kinds of questions to make sure that I don't make any assumptions about what is important for Tom. I acknowledged that Tom seemed to have had people in the past make judgements about him or try to impose their ideas upon him or his family. To have any chance of helping Tom and Judith help Peter to put an end to sexual abuse, I needed to understand what they believe in for their family, the efforts they have put in and any disappointments they have faced. I needed to be a hundred per cent clear on what Tom believed in as a father, what he valued in his family and to respect these things, to make sure I don't misunderstand or disrespect these values. I needed to be sure that I didn't come in with my own ideas and try to impose them on Tom's family.

Having re-focused on a just purpose for a collaborative project, we were able to continue with clarification of Tom's ethical strivings, their significance and history in his relationship with Peter.

Ethical appeals with Kevin

As the inevitable experience of shame is named and legitimised, space can be opened for ethical conversation with Kevin. Ethical recognition and clarification is then informed by the following themes of enquiry:

- *What have been Kevin's hopes and visions regarding his contribution as an elder in his extended family?*
- *How has Kevin wanted to relate to his partner, his children, his grandchildren?*
- *What kind of grandfather has Kevin wanted to become?*

Listening for intent

My initial enquiries focused on Kevin's expressions of shame in relation to his abuse of Susie. Kevin declared that he would be a '*cruel*' and '*heartless*' person if he did not feel enormous shame in relation to his abusive behaviour. I began to enquire about Kevin's strivings as a grandfather:

What have you wanted to contribute in your family, as a grandparent?

What have you wanted to offer as an elder in your extended family?

What have you wanted to provide for your grandchildren?

How have you wanted your grandchildren to regard you?

How did these qualities become important to you?

Ethical clarification

Kevin referred to his '*life experience*' in having faced and dealt with a broad range of hardships and challenges over his life. He regarded himself as having '*common sense*' to offer family members in times of difficulty, to help them '*stay on the right track*'. Kevin believed that this was the role of an elder in the family. He spoke of having to '*learn things the hard way*', as a young person and cited examples where he believed he had offered helpful practical advice and moral guidance to family members, thereby earning their '*respect*'.

Connections through difference

Kevin stated that he had tried to be a grandfather who was '*protective*', '*trusted*' and '*fun to be with*'.

He felt that his grandparents had been '*stand-offish*' and removed, but believed that his own grandchildren '*love*' and '*adore*' him. In this conversation, Kevin appeared to lose sight of the fact that his actions had compromised '*respect*' and '*trust*' and violated his own principle of '*protectiveness*'. The complexity of Kevin's experience became evident in the contradictions in expressions of shame and recognition of violation, on one hand, and reification of his ethical ideals, on the other. The process of ethical clarification holds this paradox and helps to prevent self-righteous intoxication by enabling reflection upon ethical preferences within a specific context in which abuse has been acknowledged:

What has it meant to you as you realise that there are times:
– when you have not lived up to these responsibilities?
– when it has been more do as I say rather than as I do?

How important is it for you to face this head on and not to run away from it?

How hard has it been to do this?

How might this fit with the kind of man you are wanting to become?

How important is it to you and to others:
– that you stand on your own two feet,
– face fully what you have done,
– try to earn respect, and
– that you don't rely on quick reassurances, forgiveness from some family members or your priest?

What does it say about you that you are prepared to face it head on?

What are you having to find in yourself to do this?

What difference will it make to others and to yourself, as you stand your ground?

Can you respect this stand?

How might this fit with the kind of man you are wanting to become?

Kevin was invited to consider an ethical position which respected his preferences and strivings alongside his realisations of violation. In this way the process of ethical clarification could privilege evidence of agency and independence and allow for interplay and exploration of consistency between programme goals and Kevin's ethics.

Ethical appeals with Barry

As Barry began to focus upon realisations he had made about his abusive behaviour, space could be opened for ethical conversation. Ethical recognition and clarification could then be informed by the following themes of enquiry:

- *What has Barry been striving for in his own life?*
- *What have been Barry's hopes and visions for his family?*
- *How has Barry wanted to relate to members of his family?*
- *What kind of partner and father has Barry wanted to be?*

Listening for intent

Barry appeared caught up in a cycle of criticism, violence, remorse, apology, promises of change and disappointment. He exuded an almost palpable sense of failure as he spoke of his experience. As I enquired about what he had been striving for in his life, Barry spoke of *'trying to get things right'*. He worked as a foreman in a building company where he appeared to hold high standards for his and other's performance; *'They say I'm a perfectionist but you often have to do it yourself if you want the job done properly.'*

Barry was critical of his workmates and would *'lie awake at night worrying'* about the quality of their work. Eve had previously informed me that she was concerned about Barry's criticism of herself and their son, Colin.

When asked about hopes and visions for his family, Barry told me that he *'hated violence'* and that he felt *'disgusted'* at having engaged in such behaviour within his family. He could readily reflect on how much he was *'hurting'* and *'frightening'* Eve and Colin, and was clearly distressed and ashamed about his violence towards them. He declared that he wanted Eve, and especially Colin, to *'achieve'* and *'to be successful in what they do'*. Barry wanted Eve and Colin *'to feel safe and protected'* and *'to feel accepted'* by him.

Ethical clarification

I became increasingly curious about the meaning of the term *'accepted'* and enquired:

> *What does 'feeling accepted' look like?*
>
> *How have you wanted to contribute to Eve and Colin 'feeling accepted'?*
>
> *How has this become so important to you?*
>
> *What times have you felt you have been able to help Eve and Colin 'feeling accepted'?*
>
> *How did you manage to do this?*
>
> *How has this taken you forward in your life?*

Connections through difference

Barry spoke of never feeling approved of by his parents; *'Nothing I did was ever good enough for them.'* He especially wanted Colin to feel approved of and *'accepted'* but felt that he had failed in this regard. There were, however, times when he could acknowledge that he had *'listened to Colin, without jumping in'* or *'backed off from picking him up about every little thing'*. Barry recalled times when he had *'bitten my tongue'* rather than criticise something that was important for Eve.

The processes for ethical clarification can help privilege evidence of agency and competence in a context where the restraining experience of failure is pervasive and dominant.

CHAPTER 5

Addressing Abusive Behaviour

Addressing contradiction – windows to shame

When a man begins to recognise, clarify and acknowledge his ethical preferences, he becomes enabled and in a position to address abusive behaviour, particularly when this behaviour has violated his ethics, subverted his hopes and ideals, and is inconsistent with his preferred code of conduct in a relationship. The man's stated ethics provide an immanent reference point from which he can evaluate his own actions. Accordingly, any acknowledgement of abusive behaviour becomes an acknowledgement that he has made of his own accord rather than one he has conceded under external pressure.

Two extremely significant yet somewhat paradoxical developments are promoted by the processes and enquiries which appeal to ethics:

1. The man is likely to recognise, recall and clarify personal strivings and qualities associated with the kind of person he has wanted to become. He may begin to re-invest and to experience a sense of re-commitment to this sense of becoming. On one hand, this fosters a sense of agency and self-respect.
2. On the other hand, a reconnection with ethics is likely to heighten a sense of contradiction between his ethics and preferences and his actions that do not accord with them. This produces an increased awareness of having violated his own code of conduct and brings forward a pervasive sense of shame.

Invitational practice requires ongoing vigilance for evidence that points towards these *windows to shame*. Such windows can provide opportunities to assist the man to resolve this dissonance by beginning to hold an ethical position, first by naming the abusive behaviour as such and by considering further principled steps to face up to the behaviour and its effects. This process becomes one of establishing *integrity through facing shame*.

Windows to shame often become apparent during the clarification of ethics, without any specific enquiry which directly relates to the abusive behaviour. Evidence of shame is initially likely to be non-verbal. The man may avert his eyes downwards, whilst expressing his commitment to ensuring safety in his relationships or whilst describing the effects of injustice that he himself might have experienced. At such times, it is likely that he may also be recalling and reflecting upon similar actions of his own which have been unjust and abusive. These experiences of dissonance and shame are likely to be fleeting due to their highly confronting nature. However, these windows to shame are indicated by gestures and signs which include briefly averted or watering eyes, faltering or hesitant speech, held breathing, swallowing and small movements of turning away.

Windows to shame can also be signified by behaviour which appears to be defensive, dismissive and even combative or aggressive. This behaviour sometimes becomes evident when men are clarifying details of their own ethical strivings and positions. When dissonance is experienced, the man may appear to move away from a previously stated respectful position or attempt to withdraw from a conversation in which he has seemed highly invested. He may challenge and become dismissive of the counsellor's ethical enquiries or revisit a previously abandoned story of blame or minimisation. Such avoidance reactions are not uncommon reflections of dissonance and should not be misinterpreted as evidence of the man showing his irresponsible 'true self'. A window to shame allows an opportunity to assist the man to consider and explore contradictions and paradoxes always with the possibility for new forms of resolution which can enhance a sense of integrity.

Such experiences of contradiction and shame are inevitably disturbing, can feel toxic and disabling and are likely to promote attempts to avoid or escape. Our major responsibility in Invitational practice is to help reposition experiences of shame from a *disabling* sense to one that feels *enabling* towards a respectful and ethical journey with an enhanced sense of integrity. This requires ongoing openness and vigilance for windows to shame throughout the processes of ethical clarification. Once a man has demonstrated a sense of connection with his ethical strivings and preferences, we can safely enquire about incidents of abusive behaviour and enhance or *provoke* his awareness of dissonance through windows to shame.

Invitational practices which can enable men to address their abusive behaviour in ethical ways include:

- Contrasting intent and action
- Promoting a sober conversation
- Opening a window to shame
- Repositioning shame

Contradiction and windows to shame – Jack

Contrasting intent and action – Jack

A bridge or connection between naming ethics and addressing abusive behaviour is assisted through enquiries that draw distinctions between the man's intent and his actions. Such enquiries refer to abusive behaviour with concepts that suggest there may be *times when you have acted*:

– *in ways you regret.*
– *against your better judgement.*
– *in desperation.*
– *in ways that have hurt the ones you love.*
– *in ways you don't approve of.*
– *in ways that don't fit the person you really are.*

As we *listen for intent*, these concepts are developed from evidence of the man's stated ethical strivings and preferences. They privilege the possibility that he may hold respectful intentions but has acted in ways that have violated his own code of ethics. Such descriptions create manageable opportunities for the man to begin to take steps towards naming abusive behaviour. His steps are therefore ethical and can foster a sense of integrity.

A conversation with Jack which contrasts intent with action, might be informed by this form of inquiry:

Jack, you have made it clear that you have wanted a family where you stand by Sue and Paul, and where

they feel safe, cherished and respected. You have made it clear that you have tried to make a family where everyone feels they belong. Hurting or frightening Sue and Paul is not what you are on about – in fact just the opposite – you have wanted a family like the one you never had.

Have there been times when you have really wanted closeness and togetherness but somehow wound up acting in ways you regret which have pushed them away?

I can only imagine there must have been times when you have wanted closeness but have somehow wound up hurting or frightening Sue and Paul?

A man will often respond to these enquiries with some acknowledgement that he has at times acted against his better judgement and hurt the very people he cares about. If this was the case, we might assist him to begin to appreciate his openness and to consider the ethical implications of this position, where it might take him and what this might mean for his family. This requires patient enquiry which is sensitive to preventing the possibilities of overload:

You seem to be making it clear that you don't feel proud of some of your actions?

Would anyone understand this about you; that you don't need anyone to tell you that you have made mistakes – you have realised this yourself?

What is it that you have realised?

What does it say about you that you can stop and think about your actions?

Would anyone else appreciate that you feel bad about some of the things you have done?

Have you felt under estimated about this?

What is it that others haven't understood about you?

How does it affect you when you stop and think about your actions?

How much has it worried you? Over what time period?

Have you been trying to get close and connected but wound up hurting the people you love?

How much has it felt like you have been trying hard but are going round and round in circles?

How much have you wanted to find a better way?

Who has recognised this about you?

This context for openness and reflection will gradually be broadened into a more detailed discussion of the nature and effects of abusive behaviour. An ethical journey will generally require the man to examine and reflect upon recent and salient incidents of abusive behaviour, in order to understand its nature and impact upon others – to begin to *see it like it really is*. In this way the man can resist the temptation to skip over the harmful consequences of abusive behaviour, make shallow promises and engage in the self-centred quest for forgiveness and forgetting. A detailed examination of an incident of abusive behaviour can open *windows to shame* towards gaining a deeper understanding and a sense of remorse which fosters ethical realisation and development.

Promoting a sober conversation about abusive behaviour – Jack

Jack's response to initial enquiries contrasting intent and action was actually somewhat ambivalent. He appeared sad and resigned for a moment whilst he acknowledged that he was not achieving the kind of relationship towards which he had been striving. He quickly reverted to a familiar pattern of complaint about Sue's actions, in particular her decision to leave with Paul.

Conversations about violence and abusive behaviour can rapidly become *intoxicated*, whereby the man escalates a sense of self-righteous indignation and blame which allows little opportunity for ethical reflection. These restraining patterns of thinking and expression constitute well-rehearsed habits of avoidance of responsibility which are likely to be exacerbated by experiences of shame, especially when dissonance arises from ethical clarification in the face of references to violence. Processes which enable a *sober* conversation tend to disrupt *self-intoxicating* habits and create opportunities for new realisations.

These processes begin with requesting the man's *permission* to enquire about a recent incident of violence or abusive behaviour. *Asking permission* is a simple courtesy that requires us to knock on doors and wait to be invited in rather than barge through, with a sense of entitlement, and forcefully attempt to open up a sensitive and shameful issue. Asking permission models respect of boundaries and consideration of the feelings of others:

Jack, you have helped me to understand a lot more about the kind of relationship and family you have been striving for and a lot more about the ways you have wanted to help build this family. Yet somehow, despite your hopes and your efforts, it's not working out. What isn't clear is what is going wrong.
– Jack, would you help me understand what led up to Sue leaving?
– Can I ask you about what happened last week when you hurt Sue?
– Will you stop me if I ask you something that you don't want to talk about?

Jack agreed to discuss this incident and rapidly became caught up in a familiar cycle of self-intoxicating, righteous indignation about Sue's *'unreasonable'* and *'uncaring'* actions. A sober conversation could be facilitated by interrupting this self-intoxicating flow and by slowing down the process of telling with detailed enquiry about specifics of time, place and experiences of those involved.

Jack had condensed the incident into a brief story of personal injustice whereby he had tried, on two occasions, to telephone Sue from work but the phone was engaged. He arrived home, asked Sue about who she had been talking to and she told him to *'fuck off'*. Whatever (violence) followed was therefore provoked by Sue's unjust and uncaring attitude and behaviour. Jack had frequently rehearsed and edited this account, to the point where any enquiry about this incident would rapidly trigger an emotionally intense and self-righteous outburst of expression which would rapidly escalate into intoxicated outrage.

In this context, it is not uncommon for men to appear to almost re-experience the (condensed) events with passionate intensity as though they were reliving them. Further telling of an intoxicated account serves only to buttress a rigid and limited version of events which precludes any opportunities for new discoveries or alternative ethical possibilities.

I interrupted Jack's intoxicating flow by acknowledging his emotional intensity and invited him to slow down, pointing out that I was unable to keep up with him:

Jack, whatever happened really upset you. Can we slow things down so I can understand how this happened?

My frequent interruptions or *declinations* took the form of enquiries, first about time and place:

When did this start? When did you first start to feel upset?

Where were you? What were you doing?

Was it when you got home or before you got home?

Had you been worried or upset even before this?

Jack told me that he felt *'pissed off'* and *'annoyed'* at work, on the day of the incident, when Sue's phone was engaged. I asked him about the number of phone calls and the times of day that he had made these calls. I asked whether he had been feeling this way prior to going to work. Jack recounted an incident, two days earlier, where he had argued with Sue about *'how her parents were interfering in our lives'*. Jack said he had still been *'annoyed with Sue about her attitude'*. Such enquiries about time and place help to broaden the account of events and their context and create opportunities to explore alternative understandings of events.

I patiently began to enquire about Jack's telephone calls and their meaning to Jack, especially when Sue was not available:

What did it mean to you when Sue was not available?

What were you thinking?

What were you thinking about Sue?

How did it affect you? At this time? Later on?

These enquiries concern events which precede incidents of violence. They can enable clarification of characteristic and long standing patterns in the man's thinking and experience which are associated with the development of abusive behaviour. In particular, clarification and appropriate naming of the man's emotional experience is enabled.

Jack described patterns of thinking about Sue being unavailable when he called; *'I was really angry'*; *'She's always on the bloody phone to her friends'*; *'They put stupid ideas in her head'*; *'She knows I ring at that time'*.

I wondered about Jack's emotional experience. He appeared to be describing a context for feelings of *disappointment, worry or hurt* as opposed to *anger*:

Jack, how much have you worried about Sue's contact with her friends?

How worried were you when she wasn't available on the phone?

How much did you feel let down?

I began to enquire about the nature and intent of Jack's telephone calls to Sue:

These phone calls sound important to you?

How often do you make these calls to Sue?

What is the reason for making the calls?

What is important to you when you call Sue?

What is it you are trying to connect about?

Do you think Sue sees the calls the same way that you do?

We clarified that Jack telephoned Sue up to four or five times each day. Jack regarded these phone calls as expressions of love and connection; *'reminding that I care about (Sue and Paul)'*. He recognised that Sue saw this very differently, often regarding the phone calls as intrusive. I took care to name clearly and without any judgment, this difference in perception. Jack acknowledged that he did *worry* about Sue's commitment to the family when he considered her unavailability on the phone, her desire for contact with friends and the fact that she found many of his calls unwanted and intrusive.

It is vital that we take time to patiently explore and understand the man's experience and perceptions without judgment or evaluation. Tempting as it may be to advise him that his thinking and actions are possessive and controlling, our role is to broaden the context and the accounts of events by opening up possibilities, differences and alternative versions; to establish conditions whereby he can make his own judgments based on his own ethics:

Jack, you are wanting to connect with Sue; trying to show love and caring through your phone calls. You are making it clear that you worry about Sue's commitment and about your relationship and you try to make a connection.

Sue seems to see it differently. She worries about your phone calls and finds them smothering. They have the opposite effect to connection.

What were you thinking? How worried were you? How disappointed? How hurt were you feeling on that day when you left work?

Through declination and detailed enquiry, we can gradually enable a broader and more sober reflection upon events and experiences. I enquired about Jack's experience as he was driving home from work. Jack made it clear that he was becoming increasingly preoccupied with thoughts such as; *'She thinks more of her friends than her family'*. I asked him to rate the intensities of feeling *disappointed*, *let down* and *hurt* on a 10 point scale. Jack rated himself nine out of a possible 10, with regard to feeling *hurt*, before he had even arrived home.

Jack was invited to describe in detail his experience and actions after getting out of the car and entering the house. He was also invited to try to imagine Sue's experience and to recall her actions at each discernable point leading up to and including their dispute and the incidents of violence. When a condensed version of events is expanded and detailed, a broader range of possibilities becomes apparent. Such enquiries take the form:

What were you thinking?

What were you feeling?

What did you say?

What did you do?

What did Sue say?

What did she do?

What do you imagine she was thinking?

What do you imagine she was feeling?

Given his previously stated ethical commitments, I continued to wonder and enquire about what it was that Jack had hoped to establish apart from dispute and violence. Accordingly, I maintained a focus upon Jack's intent in my enquiries:

What was it that you were really wanting when you phoned?

What were you really hoping to achieve when you arrived home?

What was it that was important for you to try to bring about?

How worried were you feeling?

How frustrated and hurt were you feeling?

These enquiries help to punctuate and extend Jack's account of events and by enabling sober reflection. Jack could identify familiar patterns of thinking which included, *'She doesn't care about me'*; *'She doesn't give a shit about the family'*; *'She thinks more about other people'*. He could begin to name patterns of familiar intoxicating feeling states which escalated from *worry* to *hurt* and

frustration, eventually culminating in *indignation* and *contempt*.

Jack recognised that Sue was probably feeling *'pressured'* by him and *'frustrated'* at first and eventually *'scared and hurt'*. I invited Jack to consider Sue's actions and to speculate her likely intent:

What do you think Sue was trying to make happen when she said . . .?

Many men will begin to notice events, actions and reactions of others that they had never previously recognised whilst under the influence of self-intoxicating preoccupations and feelings. On noticing a man appearing to engage in sober reflection, I might enquire:

What are you seeing?

What are you realising?

What are you opening your eyes to?

What are you noticing now that wasn't clear before?

In sober reflection and conversation, men will frequently make new realisations about their partner's likely experiences, including their feelings of fear and intimidation and attempts to placate, avoid further conflict and violence, and protect their children.

In the course of this conversation, Jack complained that Sue had refused to answer his questions about who she had been talking to and that she swore at him. Sue then picked up Paul (who had witnessed these events) and went to leave the room. Once again, Jack became increasingly agitated and righteously indignant as he related these events; *'She told me to fuck off!'*; *She just walked away!'* I interrupted this flow, noting Jack's likely hopes and intent and enquired further about his experience and how he imagined Sue's experience:

You sound like you were really wanting reassurance from Sue more than anything; you were really wanting connection but headed in a totally different direction.
– What do you think Sue was thinking and feeling?
– Why do you think she went to leave?
– Why do you think she took Paul with her?
– What did you wind up thinking at the time?
– What did you think about Sue then?
– How big was the hurt feeling at that time?

Jack imagined that Sue was probably feeling *'frustrated'* and thinking, *'she'd had enough'*. He began to speculate that perhaps, *'She didn't want Paul to see any more (of the dispute)'* but quickly reverted back to righteous indignation, *'She said (fuck off) in front of Paul!'*

Once again, I interrupted this flow and enquired about Jack's experience at this time. He rated his levels of *hurt* and *frustration* as *'over the top (of the 10 point scale) – about 15'*; *'I needed to teach her a lesson'*. Jack said that he tried to talk to Sue. Once again, I acknowledged his hopes and intent and enquired about what he said and how loudly he was speaking. Jack acknowledged that he was shouting at Sue and that he called her a *'stupid bitch'*. He told me that he, *'might have pushed Sue a bit'*; *'I can't really remember what happened'*. I acknowledged the difficulty in recalling events that are so hurtful and shocking:

I know it's not easy to look back at times when things are going exactly the opposite to what you are trying to do; when there is so much hurt. Nobody would want to remember these times. But how can you understand where it's going wrong if you don't take a really close look?

Once again, the aspect of Jack's intent with hopes for connection with Sue is kept in the foreground along with what appears to be vengeful feelings and thoughts of retribution. A sober conversation is greatly facilitated when we can appreciate this complexity in Jack's experience.

Opening a window to shame – Jack

Jack acknowledged that he grabbed Sue, started to shake her and then slapped Sue's face. He once again appeared somewhat indignant as he began to recall feeling hurt whilst describing this physical violence. Rather than invite further descriptions of the violence, I thought back to recent conversations about Jack's aspirations as a father, his recognition that Sue may have tried to protect Paul in this dispute and his stated concern about Sue swearing in Paul's presence. I decided instead to enquire about Paul's likely experience but in the form of a *provocation*:

Where is Paul as you are shouting at and grabbing Sue?

Jack immediately looked shaken and averted his eyes downwards. Not surprisingly, this enquiry appeared to open a window to shame.

An Invitational *provocation* is a timely enquiry which is informed by knowledge and understanding of the man's ethics and an emerging awareness of a substantial contradiction between ethics and actions. A *provocation* points boldly and directly towards a shocking incongruity; in this case Jack's striving to be a respectful and protective father whilst at the same time acting in ways that will clearly make his son frightened of his father. A *provocation* can be distinguished from a *confrontation* by virtue of its origins which are centred in the man's own stated ethical commitments and his growing willingness to face and consider his unethical actions. He must be ready to hold and appreciate this contradiction or paradox. He confronts himself rather than being subjected to confrontation.

An alternative *provocation* might attend to Jack's previously stated ethics about wanting Sue to feel safe and respected, alongside his recollection of feeling 15 out of 10 hurt and *'need(ing) to teach (Sue) a lesson'*. As Jack recalled grabbing Sue, I might have enquired:

You are feeling 15 out of 10 hurt; how much are you wanting to hurt Sue right now?

In this case, Jack would be invited to imagine being there at the time of the incident but also being present here and now. Once again, a shocking contradiction that expresses two truths is highlighted. Jack does not want to hurt the woman he loves, yet he clearly has entertained vengeful thoughts of causing her harm.

Repositioning shame – Jack

Opening a window to shame enables possibilities for Jack to experience a deeper sense of remorse; *to look shame in the eye; to see (abusive behaviour) like it really is*. However, this experience can also be disabling, promoting a sense of diminishment, humiliation and avoidance. Our role must now be to provide *safe passage* for the man to gain an ethical experience of remorse. I wanted to assist Jack to name and explore this experience along with its meanings and possibilities for ethical reclamation; to assist him to reposition the experience of shame from one which feels disabling to one which is potentially enabling of respect and integrity.

Jack looked shaken with his eyes downcast. He looked ashamed. I gently commented on my observation and enquired:

I can see you don't feel proud about what you did.

What are you seeing?

What are you realising when you look at Paul?

His eyes watered and Jack replied falteringly that he could '*see*' Paul because Sue had been holding him when he grabbed her. I continued:

What are you seeing?

What is happening with Paul?

Jack's eyes filled with tears as he responded, '*He is shit scared – terrified*'.

What tells you that he is that scared?

Jack described Paul '*cowering on the floor*'. He could tell by '*the look in his eyes*'.

Who is he frightened of?

Jack acknowledged he had made his son afraid of him. I returned to Jack's stated hopes and intent as a father:

That's just the opposite to what you have been striving towards for Jack.

I then acknowledged Jack's openness and initiative:

Jack, you don't need other people telling you that what you did was wrong, you can see this for yourself; you know it in your own heart – and you can face it too.

Here was an image with the capacity to haunt Jack; its shocking nature evoking intense shame through the contradiction represented in the violation of certain ethics that are precious to him. Jack was now experiencing intense feelings of shame with the recognition that he has exposed his son to terrifying violence. This moment of recognition and realisation is akin to Deleuze's description of the *stutter* – a moment of shock, disturbance and disruption of the familiar – and points to an ethical form of remorse, as described by Gaita (Deleuze, 1997; Gaita, 1991). Such recognition has enormous potential to connect Jack with his own ethics and motivate him to take action.

Jack's initial reaction to this shocking incongruity was to discount his own ethical capacity; '*I'm just like my old man*'. This characteristic *cycle-of-violence* identity conclusion (*I'm worthless, just like my father*) which follows an unbearable experience of shame is likely to be disabling and to promote familiar patterns of avoidance, minimisation and justification of his actions. We must assist Jack to find an enabling way to stay with the experience of shame; a way which might foster accountability for his actions and an ethical reclamation with a sense of integrity. Further enquiries are made in ways which allow for ethical possibilities and meanings to be considered and acknowledged:

Jack, you are seeing Paul terrified of his Dad.

Have you stood your ground – Have you let yourself look closely at this before?

How is it affecting you?

Jack responded; '*I've never felt so low*'; '*I'm an arsehole*'. These responses reflect levels of disgrace that would appear inevitable, given his stated ethics, but lead Jack towards identity conclusions about worthlessness. Could this intense experience of shame not also reflect an affirmation of ethics and a potential reclamation of integrity? I wondered and enquired:

Jack, if you could see Paul terrified of his Dad and you didn't feel low and ashamed; What would that say about you? What would it say about you as a Dad? What kind of person would you be?

Is this the first time you have taken such a close look?

Is this the first time you have stopped to think and spoken out?

How much does it hurt? What is it taking for you to stay with that picture of Paul and not run away?

Would an 'arsehole' stand his ground and face it?

What would an 'arsehole' do in a situation like this?

What does it say about you that you are taking a close look, that you are not running away, even though it hurts like hell – that you do feel so low and ashamed?

The aim of these enquiries is not to diminish or remove the experience of shame. This experience will be pivotal for any possible ethical reclamation. Repositioning shame simply points to or opens possibilities for ethical consideration and action which might promote investment in the difficult journey of reclamation. Jack would rightly protest if he felt we were attempting to exonerate him from shame. He might, for example, contemptuously assert; *'That isn't going to make me feel OK!'* We would need to address this misunderstanding by returning to the ethical dilemma and the necessary experience of shame:

> *You have just begun to take a close look at actions you could never feel good about and it has shocked you to your core. If you could sit here now and feel OK, what would that mean?*
>
> *This is not about feeling better, it's about what you might do about it – whether you face it or run from it and leave it to others to feel bad about. It feels unbearable when you stand your ground.*
>
> *Wouldn't everything you have told me you believe in be bullshit, if you were feeling OK, after what you have just taken a close look at?*

Given Jack's initial tendency towards disabling identity conclusions, that he might possess an abusive nature 'like his father', we can pursue further enquiries which are informed by the Invitational concept, *connections through difference*:

> *Do you think Paul would have any idea that his Dad can stop and think – and feel bad about what he put him through that night?*
>
> *What might it mean to Paul, that you do feel so bad – and you are facing it?*
>
> *How are you managing to stop and think about his feelings?*
>
> *Did your Dad ever stop and think about what he put you and your Mum through?*
>
> *What difference might it have made if he did?*
>
> *How different is the path you are taking right here and right now?*
>
> *Where might this take you?*
>
> *How does it fit with the man, the father, you are wanting to be?*

This process of enquiry should always remain sensitive to potential restraining influences which constitute *responsibility overload*. We should never take Jack's preparedness to face his abusive actions for granted but maintain a sense of curiosity and wonder about his maintenance of *ethics in the face of adversity*:

> *Would anyone else have any idea about how bad you feel about what you put Paul through?*

> *Would anyone understand how much it hurts you inside to look at what you did?*
>
> *What is it taking, to stay with that picture of Paul in your mind?*
> *– to try to see it like it is?*
> *– to make no excuses?*
> *– not to run away from it?*
> *– to face it yourself, not just leave it for Paul to worry about?*
>
> *How are you managing to do this, when it hurts so much? When you have been through so much yourself?*
>
> *What are you proving to yourself?*
>
> *How does this fit with the person you want to be?*

Jack is invited to consider the ethical meanings and implications of his feelings of shame and remorse and his preparedness to *stand his ground* and begin to face up to the nature and effects of his actions. He can be assisted to relate these steps to his previously stated ethical strivings and preferences:

> *Jack, it would be a lot easier to turn away from this and leave it for someone else to worry about. What is it taking to stand your ground? What are you finding in yourself? Is it strength? Is it courage? Is it love?*
>
> *Have you ever taken a stand like this before?*
>
> *Has anyone else you know ever taken such a stand?*
>
> *What tells you that this is the right path for you to take?*
>
> *How do you know that facing such unbearable pain is going to help you and help Paul?*
>
> *What tells you that this fits for you as a man and as a father?*

Jack suggested that it was *'standing by Paul'* and wanting to be a *'proper Dad'* that was moving him to take this stand. He recognised he was in unfamiliar territory and unsure about what to do. I invited Jack to consider the vital importance of the step he was now taking:

> *You are speaking out about your commitment to stand by Paul and you are beginning to take a huge step to act on that commitment; to walk the talk – Can you see that?*
>
> *I guess that it is not the first time you have hurt Sue and frightened Paul?*
>
> *How important is it for you to put a stop to this?*

It will mean continuing to take an even closer look at your actions? How strong is that commitment?

Jack rated his commitment to stand by Paul as 10 out of 10. I then invited him to try to locate this experience physically in his body. A corporeal ethical experience might helpfully sit alongside the experience of shame and assist Jack with ethical realisation through a connection between thinking and feeling; a bringing together of head and heart:

Where can you feel that commitment, that strength in your body?

What tells you that it is there?

Where can you feel the shame in your body?

How strong is the feeling of shame?

How much commitment?

How much strength is it taking to face that much shame?

The feeling of shame will be strong when you leave today.

How will you keep that strength of commitment alive and strong when you leave here today?

Timely enquiries and provocations which open windows to shame in order to make ethical meaning of remorse, are vital in Invitational practice. Such invitations are likely to be accepted when they are attuned to the man's stated ethics and his own developing awareness of shame and remorse regarding his actions. When shame is named, contextualised and repositioned in terms of its ethical salience, there is little reason to be concerned about escalations which might lead to harm to self or others. Such desperate actions tend to be associated more with shame avoidance, whereas the repositioning process enables a sense of possible direction which might allow for accountable forms of atonement, ethical realisation and a reclamation of integrity.

Contradiction and windows to shame – Tom

Contrasting intent and action – Tom

Tom's strivings to assist Peter's responsible development and for a mutually respectful and supportive relationship with his son have been named and acknowledged along with his sense of

disappointment and frustration at feeling he has failed to achieve either ethical goal. In this context, he might similarly be invited to contrast respectful intent with desperate or misguided actions:

Tom, you've been worried and disappointed about Peter for years. You have made it clear that you have tried everything you can think of to help get his life on track.

I imagine there must have been times when you felt so worried and frustrated:
– that you found yourself acting in desperate ways?
– that you went over the top and acted against your better judgement?

I felt that Tom was not ready to engage in such sober conversation about his actions. I had noted Tom voicing concerns about *'the bloody welfare'* on several occasions and recognised that he still appeared very concerned that he might be subjected to further coercive and judgmental treatment. I was aware of a Child Protection notification which had been raised when Peter was assaulted by his father at the age of 10. I wondered about the potential for *responsibility overload*:

- *Might Tom feel that no-one has considered, let alone respected his ethical strivings as a father?*
- *Might he be concerned that others, especially those concerned with the protection of children, will judge him as uncaring, unprincipled or even monstrous?*
- *Might his intent in situations where he has hurt Peter need to be further acknowledged and clarified, if he is to face the nature and effects of hurtful actions?*

I decided to address Tom's concerns about judgement and invite reflection upon the incident that had led to Child Protection involvement, but in the light of his stated ethical strivings. I had previously viewed a Child Protection report which stated that witnesses on a public beach had observed Tom hit and kick his 10-year-old son, causing bruising and a cut to his head. Police intervened and Tom was eventually cautioned about his actions. It appeared that no further Child Protection action was taken after an interview where Tom was described as uncooperative, having sworn at the workers and then stormed from the room. I commenced this enquiry by wondering whether anyone else could have recognised that there might be more to Tom, as a father, than his violence and criticism of Peter:

> *Who do you think understands how important your hopes and plans for Peter have been?*
>
> *Who would know how hard you have worked to try to achieve them?*
>
> *When welfare was involved in your life, I know you didn't find this helpful.*
>
>> *Did they know about or ask you about your hopes and plans for Peter?*
>>
>> *Did they understand the worries and frustrations you had with Peter?*
>>
>> *Did they seem interested in the problems you were having with Peter or only in what happened on the beach that day?*
>>
>> *Did you feel that they wanted to help you deal with these problems or did it feel like they wanted to blame you for these problems?*

Promoting a sober conversation about abusive behaviour – Tom

These conversations about perceived intent are not aimed at promoting criticism of Child Protection workers or suggesting that their intervention was not required. They do, however, hold together the serious issues of Child Protection and the implication that Peter has been harmed, with Tom's concerns and intent and the possibility that he may not want to cause harm to his son. They highlight potential *responsibility overload*, in Child Protection work, when men are expected to consider the effects of their actions and the experiences of a child they have harmed, in the absence of having their own experiences and concerns acknowledged by the worker.

Having established Tom's perceptions of the intent and interests of the Child Protection workers, I first asked permission to discuss the incident which led to their intervention:

> *Is it okay for me to ask about what actually happened that day?*

Tom snapped back, *'You've got their report, why ask me?'* At this point, I wondered not only about Tom's concerns of external judgement, but about the possibility that he may have judged himself unfavourably and have felt considerable shame about his actions. I expressed my interest in his views rather than those of others:

> *I have seen the welfare report about how they saw what happened but that doesn't tell me anything about how you see it.*

As with Jack, I continued to invite a *sober* conversation by *listening for intent* with frequent interruptions of intoxicating escalation and detailed step-by-step enquiries about time, place and experience. By maintaining a focus of curiosity on Tom's intent and hopes on the day of the incident, potential escalations of self-intoxicating, righteous indignation could be prevented.

I discovered that the incident had taken place on Peter's 10th birthday, which was to be celebrated with a beach picnic. I wondered about Tom's hopes and expectations for this day:

> *What had you planned for the day?*
>
> *Was it going to be a special day?*

Tom and Judith had, in fact, made special plans for a *'surfing birthday party'*. Tom had planned to teach his son to surf and had expectations that this might become an activity that they would engage in together on weekends. I enquired about the preparations for the party and was told that Judith had made a special *'surfer cake'* while Tom had borrowed money to buy Peter a particular surfboard which was decorated in a way that *'Peter would love'*. I explored these preparations in detail and wondered about the caring, excitement and anticipation that went into these preparations:

> *You put a lot of thought into trying to make this a special day for Peter. You had high hopes about what might come of it for you and Peter.*
>
> *Did the welfare people know about this?*

Tom retorted angrily, *'Those bastards wouldn't have given a toss'*. However, as I gradually enquired about how the day had unfolded, following this period of preparation and anticipation, Tom quickly began to engage in some sober reflection. He sighed regretfully and lamented, *'I just don't know what happened that day'*. Tom was slowly becoming open to consider the events of that day from perspectives other than the perceived injustice of the Child Protection intervention.

Tom became agitated as he described how, *'Peter just upped and disappeared'*, as he and Judith were setting up the picnic. Peter's disappearance led to a lengthy search. My early enquiries established that Tom was initially *'annoyed'*, and thinking, *'where the hell has he gone'*. This gave way to concern and Tom became *'worried sick'* about Peter's safety; *'something could have happened to him'*; *'there are all kinds of weirdos about'*. I maintained a focus on Tom's worry and concern, with their ethical implications, rather than allow his sense of annoyance and anger to dominate the conversation. In a sober conversation, Tom may be able to begin to appreciate the breadth and complexity of his emotional reactions rather than interpret all of his emotions as expressions of injustice and anger.

Tom's worry escalated over quite some time of searching until later he found Peter who was playing in the sand under the jetty, *'like he didn't care that we were worried sick'*. Tom appeared quite agitated as he asserted, *'that's when I really saw red'*. I interrupted his flow and enquired further about his thoughts and feelings at this time. Tom elaborated that he thought Peter *'didn't care that we'd been looking for him for over an hour'* or *'all the effort we'd put into his birthday'* and that *'this is typical of him'*. These enquiries lead to a shift in the conversation from agitated and intoxicating descriptions of anger and *'seeing red'* to acknowledgements of extreme *disappointment* and feelings of *hurt*. Tom had interpreted Peter's wandering off and apparent disinterest in surfing as a personal rebuff. He regarded his 10-year-old son's apparent lack of concern that others had been worried about him as deliberate and wilful. Tom felt this meant that Peter had *'no time for his Dad'* and experienced an intense sense of rejection. These experiences reflect Tom's hopes and strivings in relation to his son and are vital considerations if we hope to assist him to acknowledge and address any abusive behaviour. As Tom described his experiences of worry, disappointment and hurt, his affect became more sad and he became more soberly reflective.

Opening a window to shame – Tom

Once again, I enquired about his perceptions of the Child Protection workers in order to assist a separation between this perceived injustice and an injustice that Tom had carried out towards his son, despite having hopes for respectful connection. Given the sad and reflective shift in Tom's affect, I felt that he might be ready to consider his own actions in this light; that the experience of shame might be accessible for him:

Were the welfare people interested that you felt worried, disappointed and let down or did they only seem interested in what you did to Peter that day?

What did you do then after you found Peter?

Tom was reluctant to describe his assault of Peter; *'I don't know what happened'*; *'I just lost it'*. The concept of *losing it* might be regarded as a vague minimisation of responsibility for one's actions. However, this concept might also imply a recognition by Tom of an ethical quality that he perhaps lost sight of on that day. I acknowledged the difficulty in facing the shame that accompanies recognition of unethical actions:

I guess it is not something that anyone would want to remember.
Did you wind up doing something that really shocked you?

Tom averted his eyes and looked ashamed, but quickly protested; *'I couldn't let him get away with it'*. Despite his protest, I decided to attend to evidence of shame:

You don't look at all proud about what you are seeing.

I get the feeling that you didn't need welfare or anyone else to tell you that what you did was wrong. You could work that out for yourself.

I imagine you felt pretty terrible afterwards.

What are you realising? What are you seeing?

Tom looked down towards his feet and responded quietly. He acknowledged, *'(Peter) was only a little guy'*; *'I beat him up'*. Like Jack, Tom is accessing a shocking and shameful image or memory in which his son's vulnerability and the injustice of his actions is all too apparent. Tom had begun to shout at Peter (*'Why did you take off like that?'*) who became quickly terrified. When Peter didn't respond to his questions, he began to punch and then kick Peter until people on the beach intervened and called the police. I recalled an image of Peter telling me about covering his mouth when it was bleeding because he felt ashamed at his father's actions and cautioned myself to maintain a position of *listening for intent* and monitoring my own feelings of outrage and possible vengeful actions.

Tom attempted some rather unconvincing justifications for his behaviour (*'You have to teach* kids to respect you') but was quickly re-focused towards the actual nature and impact of his actions:

Can you take a close look at Peter? What are you seeing?

How is it affecting him?

How is he seeing his Dad?

How much did you hurt him? Frighten him? How can you tell?

Tom could see Peter *'cringing and trembling on the sand'*; *'just like me and my Dad'*. As Tom was invited to hold his memories of hurting Peter, I acknowledged his dashed hopes for connection that day:

This is just the opposite outcome to what you had planned.

How does it affect you now when you look at what happened?

How heartbreaking is it to look back at this?

Repositioning shame – Tom

As with Jack, the gradual process of repositioning shame begins with invitations to attribute meaning to Tom's willingness to face his actions and their effects on Peter; *to begin to see them like they really are; to look shame squarely in the eye*:

Would the police, welfare, anyone, have any idea how bad you felt or how much you hurt inside, about what you did to Peter that day?

Would anyone know that you still feel this way?

Have you ever spoken out about this before?

It isn't easy to look back at times when you've let Peter and yourself down?

What is it taking for you to find that kind of honesty? To try to see it like it really is?

What does it say about you as a Dad that you are prepared to face it?

These enquiries can enable Tom to recognise that he is in fact actualising previously stated ethics such as, 'honesty' and 'facing up to responsibilities in life', when holding this stand about his abusive behaviour. His strivings and hopes as a parent might similarly be invoked, along with *connections through difference* with his own father:

Would Peter know that his Dad feels really bad about the way he treated him on the beach that day?

What would it mean to him if he did know?

Did your Dad ever take the trouble to stop and think about how it affected you when he let you down?

Could you imagine him sitting here and doing what you are now doing?

What might it have meant if he had taken the trouble?

This *connection through difference* was further explored in a subsequent meeting when Tom began to describe how his father appeared to favour his sisters and either ignored Tom or *'treated me like shit'* by *'putting me down'* and *'calling me stupid in front of everyone'*. He returned to the consideration that if his father had stopped and thought about the effects of his actions, *'he would have done something about it'*.

The process of *repositioning shame* is ongoing throughout Invitational intervention as men are assisted to find evidence of ethical possibilities which might enable reclamation of a sense of *integrity through facing shame*.

Contradiction and windows to shame – Kevin

Kevin's presentation provides some contrast to the presentations of Jack and Tom, both of whom initially showed considerable reluctance in acknowledging abusive practices and their effects. Kevin appears to be more open in the initial stages of intervention, acknowledging the *'terrible thing'* he has done, that he had let others down and expressing a degree of remorse. However, despite this apparent openness, Kevin has not yet examined closely the nature of his abusive actions or their potential impact upon others within his family. His sense of remorse appears shallow and attuned to avoidance of shame or corrupted forms of shame which are concerned more with seeking reassurances and forgiveness from others than facing up to his abusive actions:

- *How might we assist Kevin to see (his abuse) like it really is?*
- *How might we assist Kevin to look shame squarely in the eye?*

In this context, Invitational practice brings forward some contrasts with the work with Jack and Tom. However, the processes which begin with *curiosity about restraint* and *listening for intent*, flow through to *ethical appeals and clarification* and on to *addressing abusive behaviour* via *windows to shame*, are identical in this practice.

Contrasting intent and action – Kevin

Kevin has defined the person he wants to become as a *protective*, *respected* and *trusted* elder who can offer guidance to help family members *stay on the right track*. He can recognise that he has violated all of these ethical principles, but has probably not dared to consider just how he has done this, to what extent and with what possible effects. He will most likely try to skip over these details in desperate attempts to 'move on' and achieve pardoning and reconciliation with family members.

Our enquiries might assist Kevin to consider how he might himself, '*stay on the right track*', if we invite him to remain connected with his ethical strivings whilst remaining vigilant for evidence of small steps that he takes towards facing up to his abusive actions. Our vigilance and occasional *provocations* can assist Kevin to recognise and appreciate how these steps are consistent with his ethics and lead him towards possibilities of a more accountable and respectful restorative action. If we can slowly and gradually help provide *safe passage* for Kevin to consider and take these steps, he may be able to appreciate that whilst he acted monstrously, he can face his actions and establish, through accountable restorative action, that he is not becoming a monster. These steps might lead him towards actualising his ethical strivings.

We must remain consistent and patient in this endeavour. Kevin's prevarications and self-centred appearances of wallowing in corrupted shame can provoke feelings of urgency and contempt in counsellors. We can easily and unwittingly *underestimate* Kevin by encouraging or advising him to take steps to address abusive actions that he is unready for, particularly as we become more aware of the confusion and distress of family members.

As I became curious about what was restraining Kevin from addressing his abusive actions and their effects, it became apparent that he projected a sense of pathetic helplessness which carried an implicit invitation to others to take initiative or responsibility on his behalf. Through his somewhat self-centred expressions

of remorse, Kevin seemed to plead for reassurance, forgiveness and affirmation that he was really a good person. He appeared to be highly reliant on family members and his parish priest for such reassurance.

Indeed, family members had become polarised in their views and reactions. Kevin's partner, May, felt highly distressed and confused. On one hand she felt deeply hurt and betrayed. However, she had been married to Kevin for 38 years and had regarded him a '*good man*'. She did not know what she should do. Moreover, she felt blamed by her daughter who wanted her to separate from Kevin. At the same time, she was worried about Kevin feeling '*depressed*' and having talked about '*taking his own life*'.

Susie's parents felt hurt and outraged and wanted no contact with Kevin or May. Other family members tended to minimise Kevin's abusive actions and argued that he be forgiven for his '*indiscretions*'. Kevin sought support and reassurance from these family members and from his parish priest who had spoken of forgiveness from God.

I decided to make contact with all adult family members and the parish priest. They all expressed an interest in meeting with me to discuss their reactions and needs, the nature of my intervention with Kevin and how they might contribute towards meaningful restorative action.

These conversations were vital in clarification of family member's perceptions of Kevin's ethical strivings and the nature and impact of his abuse of Susie. Moreover, most family members expressed confusion and uncertainty about the schism that had developed in the family and concern about how to address this. Some were confused and unsure about the nature of the abuse and its effects. All welcomed an opportunity to consider how they might understand and address these issues. I raised topics which included:

- *How has Kevin conducted himself as a partner, father and grandfather?*
- *What has his abuse of Susie meant to each family member?*
- *What might need to happen to address problems and concerns?*
- *What concerns might each family member have about Kevin?*
- *What responsibilities might Kevin need to take to address these problems?*
- *What steps and signs might indicate that Kevin is facing his responsibilities?*

- *What signs might indicate that Kevin is avoiding his responsibilities?*
- *What kinds of support might Kevin require from family members?*
- *How might family members support each other?*

As family members began to consider the nature and impact of Kevin's abusive behaviour, they started to distinguish separate expectations and responsibilities of each person. In particular, this allowed for greater clarity about what might be expected of Kevin for accountable and meaningful restoration. Some family members could begin to support ethical action by Kevin, rather than inadvertently excuse or overlook his abusive behaviour. The priest welcomed the opportunity to discuss his support of Kevin and admitted that he was unsure about how to respond. He eventually became actively helpful in assisting Kevin to challenge patterns of avoiding responsibility for his actions.

Given these restraining patterns of reliance, it would have been very difficult to assist Kevin to hold an ethical position, *to stand on his own two feet*, without addressing unhelpful family interactions.

Promoting a sober conversation about abusive behaviour – Kevin

Whilst Jack and Tom tended to intoxicate themselves with preoccupations of righteous indignation, personal injustice and external blame, Kevin rapidly became preoccupied with his own escalating, self-centred expressions of remorseful sentiment. These forms of shame appeared shallow and corrupted by fears of the possible consequences of his abusive actions. They tended towards expressions of self-pity with implicit pleas for forgiveness. As Kevin's experience became increasingly captured by self-centred preoccupations, self-pity and self-deprecation, he became increasingly distanced from any sense of agency or capacity to take authentic ethical action. He seemed to be wallowing in a shallow form of remorse which appeared strangely comforting, perhaps through avoidance of the realities of the nature and effects of his actions.

A sober conversation requires interruption of these escalations with enquiries which focus upon ethical action and which hold Kevin accountable to his hopes and strivings to become a *respectful, trustworthy* and *protective* elder.

Of course, attempts to invite a sober conversation might provoke *responsibility overload*, without first having conversations which have explored and acknowledged Kevin's fears and anxieties about criminal consequences, relationship and family disintegration and the potential loss of his position and status as a favoured grandparent. Kevin clearly found the idea of him being a perpetrator of abuse to be unbearable and struggled to avoid a sense of judgment and shame. These concerns and worries must be acknowledged if we hope to invite Kevin to appreciate the concerns and worries of other family members. In fact, Kevin's anxieties would most likely escalate in the face of premature attempts to invite him to address his abusive actions, as he retreated into the isolation and detachment of self-pity. If we can gradually invite consideration of Kevin's anxieties and fears, his ethical strivings and the small steps he has taken towards facing and addressing abusive actions, in a respectful and sober manner, he may eventually find courage to face these fears, stand his ground and recognise how they have displaced his awareness of the distress and worries of other family members.

With both Jack and Tom, it proved helpful to focus upon a specific salient incident of abuse and invite a sober description in detailed retelling and later broaden the focus to include other incidents and acts that constitute a course of abusive action. With Kevin, I wanted to attend to any evidence of agency he demonstrated and decided to make his early initiatives the focus of enquiry. I was especially concerned to avoid establishing a paradigm whereby I set a facing up agenda to which Kevin might then respond in a reactive manner, either by attempting to gain my approval or by withdrawing further into a state of avoidance.

I took note of one of Kevin's early acknowledgements, *'I've done a terrible thing to an innocent little girl'*, and wondered about his use of the two adjectives, *terrible* and *innocent*:

When did you make that realisation that it was a 'terrible thing' that you did to Susie?

What was it that made you see it as 'terrible?'

What is it that is 'terrible' about what you did to her?

What is it that you realised about Susie being an 'innocent little girl?'

What are you beginning to understand about her 'innocence?'

Kevin struggled to clarify these concepts, as I encouraged him to think and not just feel about his realisations. He acknowledged that Susie was *'only 9 (years old)'* and that she *'trusted me to look after her'*. As he began to describe a context for exploitation, he began to cry and appeared to become caught up in a self-deprecating escalation. I interrupted this emotional expression and invited Kevin to stop crying and think about the steps he had begun to take:

> *Have you let yourself stop and really take such a close look at what you did to Susie?*
>
> *What is the hardest thing to look at?*
>
> *What is it taking to begin to see it like it is?*
>
> *What are you having to find in yourself?*
>
> *How might it help you to study what you did, to really understand how it can harm an 'innocent little girl'?*
>
> *How might it help you to stand your ground, not to hide behind tears and fears?*
>
> *What might it mean to put Susie's feelings first?*
>
> *Why do you need to look so closely?*
>
> *What would it mean to May, Susie and your family?*
>
> *What does it say about you? How does it fit with the man you want to be?*

Opening a window to shame – Kevin

These kinds of enquiries were continued, but with a sense of patience and willingness to proceed with gradual developments. Kevin was unready, at this time, to open a substantial *window to shame* and experience a deeper sense of remorse which might motivate profoundly new forms of restorative action. However, he could be assisted to discover his own capacity and initiative to think in accountable ways about the experiences of others and to plan ethical actions.

Repositioning shame – Kevin

With the support of family members who maintained expectations of Kevin for accountable and responsible actions, Kevin could gradually be assisted to develop and hold a mindful and ethical position. At a later point in his journey, whilst considering the deception or *'tricks'* he used to secure Susie's participation in the abuse, Kevin appeared shocked when he suddenly

regarded his actions from a new perspective which led him into a deeper sense of shame and remorse than he had previously experienced. This *window to shame* is described in Chapter 10 (see pages 118 and 124) and could only take place once Kevin was ready. We must patiently strive to provide opportunities and *safe passage* to assist readiness for further development which takes place when the man is ready to take new steps that he determines to be ethical.

Contradiction and windows to shame – Barry

Barry appeared willing to acknowledge and name his violence as unacceptable. He *'hated'* and felt *'disgusted'* at his physical and verbal abuse which he recognised was *'hurting'* and *'frightening'* Eve and Colin and destroying his family. Barry appeared to be in a constant state of shame which seemed to promote only a sense of incompetence and insufficiency which made him increasingly reliant upon family members to try to prevent and deal with the consequences of his violence.

Barry differed to Kevin in that he was constantly striving to change his behaviour, only to find he had made hollow promises and let himself and his family down once again. He seemed to allow himself no respite from responsibility for his actions; he would accept no justifications or consolations and certainly was not seeking any kind or pardon or forgiveness. Yet paradoxically, he appeared to resign himself to justification by drawing the conclusion that he could not help himself; that he was somehow limited or incapable of changing his behaviour.

I wondered about this identity conclusion which produced a sense of insufficiency and seemed to pervade most aspects of Barry's life and experience, regardless of his levels of achievement. Barry appeared competent in many areas, yet he seemed to believe, almost constantly, that he was *'not good enough'*. My *curiosity about restraint* led me to wonder about what might be preventing Barry from acting on his experience of shame:

- *Perhaps Barry has not sufficiently faced his actions, their impact and their shamefulness, to stop hurting family members?*
- *Perhaps Barry has not yet discovered an enabling way to process his experiences of disgrace?*

- *Perhaps he has established a habit of becoming overly reliant upon family members to face responsibilities that are rightfully his own?*

I began to wonder about the nature of Barry's pervasive sense of shame. Barry had previously related a long-standing history, from childhood, of self-doubt, worry about his performance and of *'never (being) good enough'*. He was constantly, *'trying to get things right'* but always facing a sense of failure and insufficiency. Much of the shame that Barry experienced was a form of *mistaken shame*; a sense of inappropriately attributed shame that comes from feeling he has not lived up to the expectations of others, including his parents and perhaps certain cultural blueprints about masculinity. When mistaken shame is conflated with disgrace, the combination can become confusing and overwhelming. *Mistaken shame* needs to be resisted and re-attributed back to its appropriate site of ownership. *Disgrace* needs to be faced and experienced with appropriate remorse, in order to enable ethical and restorative action:

- *Perhaps Barry has confused mistaken shame with disgrace leading to ineffective attempts at addressing his reactions to abusive behaviour and an overwhelming sense of failure?*
- *Perhaps Barry's extreme mistaken shame has resulted in a pervasive sense of self-doubt which prevents him from recognising any capacity to take effective ethical action?*

Contrasting intent and action – Barry

Barry had already clarified his strivings *'to get things right'*, and in particular to treat Eve and Colin respectfully, to help them *'feel safe and protected'* and *'accepted'* by him. He declared that he wanted to *'listen'*, to *'back off from criticising'* them and could even recognise some successful attempts to actualise these strivings. Barry did not want to continue to *'hurt and frighten'* members of his family.

Barry did need to find enabling ways to address and process feelings of disgrace, in relation to his abusive actions. He would most likely need to take a closer look at his actions, open *windows to shame* and face levels of disgrace he had not previously imagined. However, we first needed to address the restraining effects of his *mistaken shame*, in order to enable an effective focus on *disgrace*.

Promoting a sober conversation about abusive behaviour – Barry

With Jack, Tom and Kevin, early enquiries focused directly upon abusive behaviour and its effects. This direct focus would eventually enable access to disgrace shame and an ethical sense of remorse. An interplay between each man's intent and his contrasting actions was kept in the foreground of my enquiries. Such a direct conversation with Barry would be likely to lead towards experiences of overwhelming disgrace and a further sense of humiliation, helplessness and inadequacy. Conversations about violence and abusive behaviour can only be helpful when they promote a sense of ethical possibility and agency. Early intervention with Barry initially required a more indirect approach which explored an interplay of intent and action within his experiences and practices associated with *mistaken shame*, whilst not losing sight of his abusive behaviour.

I began by enquiring about the ubiquitous presence of *criticism* and *judgement* in Barry's life:

> *How and when has 'criticism' entered, or been present in your life?*
>
> *In what ways has 'judgement' shown itself within your life and your family?*
>
> *What effects have these notions had in your family?*
>
> *What hopes and visions have they limited or interfered with?*
>
> *How have they influenced 'feeling safe', 'feeling accepted' and 'feeling listened to' etc?*
>
> *Where did these notions come from?*
>
> *How have they developed their influence over time?*
>
> *Where have they been taking your family?*
>
> *Where have they been taking you?*

These enquiries are informed by the Narrative Therapy concept, *externalisation*, which enabled Barry to draw a distinction between ideas and practices which have external origins, traditions and histories and Barry's own ethical strivings and preferences. These notions were not invented by Barry, nor are they essential components of his being; he has perhaps unwittingly subscribed to their tenets and become captured by their influence (White, 2008).

It soon became apparent that Barry had learned to subject his own experience and behaviour to

criticism and *judgement*. He appeared to have
become a harsher judge of himself than any
family member might have been in the past. We
gradually explored the influence of *self-criticism*
and *self-doubt* in Barry's life and experience.
Barry related a history of feeling disapproved of
and *'never good enough'*, commencing in his
childhood; of striving to be *'accepted'* but *'never
making the grade'*. He began to consider how
much he had taken this, *'never good enough'*
concept to heart; how he had come to believe
this sentiment as a truth about him and invest in
it through practices of *self-doubt*. Barry could
recognise that he would find flaws in whatever
he did; that he would *'raise the goal posts'*
however high the achievement and regardless of
how much positive feedback he received from
others. He considered his complicity with
influences of his parents and cultural interests
about masculinity which concerned, *'What a
man's gotta do.'*

I enquired further about the effects of
constantly living under this burden of *self-doubt*
and invited Barry to question its legitimacy:

> *How has living under the influence of 'self-doubt'
> for so long affected you?*

> *How have you tried to deal with the kind of shame
> that 'self-doubt' brings?*

> *Whose shame actually is this? Where does it really
> belong?*

Barry protested, *'I've done some pretty terrible
things to my family.'* I responded by agreeing with
Barry, but invited the consideration of a
distinction between forms of shame:

> *Which shame is your shame? What you put Eve and
> Colin through or not living up to someone else's
> expectations?*

> *What are you responsible for?*

> *What do you need to face? What could you afford to
> throw off?*

Opening a window to shame – Barry

Barry had returned to his abusive behaviour
towards Eve and Colin and rightly declared his
sense of disgrace at his actions. He seemed to
hone in on this behaviour as he exclaimed, *'That's
just it; that's what I do; I take out **my** shit on them!'*
Barry appeared agitated but purposive and
directed. When I enquired about what he was

realising, Barry replied, *'I feel like crap so I make
them feel like crap'*. Barry was intensely caught up
in his recognition of injustice embodied in the
vengeful metaphor of feeling *'shitted on'* and
'shitting on' others in return. He appeared to have
shocked himself with this realisation which
exposed a terrible truth about the injustice of his
actions.

Repositioning shame – Barry

Barry did not appear resigned or paralysed with
helplessness, as I discovered when I enquired:

> *What will you do with this realisation?*

Barry looked shaken but expressed determination
to, *'clean up my own back yard, before getting stuck
into others'*.

I continued my enquiries with the aim of
developing further *sober* conversation which
might help enhance Barry's agency and
determination towards ethical action. These
enquiries included many of the kind already
documented which invite consideration of the
experience of disgrace from an enabling and
ethically moving perspective. Some specific
enquiries included the following:

> *Will this mean 'getting stuck into' yourself or might
> you be kinder to yourself?*

> *How might this help you to be more respectful to
> Eve and Colin?*

> *How has self-doubt tried to hijack your best efforts
> and bring them down?*

>> *What does it get you thinking about yourself?*

>> *What does it get you thinking about others?*

>> *How does it trick you into turning on others?*

>> *How does it try to justify criticism of others?*

>> *How does this masquerade as constructive
>> criticism?*

> *When have you stood apart from self-doubt and
> stood your own ground?*

>> *How did you manage to refuse to follow its
>> direction?*

>> *What difference did this make for you? How did it
>> suit you?*

>> *What did you discover about yourself?*

*When have you tried to stand back from criticism
with your family?*

What did you try to do instead?

What did this mean to Eve and to Colin?

What difference did this make for you?

What did you discover about yourself?

Like Jack, Tom and Kevin, Barry later opened
other *windows to shame* as he examined more
closely his abusive actions and their
consequences in the light of his ethical strivings.
These experiences of remorse are considered vital
in moving forward in the journey towards
becoming ethical. Ethical reclamation and
accountable, restorative action require
experiences of both remorse and generous love
which are in turn constituted by two forms of
encounter with the humanity of others; the shock
of realisation of having wronged the other and
the renunciation of personal privilege which
accompanies restitution and reaching out
towards the other.

Establishing readiness for the journey

Readiness has been described as a key concept in
Invitational practice which concerns motivation
and a sense of agency. A sense of *readiness* to
invest in the journey, *becoming ethical*, requires an
emotional or affective, as well as an intellectual,
commitment. This entails a commitment which is
made using both the *head* and the *heart*. The man
is invited to make a commitment which fits with
his ethics and which feels authentic; a
commitment which demonstrates and enhances
integrity.

This sense of commitment and readiness for
the journey is initially enabled through our
appeals to ethics but becomes 'real' as the man
opens the *windows to shame* and begins to process,
both intellectually and emotionally, the
contradictions between his ethical strivings and
his actions. *Windows to shame* are vital in enabling
an ethical remorse that constitutes the emotional
component of this processing and promotes
integration of *head* and *heart*. I have consistently
found that commitment and investment in the
journey remain limited when these experiences of
shame and remorse seem inaccessible.

Readiness for the journey is reflected in the man's
stated commitment to:

– cease abusive behaviour.
– make restitution for harm done.
– reclaim a sense of self-respect and integrity.

The man understands the importance of
continuing to take steps to examine abusive
practices and their effects upon others. He
recognises that each step will challenge him and
he may have to face emotional pain. However,
each step has meaning and integrity in promoting
the cessation of abuse, restitution and ethical
reclamation. He is rightfully apprehensive, but
ready to proceed.

Broadening the focus on abusive behaviour – Jack

Jack had opened a *window to shame* and
experienced intense remorse in relation to his
son, Paul. Through processes of *repositioning
shame*, he began to perceive an ethical direction
that had integrity; a need to face and address his
abusive behaviour and its effects upon Paul.

At this stage, Jack's attention had been focused
upon his physical violence and its effects upon
Paul. Other types of abuse which include forms
of restrictive, possessive and controlling
behaviour had been only alluded to. In particular,
Sue's experience of Jack's abusive behaviour had
not yet been addressed at all. Sue appeared
almost invisible in these initial conversations with
Jack.

Invitational practice requires that we *listen for
intent* and proceed at a pace that is informed by
the man's ethical realisations and his readiness to
take new steps. As Jack clarified his ethical
strivings and preferences, it became apparent that
windows to shame would be more accessible in
relation to his son than his partner. Jack's
physical violence appeared to provide a more
obvious and unequivocal focus than his other
abusive practices. Once Jack had begun to take a
significant step in facing the effects of his abusive
behaviour upon Paul, I decided to invite Jack to
broaden his focus on abuse:

*Have you noticed, Jack, that you are now talking
much more about your own behaviour and what you
need to do and much less about what you think Sue
needs to do?*

*You seem to be making a lot fewer excuses for
yourself; how are you managing this?*

Does this direction feel right for you?

Can I ask more about how it affected you when you hurt Sue?

You made it clear that this was not what you wanted; you wanted to connect with Sue, not to hurt her?

How much has this been happening for you?; You want to connect with Sue, you want to be close to her, you start to feel hurt and then you wind up hurting Sue and driving her away.

Following this clarification of intent, Jack declared once again, that he did not want to hurt Sue; '*I love her*' but '*she doesn't respect me*' and '*I guess I just lose it*'. I noted the complexity in these statements which reflected a desire for intimacy, blame of Sue and a degree of recognition that his violence is not acceptable. I began to enquire about the impact of violence upon *respect*:

You have made it really clear that 'respect' is really important to you. What do you think it does to respect when you hurt Sue?

These enquiries explored and clarified the concept of *respect* via *connections through difference*:

How did it affect your 'respect' when your Dad hurt your Mum?

How was it affecting your Mum's 'respect' of him?

Did your Dad just hurt your mum physically or did he also hurt with words or in other kinds of ways?

What worried you the most?

What do you think affected your Mum the most?

Do you think your Dad ever stopped to think about what he was putting your Mum through?

How much did your Dad try to 'respect' your Mum's feelings and ideas?

Do you think he ever stopped to think about it from your Mum's point of view?

Did he ever take responsibility for his behaviour or was he more inclined to blame your Mum?

What have you realised that he might never have even considered?

You were able to stop and think about Sue's feelings earlier; you know she sees your phone calls differently to you, you reckoned she was 'frustrated' and 'she'd had enough'. You could even see that she might have been trying to protect Paul – you could think about all this even though you were feeling really hurt and frustrated.

How are you managing to try to understand and 'respect' Sue's feelings as you remember this incident?

How have you managed to move away from just thinking of yourself and think more about Sue's feelings?

How important is it for you to try to 'respect' Sue's views and feelings – even if you are not feeling respected yourself?

I decided to broaden the focus by making reference to the likelihood of a pattern of abusive behaviour which included non-physical violence:

I guess that this isn't the only time that you have hurt Sue and frightened Paul?

Is it the first time you have been prepared to take a really close look at it – not just say sorry and hope it never happens again?

What is different that you can speak out now?

Has the hurting been mostly physical or has it been more with words or other ways?

Would it be fair to say that last week wouldn't have been the first time that you have acted in ways that you regretted;
– where you have gone over the top in checking up on or challenging Sue?
– where you have come on to Sue in jealous or possessive ways?
– where you have wound up hurting the people you love?

What kinds of hurting worry you the most?

What kinds of hurting do you think might worry Sue the most?

Jack stated unequivocally that he wanted to stop physical violence. He struggled as he considered Sue's experience of his behaviour as '*possessive*' but acknowledged that his '*jealous*' actions did escalate to the point where he would '*go on and on at her*'; '*with a thousand questions*' and seeking reassurance. Jack recognised that this left him feeling worried and '*a bit paranoid*'. In this context he did not show '*respect*' to Sue. He acknowledged that this was the context in which he had '*put down*', threatened and actually assaulted Sue.

Jack recognised that Sue regarded his '*possessive*' behaviour as abusive, but was clearly not yet ready to label it as such himself. Such a realisation would require opening a *window to shame*, along with viewing aspects of this behaviour and its effects upon Sue from a shocking and new perspective. Jack had begun to address his abusive behaviour towards Sue but still struggled with a competing sense of reciprocity; that perhaps Sue contributed to or provoked his actions by *'disrespecting'* him. Once again, the importance of patient enquiry informed by *listening for intent* cannot be over-emphasised. If we become impatient, allowing a sense of urgency for Jack to experience understanding or a sense of shame and remorse equivalent to that which he felt in relation to Paul, we are likely to under-estimate Jack's own capacity and agency for ethical realisation. We reproduce violence and restrain Jack's progress in his own journey.

Mapping the effects of abuse – affirming ethical preferences – Jack

When the man has begun to engage in *sober* reflection on abusive behaviour; when he can acknowledge that his actions have hurt family members and is becoming open to experience them as shameful, it can be helpful to return to further consideration of his ethical strivings. In particular, he may be invited to consider the impact of abuse, over time, upon personal and relationship qualities and ethics that he has valued and striven for and to re-confirm the continued importance of these qualities.

The process of *mapping the effects of abuse* becomes established in relation to the reference point of Jack's ethical strivings:

> *You have been trying to make a family where Sue and Paul feel respected and cherished, where they feel safe and they belong, but at times you have wound up acting in ways that have hurt and frightened them, even driven them away.*

I had already begun to invite Jack to consider the effects of his abusive behaviour upon *'respect'* within his relationship with Sue. This enquiry arose out of Jack's expressed concern that Sue might not *'respect'* him. Similar enquiries were extended towards the effects of acknowledged hurtful actions and words on other valued ethical relationship preferences. The following binary forms of enquiry hold and contrast abusive and ethical possibilities in relation to personal and relationship qualities:

> *Have Sue and Paul been feeling safer or more fearful of you over time?*
>
> *Is Sue more trusting or fearing of you over time?*
>
> *Would she be feeling more cared about or more hurt by you, as time goes by?*
>
> *Would Sue have stayed with you more out of desire for you or out of duty?*
>
> *Have you been gaining Paul's respect or his fear, over time?*
>
> *Is he becoming more safe and secure with, or more afraid of, his Dad?*
>
> *How has hurting Sue and Paul affected how you feel about yourself over time?*
>
> *Have you been gaining or losing respect for yourself?*
>
> *Have you been more into trying to manage your own actions or trying to control Sue's actions?*
>
> *Has this been moving you closer to or further away:*
> *– from what is important to you?*
> *– from the kind person that you want to become?*

Such an examination of time trends in a relationship can bring a sharper focus on the level of deterioration and extent of loss of valued personal, relationship and family qualities. Jack felt concern as he considered what he had been losing and worried about the kind of person he felt he had been becoming. He experienced two contrasting reactions as he began to recall actions which had caused considerable distress and hurt to both Sue and Paul.

Jack recalled an incident where he *'trashed her things'*, again in Paul's presence. He recalled *'putting Sue down'* with a particularly offensive name that he knew would hurt her. Jack appeared to experience shame as he recounted details of these incidents and as I invited him to explore the ethical implication of these realisations, he returned to the haunting image of Paul, terrified of his father, and restated his determination to stop hurting Sue and Paul.

However, Jack did not hold his experience of shame regarding his actions towards Sue for long. He leapt rapidly from shame to an urgent and desperate desire to reassure and reconcile with Sue; *'She needs to know that I love her and that I'll never hurt her again'*; *'I can't make things right if we're not together'*. I interrupted Jack's flow, acknowledging the importance of his need to try to make amends for his actions:

> *Jack, you want to try to put things right.*

How often have you tried to do this – to make apologies or give reassurances before?

What have these hasty attempts meant to Sue?

What difference have desperate attempts made for you?

What is more important, stopping violence and hurting Sue and Paul once and for all or trying to reassure Sue?

What needs to come first, making sure you have changed your own behaviour or trying desperately to change Sue's mind?

This conversation was developed further on several occasions (see Chapters 11 and 13) as Jack struggled with possessive thinking with an accompanying sense of desperation and urgency. I invited Jack to slow down, to consider the need to study his abusive actions and their effects closely, to deal with his own challenges before considering reconnection with Sue.

This consideration must be based on an ethical reference point which is meaningful for Jack. I invited him to return to the recognised effects of abusive behaviour and to affirm his personal and relationship preferences by reconsidering and restating the importance that he placed upon the qualities such as *safety, respect, trust, fairness, tolerance,* etc.

In this context, Jack might be invited to reconsider and affirm the kind of relationship he has wanted with Sue:

Would you want Sue to return to be with you out of a sense of duty or because she desires to be with you?

Do you want her to want to be with you or to feel obliged to be with you?

Would you want her to feel desire to be with you and have respect for you, or to pretend?

How important is it for you to manage your own actions rather than try to influence Sue's actions?

Would you prefer to demand Sue's respect or to try to earn it?

How important is it to you to now show respect, rather than demand it?

These enquiries are vital considerations for Jack in deciding about a commitment to address abusive behaviour as opposed to continued participation in a cycle of desperate reconciliation and further violence. They might be extended to invite affirmation of the importance of qualities such as *safety, trust* and *partnership*.

In particular, Jack was invited to consider whether violence might have any place in his relationship or family:

Would it be possible to have the kind of relationship you are wanting if you continued to hurt Sue and Paul?

Do you think there is any place for violence within a relationship or family?

How important is it for you to stop violence once and for all?

Are there any kinds of hurtful actions you would want to maintain?

How important is it for you to be able to manage your behaviour in disagreements or arguments, without resorting to violence or hurting Sue?
– Even if Sue does something that you think is totally unreasonable?
– Even if you feel disrespected by Sue?
– Even if you feel that Sue is totally in the wrong?
– Even if Sue says or does something that hurts you?

How important is it for Sue to feel 100 per cent safe with you, regardless of what she thinks, says or does?

How important is it that Paul feels 100 per cent safe in your family?

How does this kind of commitment to non-violence, showing respect and tolerance fit with the kind of man and partner you are wanting to become?

These Invitational enquiries have referred to both personal and relationship hopes and preferences. I was mindful that Jack was preoccupied with reconciliation with Sue and Paul and still struggling to set a priority on addressing his abusive behaviour. Jack was not 'required' to cease or suspend his interest and hopes in reconciliation. These interests can be respected and enquiries can be initiated about relationship preferences which can also introduce invitations to set personal ethical priorities which challenge a sense of entitlement to reconcile or hasty and desperate decisions or actions which might privilege nostalgic forms of restorative action.

The focus of these enquiries gradually shifts from relationship preferences to clarification of personal ethical strivings in relation to qualities such as *respect, trust, partnership and fairness*:

How are you wanting to be in this relationship?

How are you wanting to show respect?

How are you wanting to practise tolerance?

How are you wanting to be as a partner?

How do you want to place trust in Sue?

Jack might also be invited to reconsider and affirm the kind of relationship that he wants with Paul and the kind of father he is wanting to become. Examples of this kind of Invitational enquiry are detailed in the following description of intervention with Tom.

Establishing commitment – Jack

As experiences of shame and remorse are complemented with sober conversation about the effects of abusive behaviour and affirmation of ethics, Jack could be invited to consider and state an ongoing commitment to facing and addressing abuse. This commitment might then constitute his own reference point for the journey towards *becoming ethical*. Such a commitment is an expression of readiness to study abusive behaviour and its effects in order to cease abuse, make restitution for harm done and reclaim an ethical sense of becoming.

I was disinclined to encourage Jack to take further steps towards naming abusive practices, facing shame and developing ethical alternatives. Invitational practice instead aims to respect the man's capacity for initiative and to invite him to reflect upon the nature, significance and ethical implications of steps that he is currently taking and then consider his readiness in relation to new possibilities. Consequently, we might be inclined to caution or discourage taking new steps until the man has thoroughly considered their implications and feels convinced any such step is likely to be consistent with his ethical preferences and likely to further enable his journey towards respect. This process, termed *talking about talking about it*, invites reflection:

How might this step help you:
– to stop further abusive behaviour?
– to make restitution to those you have hurt and to your community?
– to become the partner and parent you want to be?
– to reclaim integrity and self-respect?

What tells you that you are ready and able to take such a step?

A man must find his own motivation to study abusive behaviour and its effects; to establish and commit to his own agenda to face up fully to his abusive actions. In this context, the ethical journey becomes an ongoing personal commitment, not just a series of time limited steps that might be instrumental in achieving forgiveness or reconciliation.

In establishing commitment, Jack was invited to reflect upon steps he had already taken towards facing his abusive actions and their effects:

Have you noticed the difference in how you are talking now, compared to when you first walked in this room?

What difference does it make when you start to look at your own behaviour and what you need to do, rather than what Sue is doing?

Have you ever let yourself take such a close look at this before?

In the past, how often have you just skimmed the surface, made shallow apologies and tried to put it behind you?

What difference might it make when you slow down and take a really close look at;
– how you have hurt Sue and Paul?
– what you have put Sue and Paul through?
– how you have wound up hurting them when what you want is love and connection?

What might be more helpful:
– to study your abusive behaviour or leave it for others to think about?
– to face up to it yourself or turn your back on it and hope that it goes away?
– to be thinking about ways to stop hurting Sue and Paul or to be thinking about how to get back with them?

How ready are you to take an even closer look and:
– to put maximum effort into stopping violence?
– to worry about stopping violence and not worry about getting back with Sue and Paul?
– to face it full on – not leave it for Sue and Paul to worry about?
– to face it fully – not turn your back or run and hide?

What would this say to Sue and Paul?

What difference might it make for Sue and Paul?

What difference might it make for you?

Which path is the hardest one to take?

What steps have you taken already?

How are you managing to take these steps?

What are you up against? What are you needing to find in yourself?

Has anyone else in your family taken such courageous steps?

What difference might it have made if your father had chosen this path?

How will this help you to:
– stop violence and hurting once and for all?
– stop making desperate and hollow promises?
– make proper amends for what you have put them through?
– feel real respect for yourself?

What tells you that you are ready to commit yourself to this path?

What will you be up against?

What kinds of challenges will you face?

What will be you proving to yourself?
– as a man?
– as a partner?
– as a father?

How does this path fit with what you respect and what you believe in?

Which path might be showing your true colours?

How might it fit with the man you want to be?

Broadening the focus on abusive behaviour – Tom

In repositioning Jack's shame, towards recognition of the terror he had caused in his son, Paul, I invited him to consider and acknowledge that this was an example of an ongoing and diverse pattern of violence towards Sue. Whilst Jack was not yet ready to label all of these actions as *abuse*, he was open to acknowledging this pattern of behaviour.

In invitational practice, it is vital to continue patiently to *listen for intent*, make ongoing assessments of the man's *readiness* and resist inevitable inclinations to urge him on towards further ethical realisations. Tom had reluctantly agreed to attend for the purpose of helping his son Peter. He has taken bold steps in discussing his own disappointments, frustrations and an incident where he judged himself that his violence towards Peter was unacceptable and that he felt ashamed.

I was disinclined to broaden the focus on abuse at this time, even though I was aware that Peter had been subjected to physical and verbal abuse

on many occasions over an extensive period of time. I was aware, from conversations with Peter, that he had experienced humiliating punishments and that he felt shamed and debased on the beach that day. I imagined, justifiably as it later became apparent, that Judith was also likely to have been subjected to abusive behaviour by Tom.

I pointed out that Peter had not forgotten the incident on the beach either and decided to invite further reflection on the ethical implications of such an event and to seek ethical affirmation, before consideration of a broader focus upon abuse. However, these enquiries did promote an implicit assumption that similar behaviour would have taken place.

I anticipated that Tom might become alarmed and confused about a continued focus upon his experiences and behaviour, particularly given their shameful nature in the context of apparent hypocrisy in the contrast between his stated ethics and concerns about Peter's behaviour. I wondered about the potentially restraining nature of Tom's reactions and wanted to prevent any possible escalation of defensive responding. Accordingly, I interrupted our conversation to reflect on its purpose and to anticipate possible misunderstandings, and in particular, that I had not forgotten that we were meeting to help Peter. I tried to imagine these reactions:

You are probably wondering why I have brought all this up?

How is talking about this going to help Peter?

Is this about making excuses for Peter or worse still blaming you for his problems?

*I want to make it clear that you are **not** responsible for what Peter did to Leanne but he is going to need your help if he is to face and deal with what he did.*

I began to appeal to previously stated ethics which concerned honesty and leadership towards responsible action:

I have been wondering how what you have just been talking about might help Peter face up to what he has done.

What would Peter think if he knew his old man had the honesty and the guts to stop, think and face up to a time when he let his son down, and when he hurt and terrified him?

What would it mean to Peter if he knew that his Dad felt worried and ashamed about hurting him?

What kind of example would this set of honesty and courage in facing up to something that is really hard?

What do you think he might learn from you in this?

Could it help him find the courage to face up to what he did to Leanne and not run away from it?

These enquiries are informed by explanatory concepts of restraint rather than direct causality, in understanding abusive behaviour. Tom's behaviour is not regarded as causally related to Peter's abusive actions, but the steps he takes to address his abusive actions will have a vital influence upon the steps his son might take. Tom is not regarded as part of the problem but part of the solution. The fact that Tom's recently stated position regarding violence towards his son might be both ethical and of help to Peter was further considered:

When you hurt or let someone down, you can either face it or turn your back and leave it for the little guy to worry about; you face it and deal with it or you run from it.

I respect the fact that you have not turned your back here.

What difference might it make if Peter knew this side of you better?

Peter has heard you talk about being honest and facing up to what he has done but do you reckon he has felt you do this for him?

What would it mean to expect him to do something you are not doing for him?

Is it what you say or what you do that can make the most difference?

Tom asserted that the incident happened long ago and Peter should know how he felt about hurting his son that day, but acknowledged that he had never spoken to Peter about it or attempted to apologise. He wondered whether Peter would even remember the incident and appeared distressed on hearing that his son did remember and did still feel hurt in relation to it. He spoke quietly and in a manner that appeared thoughtful and at this point I decided to invite him to hold with his ethic of *honesty* and to broaden his focus on abusive behaviour towards Peter:

I guess it is not the only time that you have resorted to desperate actions that you don't feel proud of?

Can we call a spade a spade here?

Tom acknowledged, 'I guess sometimes I do go over the top' and pointed out that, 'Judith says I'm way too hard on him'. Tom appeared to struggle with the contradiction between intent and action as he experienced shame and quickly added, 'Peter needs discipline'; 'He can't keep running amok like he has been doing'; 'I can't just sit there and do nothing'. I attempted to assist Tom to reposition this experience of shame:

It doesn't take much courage to set a punishment or to overstep the mark and make a mistake but it takes a lot to face up to a mistake and especially to do something about it.

How are you managing to start to face your mistakes here?

What is it taking? Is it about honesty, courage, guts; what is it that you are finding in yourself?

Did anyone in your life ever set an example of honesty like this for you? Like you are starting to do now for Peter?

Could you imagine your Dad setting an example like this by facing up to ways that he let you down as a kid?

Tom, you seem to be not just talking about honesty but doing it. Would you agree that actions speak louder than words?

What does it say about you that you can stay with this and not just tell me to butt out?

How would this fit with who you are and what you believe in?

How would it fit with your hopes and plans of your family?

Tom had begun to acknowledge a pattern of abusive behaviour towards his son although he was not yet labelling his behaviour as *abuse*. His focus was on physical violence at this stage and he had not yet considered and acknowledged forms of verbal abuse and rituals of ridicule and humiliation which had impacted significantly on Peter. Tom had not yet acknowledged his violence and abusive behaviour towards Judith. These recognitions and realisations would be gradually developed as he invested further in a commitment to address his behaviour towards his son and establish a respectful pattern of leadership as a father (see Chapters 12 and 13).

When a man begins to acknowledge and feel shame in relation to some unethical and abusive behaviour, he will inevitably begin to consider other behaviours as he extends his thinking and invests in an ethical journey. Invitational practice requires patient enquiry which respects his readiness and need to proceed at his own pace. In this way we can provide *safe passage* to facilitate new realisations and avoid *under estimation* of the man's own ethical potential and capability.

Mapping the effects of abuse – affirming ethical preferences – Tom

As Tom became increasingly reflective and less reactive, I invited him to map the effects of his abusive behaviour and affirm ethical preferences in his relationship with Peter. This began with acknowledgement of the dilemma faced by Tom in considering such a contradiction between his hopes and ethical intent and the effects of his actions:

> You have tried so hard to help Peter to make responsible decisions and you have really wanted to be mates with him.
>
> How much has it shocked you to find yourself saying and doing things that hurt him and cause him to be afraid – just the opposite to what you wanted?
>
> How has this affected you? Where has it left you?
>
> What has it done to your own self-respect?

These enquiries were extended to map the possible effects over time of the violence upon Peter:

> Do you think Peter has felt more respect or more fear for his Dad, over time?
>
> Do you think he has listened more or turned away more from his Dad, over time?
>
> Do you think he has looked to you more or ignored you more, over time?
>
> Would he be feeling more respected or hurt by you, over time?
>
> Have you been feeling you are helping him more or hurting him more?
>
> Are you bringing him closer or pushing him away?
>
> Are you getting closer or further away from what has been important to you?

In this context of consideration of loss, Tom was invited to reconsider and affirm his ethical preferences:

- In the context of *leadership*:
  > What kind of example are you wanting to set for Peter as a father?
  > What kind of leadership are you showing here right now?
  > What might Peter learn from this?
  > How might facing your own mistakes help Peter to face his?
  > Might he be more likely to do as you do or as you say?

- In the context of *respect*:
  > Are you wanting Peter's respect or his fear?
  > Would you prefer that he admired his Dad or feared his Dad?
  > How are you wanting to show respect to Peter?
  > What might it mean to Peter to know what you realise about what you put him through?
  > What might it have meant if your Dad had taken the trouble to stop and think about this?

- In the context of *mateship*:
  > In what direction might this kind of leadership and respect take your relationship?
  > What might lead towards defiance? What might lead towards being mates?
  > How would you want Peter to think about you in the future when he is older and looks back at his Dad?

- In the context of *being true to yourself*:
  > How do these ideas about leadership and respect fit with what you believe?
  > How do they fit with your ideas about honesty?
  > How do they fit with your ideas about facing up to your own responsibilities?
  > How much is this being true to yourself?

Establishing commitment – Tom

Tom was reflective and thoughtful as he declared an interest in respectful leadership, although concerned that the opportunity to '*be mates*' with his son may have passed. He agreed that honesty in facing his own mistakes fitted his beliefs and was something he needed to do. He then looked somewhat bewildered and exclaimed, '*What am I meant to do, I've never said sorry* (before)*!*' In making this plea, Tom did not appear to be attempting to avoid responsibility but making a declaration of genuine confusion. We clarified that Tom was totally unused to the practice of apology in any circumstance but most importantly he genuinely felt remorseful. He wanted to take action but did not know how to proceed. In this context, providing advice would be unlikely to *under estimate* and would most certainly not be gratuitous or unsolicited.

I asked Tom if I could give an opinion about what he might offer his son, based on what I had noticed in our conversations:

> It is clear to me that Peter needs a lot of help and guidance. He has done some terrible things that he needs to face up to *and* he is hurting a lot inside.
>
> From what I have seen here today I reckon you have a lot to offer as a Dad and as a mate. Despite all the disappointment and frustration over the years, you have been prepared to:
> – stop and think about Peter's feelings
> – face the fact that you have hurt him and let him down
> – and think about leading by example
>
> What is it that you would like to be able to say to Peter?
>
> What would it say about you as a father if you could let him know this?
>
> What might it have meant if your Dad had done this?

I invited Tom to consider his readiness to take these realisations further and make a commitment:

> Are you interested in working with me to find ways to make this happen?
>
> It won't be easy.
>
> It will mean taking a closer look at your own actions – managing your own reactions in order to help Peter learn to manage his.
>
> It will mean taking a closer look at ways that you have hurt and frightened Peter.
>
> It is not a pathway for everyone. It means finding the courage to face your own mistakes and having the guts to correct them.
>
> What tells you that you're ready to take a closer look?
>
> Do you know anyone else who has tried to take a stand like this to put their family first?
>
> What would you be proving to yourself?
>
> How does it fit with the kind of man you are?
> How does it fit with the kind of Dad you want to be?

Broadening the focus on abusive behaviour – Kevin

Kevin was unlikely, at this point, to have examined the nature of his abuse of Susie in any

detail. The details of a pattern of deception whereby he gradually set up opportunities to entrap Susie in a developing range of abusive behaviours over an extensive period of time, would have been skimmed over and conflated into his description of *'a terrible thing'*. Kevin's sexually abusive actions could have been perpetrated within a broader context of other disrespectful or irresponsible behaviour. He might have engaged in other sexually offensive or exploitative behaviour or have sexually abused another child or children at some point in his life. I was not convinced that Kevin was at all ready to consider broadening the focus of abuse by addressing any of these details or possibilities.

A more helpful focus upon the effects of abuse could instead be broadened by inviting Kevin to consider his early statement, *'I've let the whole family down'*. He was invited to expand on this statement by considering each family member and the possible impact upon that person:

> Who have you let down?
>
> How have you let them down?
>
> In what ways have you let May down? etc.

Through these enquiries, Kevin was assisted to engage in *sober* conversation about a broad range of the effects of his actions upon a large number of people.

These enquiries could be extended to significant members of a man's community or the whole community itself, if relevant and appropriate. Individual acts of abuse have a destructive and undermining impact upon the security and connectedness of communities and culture itself.

Mapping the effects of abuse – affirming ethical preferences – Kevin

These enquiries involved *mapping the effects of abuse* and were established in relation to the reference point of Kevin's ethical strivings:

> You have been striving to be a wise, protective, respected and trusted elder in your family, one who has wanted to advise and guide others responsibly through your own life experiences. Yet your abuse of Susie has violated each of these important principles and betrayed each and every one in your family.

Initial realisations about the effects of abuse and its disclosure were developed and mapped accordingly:

How much has May believed in your integrity and your strivings within the family?

How might your actions have affected her security and faith in what she has believed?

What have your actions done to her sense of family?

What different directions might she be pulled in now?

How have your actions affected what she has been striving for personally and within the family?

What example have you now set in your family?

What track have you put your family on?

How might your actions have affected the integrity of your family?

What example did you provide for Susie? What were you teaching her?

How much did Susie's parents trust that you would respect and protect her?

How much confidence and respect did they hold in you?

How might your actions have affected their faith and trust in you?

How might your actions have affected their faith and trust in people generally?

What might they worry about now in relation to Susie?

Why do you think Susie told about what you were doing to her?

How might your actions have affected her security, trust and respect for you and for others?

How might she view her grandfather and what he did to her, in the future?

What different directions might your other kids be pulled in?

How much are they entitled to be angry and outraged?

Enquiries like these tend to promote fledgling realisations about the violation and betrayal of valued family qualities and personal ethics as well as real and potential harm done to others. Kevin was initially invested in hope that he may not have caused harm to Susie; 'I didn't do things that would hurt her'; 'If she didn't want to, I wouldn't do it'. His understandings about the nature of harm and the subtle processes of attributing a sense of responsibility to Susie by seeking her 'cooperation' were extremely limited. However, he acknowledged that his actions must have distressed Susie for her to tell her parents and began to consider potential harm that might well

affect her security and trust in others. Not only had he betrayed his responsibility as a grandparent, he had begun to teach Susie behaviour that could place her at great risk in the future. Kevin recognised that he had shattered respect and trust and that the family was now divided with each member hurting and distressed. He regarded his abusive actions as 'out of character' and thought that the family would be disillusioned, perhaps wondering, 'Who can you trust?' Kevin acknowledged that Susie's parents felt betrayed, 'heartbroken' and outraged, and would indeed be worried about their daughter's well-being. He wondered whether they might even blame themselves for trusting him with Susie.

In this context, Kevin was invited to re-consider and affirm his ethical strivings and preferences. He was keen to find 'some way to make things right again'; 'to tell them how very sorry I am'; and 'that it will never happen again'. However, his ideas about restoration appeared to be somewhat nostalgic and self-centred. The following enquiries tended to invite consideration of a deeper understanding of the nature of his abuse and possibilities for more expansive forms of restitution:

Kevin, you are beginning to understand more about what you may be putting your family through and, understandably, you want to try to make amends. You have made it clear that you would 'do anything' that would help repair the damage you have done. What would it mean if you tried to apologise before:
– you understand fully how you came to take the pathway you did with Susie?
– you have worked out how you came to violate your position in the family?
– you have worked out how you came to betray your own principles so seriously?
– you have fully understood how your actions might affect every member of your family, now and in the future?
– you have studied what you might have put each person through and what they might need from you?

How might this fit with the leadership and example you want to provide?

How does it fit with trying to earn respect, offering protection, etc?

How might this move you towards being able to 'look Susie's family (others in the family) in the face again?'

How might this fit with your ideas about loyalty?

How might this fit with the track you need to be on as an elder in your family?

Kevin was invited to consider what role he might want to play in assisting his family to address the chaos and division caused by his abuse of Susie, and in particular, his readiness to take responsibility without relying upon the support or protection of others within the family:

How important is it that your family get their heads together and can support one another?

How important is it that their feelings come first at this time?

How entitled are they to feel outraged and betrayed?

What might be a healthy response on their part; showing their feelings or protecting your feelings?

How much do you want them to know that:
– you believe they are entitled to feel outraged and betrayed?
– you can handle them feeling that way?
– you don't need them to protect you by looking after your feelings?
– that you can stand on your own two feet?
– you want them to support each other?

How worried is May about the effects of what you have done on others in the family?

How much have your actions undermined May's faith in you and hopes for the future?

How worried is May about you and how you are coping?

How much do you want May to know that:
– you believe she is entitled to feel outraged and betrayed?
– you can handle her feeling that way?
– you don't need her to protect you by looking after your feelings?
– you can stand on your own two feet?
– you want the family to find support with each other?

In this way, Kevin was invited to consider an ethical stance which might try to privilege the feelings, needs and restorative possibilities for family members and which might subvert the restraining pattern of reliance which would be likely to inhibit his ethical journey.

Establishing commitment – Kevin

Kevin could now be invited to consider and state an ongoing commitment to addressing his abusive behaviour and its effects, with a goal towards accountable and ethical restorative action. This commitment required his readiness to continue to face up to abusive actions, study their actual and potential effects upon others and find accountable forms of restitution. Such a commitment also required a readiness to examine closely the development of his ethical lapse in order to enable genuine confidence in making responsible judgements in the future. As Kevin demonstrated self-reliance in these endeavours he might further open *windows to shame* and find deeper respect for the feelings and needs of others.

Kevin declared a determination to be accountable for his actions and a desire to place the feelings and needs of family members before his own, but struggled with what appeared to be a sense of impatience and desperate hope to take action which might quickly bring about forgiveness, forgetting and family reconciliation. He reiterated a desire to apologise and reassure Susie's parents that, *'I can see what they are going through'*; *'I have realised how much I have hurt them'*; *'I would never put them through anything like this again'*; *'if only they would give me another chance'*. Kevin was again encouraged to maintain his desire to consider their feelings and to find ways to make amends for his actions, but was also invited to slow down and set accountable priorities:

You are beginning to think more deeply about what you have done and how this has affected others and I respect the fact that you are keen to do something about it. However, hasty and desperate decisions usually only make things worse. You have hurt people enough and I imagine you don't want to make things any worse.

Can I invite you to slow down and think back to what it might mean to try to apologise and make amends; to try to fix things with others before you have got your own act together.

Have you yet fully faced every detail of what you did and how you set Susie up?

Have you worked out how you got yourself so far off your moral pathway?

Have you understood all the possible effects that your abuse of Susie could have upon her and others in your family?

Do you understand exactly what each person needs, how to try to provide it and whether they are ready to hear from you?

Until you have a pretty good understanding of all these things, you run the risk of adding insult to injury.

Does it make sense that you get your own act together first?

He was then invited to consider broader implications of these priorities:

Could you really be sure that you would never act this way again if:
– you didn't understand how you came to act in this 'out-of-character' way?
– you didn't see it coming and you don't know where it came from?
– you haven't worked out a good plan to prevent it?

How reassuring would your promises be to others in this case?

What would your apologies mean if you hadn't yet:
– faced up fully to every detail of what and how you did this to Susie, leaving no stone unturned?
– made sure you can face fully the parts that are most painful and hardest to take a close look at, without running away?
– thought deeply about all the possible effects your abuse could have upon Susie and others in the family?
– considered carefully what each person wants from you and how you can provide this without causing further offence?

How helpful and reassuring would apologies be if you had skimmed over any of this in your haste?

Are you ready to slow down and study fully what you have done and its effects?
– to become 100 per cent sure you have faced it fully?
– to understand fully how you got yourself into this place?
– even though it will hurt like hell?
– even though the shame might feel unbearable?

What will you need to find in yourself to do this?

What might this say to your family?

What will you be proving to yourself?

How might it fit with the elder you want to be?

Kevin was also invited to consider commitment to a path of self-reliance:

How might you demonstrate to May and others in the family, that:

– you are seriously committed to this pathway of facing up?
– you can stand on your own two feet?
– you don't need them to worry about you?
– you don't need them to protect you from their feelings?

How might you protect them from your fears and worries?

What will you need to find in yourself to take this path?

What might you respect about taking this direction?

This conversation was developed further in meetings with May and Kevin, in the context of discussion about the impact of the abuse upon May and her feelings and needs (see Chapter 10).

Broadening the focus on abusive behaviour – Barry

In previous conversations where Barry was invited to address his abusive behaviour, he quickly broadened his focus from physical violence to acknowledge a pattern of criticism and judgemental behaviour towards Eve and Colin. He could only extend his focus as he gradually began to develop a sense of agency or capacity to think creatively and productively about his behaviour and to move away from drawing conclusions about personal insufficiency.

Barry had not yet labelled this behaviour as *abuse*; however, he could recognise its destructive, harmful and frightening nature and acknowledged that it left Eve and Colin fearful, diminished and disrespected. With the assistance of patient enquiry, he would eventually come to *see it like it is*, as he examined his actions and their effects more closely and to label them accordingly (see Chapter 10).

Most importantly, Barry had begun to make his focus more defined and specific; to discriminate two important ethical responsibilities by preparing to challenge *mistaken shame* and to face the *disgrace* associated with his abuse of Eve and Colin. He had begun to hold a determined position to 'clean up my own back yard'. This distinction might allow him to become clearer and more ready to face his sense of disgrace in a productive and enabling manner; to feel a sense of agency or capacity to act ethically in challenging circumstances.

Mapping the effects of abuse – affirming ethical preferences – Barry

Barry began two separate but interconnected mapping projects both centred around his stated ethical strivings.

The first project continued examination of the effects of *self-doubt* in his own life and the impact of this upon family members. He was beginning to recognise how *self-doubt* seemed like a constant presence which questioned *'everything I do'* and culminated in him feeling, *'never good enough'*. Barry felt that he had carried this burden all his life and that it robbed him of any sense of *'acceptance'*, achievement and satisfaction. As a child, he felt criticised and disapproved of within his own family and was shocked to discover that he had himself unwittingly continued this practice through *self-doubt*. This left Barry feeling that he *'never made the grade'* throughout his schooling, with peers and in his employment, regardless of the level of his performance. *Self-doubt* had seemed to justify itself as revealing a truth about Barry. He also began to recognise how he had applied the same critical logic to members of his family with the same justifications that such criticism and judgement was fair and constructive.

Barry was invited to affirm ethical preferences by re-considering times when he had challenged or stood apart from practices of *self-doubt*:

What difference has it made when you have stood up to self-doubt?

What have you discovered about yourself?

What difference does it make to expose self-doubt like this and to see through its tactics?

Who do you want calling the shots, you or self-doubt?

What suits you best?

How could you assist others to feel accepted when you are so judgemental of yourself?

How could you tune into Eve's and Colin's abilities when you are so critical of your own?

What difference does it make when you take charge of your life?

The second mapping project concerned the effects of criticism and judgement upon Eve's and Colin's lives over time, and Barry's strivings and hopes for his family. Barry considered the impact upon valued qualities such as *'safety'*, *'respect'* and *'acceptance'*. He was particularly moved when considering how his practices of judgement and criticism might have affected Eve's and Colin's *'confidence in themselves'* and their *'sense of achievement'*.

Barry re-considered and affirmed the importance of becoming a partner and a father who is *'protective'* and *'respectful'*; who *'listens'* and *'supports'* rather than criticises and judges. He re-emphasised that he wanted to contribute in ways which might lead to Eve and Colin feeling accepted; ways which might help build *'confidence'* and a *'sense of achievement'*, rather than destroy these qualities.

It is important to note that these two projects were addressed separately despite their inter-related natures. Barry's critical and judgemental practices were not regarded as causally related to his practices concerning self-doubt. A construction of causality is not regarded as helpful in Invitational practice. *Self doubt* and *mistaken shame* might have been restraining Barry's readiness to take ethical action to cease abusive practices but they should not be regarded as having caused him to abuse. The two projects were conducted concurrently with the *self-doubt* project aimed at freeing Barry from restraint and thereby enabling him to address disgrace and his abusive actions effectively.

Establishing commitment – Barry

Barry's readiness to commit to an effective and accountable ethical journey hinged upon maintaining a sense of agency; a belief in his capacity to stand apart from long term habits and consider new possibilities. Accordingly, Barry was continually invited to reflect upon steps he had taken and steps he was contemplating, to challenge *self-doubt* and to stand apart from judgement and criticism of others.

Barry appeared to have been demonstrating agency in opening up the two ethical projects. I invited him to consider how he had been able to take these steps and what this might mean in relation to his ethical strivings:

Have you spoken out and defied self-doubt like that before?

Have you recognised that you can step back from criticism like that before?

How did you find that determination?

Where is it coming from?

Where do you feel it in your body?

What does it require of you?

What are you up against?

When have you applied it before?

What did you discover about yourself?

What tells you that you are ready to commit to this journey?

How does it fit the man, the partner and the father you are becoming?

Barry was also invited to consider his commitment to stand independently to face up to and challenge practices, without reliance upon the tolerance of family members:

You have made it clear that you hate judgemental violence and that you are determined to put an end to it.

Should Eve or Colin put up with any more of this?

Should they tolerate criticism and judgement or should they speak out about it?

What tells you that you are ready for them to speak out?

What tells you that you can handle this?

How do you know that you can listen rather than react?

How would Eve and Colin know it is safe for them to speak out?

What would give them confidence that you will listen?

CHAPTER 6

Becoming Accountable

The principle of *accountability* requires that we strive to privilege the experiences, needs and feelings of those who have been subjected to abuse or who are at risk of being abused, in all intervention practice with men who have abused.

Becoming accountable entails commitment to seeking understanding of the impact and effects of abuse and the needs of those who have been harmed by the abuse. It requires practices which respectfully access these experiences and privilege them in intervention with men. We become accountable through ongoing consideration of such experiences, reflection on what they mean for our practice and critique by those who have been subjected to abuse. Becoming accountable is a vital aspect of our *parallel journey* that entails *reaching towards the world of the other*. We reach towards the person subjected to abuse, listen to their experiences and imagine the potential effects of the abuse, in order to bring these understandings forward to inform our practice.

We develop this understanding through ongoing research by reading, viewing and listening to accounts of the impact and effects of abusive behaviour on individuals, families and communities. More specific understanding can be gained when we strive to make contact and establish a connection with the individuals, or their advocates, who have been subjected to abuse by our clients. This contact is generally established at the beginning and maintained throughout intervention with the man who has abused.

We can prepare ourselves by seeking permission to view documented descriptions of family and community members' accounts of abuse. These may include police and court records, reports of statutory investigations and assessments and victim impact statements. We must seek the individual's permission to view such documents and to establish any direct or indirect contact. Permission is generally sought via written or telephone requests in which the purpose of access or contact, for ensuring accountability, is explained.

This process for establishing a structure for **accountability to Sue and Paul**, to guide work with Jack, is illustrated below:

Contact was made with Sue, soon after the initial meeting with Jack, to:

– inform Sue of Jack's participation and the nature and aims of his intervention programme.
– gain an understanding of Sue's current assessment of safety for herself and Paul.
– gain an understanding of what Sue felt was important for herself and Paul.
– provide Sue with an opportunity to have her needs and wishes taken into consideration.
– ensure that our work with Jack would not disrespect or inadvertently be insensitive to Sue's wishes and needs.
– assist Sue to access any resources or assistance that she or Paul might require.

Consultations with women's advocacy groups had determined that an approach by letter might help reduce any sense of pressure for a woman to feel obliged to become involved in a man's intervention programme. Consequently, the initial contact with Sue was made by letter;

Dear Sue,
We are writing to inform you that Jack M is attending our programme for men who have been violent or abusive to their partners or family members.
We make this contact with partners and ex-partners of all men attending our program because we want to make sure that our work respects the feelings and needs of all family members who have been hurt by violence and abuse. One of our priorities is that you and your family feel safe and respected. We want to make sure that you have the opportunity to let us know what you think we should take into account, so that our work does not cut across or disrespect what is important for you and your son.
Our programme is aimed at stopping violence and abusive behaviour. We strive to make our work account-able to the feelings and needs of women and children as we try to assist men to understand how violence and abuse affects family members and to respect the feelings and needs of others.
We would welcome an opportunity to meet with you, or with someone that you trust, so you can let us know what

is important for you and what you might want us to take into account or consider when working with Jack.

We can inform you about the programme and answer any questions you may have.

Our job is to work with Jack and assist him to take responsibility for his actions. We do not have any expectations or requirements of you and we respect your right to your own privacy at this time. We do not wish to influence your hopes or wishes for the future, only to understand and respect them.

Jack would not be attending this meeting. This is a private opportunity for you to talk about what is important for you. We will of course respect confidentiality and not share any details of our conversation with Jack, unless you wanted this.

If you would like to meet, please contact me on (phone number).

Sue agreed to an initial meeting and the purpose of contact was reiterated. In providing an explanation of Jack's intervention programme and seeking an understanding of Sue's experiences and needs, the need for accountability was stressed with particular emphasis placed on providing a safe and respectful forum:

- for Sue to express what was important for her and for Paul.
- where Sue's and Paul's needs would be respected and not questioned.
- which was not concerned with reconnection or hopes for the future.
- where there was no expectation for Sue to participate in Jack's intervention programme or provide anything for Jack.
- where Sue could ask questions and raise concerns.

Possible concerns about safety and privacy were canvassed, before inviting Sue to discuss her feelings and needs:

This meeting involves talking about your feelings and what is important to you. It might involve talking about what has happened and where it has left you.
– Have you talked about this to anyone else before?
– How safe does it feel to talk about these things?
– What concerns might you have in talking about this here?
– What concerns might you have about being listened to or taken seriously?
– What concerns might you have about the privacy or confidentiality of what you say?

Sue was invited to express any concerns and her requirements for maintaining a sense of safety

and privacy for herself and for Paul. She spoke of feeling increasingly harassed, fearful of and 'smothered' by Jack. Sue wanted to be separate from Jack but, in the context of conflicting advice from others, expressed uncertainty about whether her actions in leaving him were reasonable and justifiable. Accordingly, some enquiries were focused on her entitlement to safety and privacy and steps she had already begun to take towards realising this entitlement:

What was it that led to you taking the stand that you did?

How hard was it to take this step? What were you up against?

How important was it for you to refuse to put up with any more violence for yourself or for Paul?

How important has it been for you to stand up for your privacy?

How much is Jack respecting your privacy?

How much is Jack respecting your right to be free of violence and harassment?

The position that violence, harassment and violation of privacy are unacceptable, along with support for Sue's entitlement to be safe and have her privacy respected, were made explicit and acknowledged as programme goals for working with Jack. The process of *limited confidentiality* was explained, whereby Sue would be informed of any concerns arising from Jack's attitude or behaviour which might put Sue or Paul at risk of further harm. Sue was invited to suggest other feedback she might want to receive about Jack's participation in the intervention programme.

As Sue began to describe her experience of Jack's abusive behaviour, she was invited to consider the implications of Jack's apparent abdication of responsibility for his actions:

How much do you think Jack has stopped and thought about what he has put you and Paul through?

How important is it that Jack faces up to and understands what he has done to you and Paul and where it has left you both?

What do you want us to take on board or consider when working with Jack?

Sue accepted an offer to meet with a separate counsellor who could address her concerns. As intervention with Jack progressed, contact with

Sue, together with her counsellor, was maintained with the additional aims to:

– provide a safe forum for Sue to express concerns or ask questions about Jack's behaviour or his intervention programme.
– monitor levels of safety and respect experienced by Sue and Paul.
– monitor the consistency of accounts of both abusive and respectful actions disclosed by Jack and Sue.
– provide Sue with feedback regarding Jack's commitment and participation in his intervention programme and any concerns about risk of further abuse.
– promote relationship boundaries which protect privacy and allow separateness.
– maintain a priority on stopping abuse before addressing any relationship hopes.
– assist Sue to establish objective, behavioural means to evaluate Jack's actions.

These accountability meetings are described more fully in Chapter 15. They are pivotal in establishing and maintaining accountable practice. However, they also serve to affirm certain fundamental principles for safety and respect within relationships, families and communities:

– that Sue and Paul are entitled to be, and to feel, safe from abuse and violence.
– that Sue is entitled to express her thoughts and feelings without intimidation.
– that Sue is entitled to privacy and separateness to pursue her own interests.
– that Sue takes responsibility to ensure her own safety but does not take responsibility for Jack's abusive behaviour.
– that Jack is not entitled to rely upon Sue to accept responsibility for his behaviour and its effects.

In this context, a history of resistance by Sue can also be recognised and affirmed; which has included acts of entitlement to set her own priorities by refusing to tolerate violence and abuse and refusing to accommodate the expectations and requirements of others as prescribed by dominant cultural interests.

As we strive to become accountable to Sue's experience of abuse and understand the dilemmas she faces concerning safety, entitlement and privacy, we can assist Jack to develop similar strivings and realisations which will expand his ethical journey. We must also endeavour to establish accountability to Paul's experience. As a child who relies upon parents for security and protection, he is perhaps placed in the most powerless and vulnerable circumstances. Children's needs are frequently overlooked in intervention with domestic abuse, and establishing practice which is accountable to children's needs poses special challenges, given their developmental status, dependency and subsequent limited options for independent action and resistance.

The principle of accountability highlights a range of complexities and dilemmas in establishing ethical practice.

I initially made **contact with Tom** in order to promote fair and accountable intervention with his son, Peter. Peter was expected to face and address his abusive behaviour towards his cousin, but was also being subjected to abuse by his father. The need to prevent increasing *responsibility overload* required a focus on the nature and effects of Tom's abusive behaviour in working with Peter.

However, accountable intervention with Tom also requires an understanding of the impact of his abusive behaviour upon Peter. Tom could eventually make some restitution for his actions and hold a more nurturing and respectful parental position, as he came to appreciate the nature and extent of his son's experiences of confusion, hurt, disillusionment, injustice, and mistaken shame, as a result of his father's abusive actions. However, my efforts to assist Tom to address his abusive behaviour and to understand its effects upon his son would be limited in the absence of my own attempts to access and understand Peter's experience.

Accountable practice with Tom also required contact with his partner, Judith, to understand her experience and needs. I suspected that Tom might also have behaved in abusive ways towards Judith and remained vigilant for opportunities to address this possibility in meetings with Judith. Judith talked about attempts to seek assistance from government agencies for Tom which arose from her concerns about his abusive treatment of Peter. She had not felt ready to disclose that she was also abused by Tom on those occasions but wanted her partner to stop hurting Peter. Judith told me that the agency workers made notifications to Child

Protection authorities and encouraged her to separate from Tom. She did not want to separate and left these meetings feeling a sense of negative judgement as *'weak'* and *'a failure as a mother'*.

Ongoing conversations with Judith appeared to gradually highlight certain ethical qualities; her concerns as a mother, her determination to try to help Peter and her capacity to *'hang in there'* however difficult it might be. Eventually Judith did feel ready to disclose that she was also subject to physical and verbal abuse by Tom. These disclosures were made at the same time that Tom had begun to recognise the need to address his abusive behaviour towards Peter. I began to enquire whether there were also *'times when you may have acted in ways you regret towards Judith'* and Tom was able to take further steps in starting to face up to abusive behaviour towards his partner. Patient ethical enquiry, in relation to the abuse of Peter, could help open possibilities for naming and addressing another arena for abusive behaviour towards Judith. Similarly, patient efforts to understand and attend to Judith's experiences of parental concern and her experiences of accommodation of and resistance to Tom's demands and expectations, could promote accountable intervention with Tom. Tom was then able to challenge a long-standing pattern of reliance upon Judith and to take responsibility to address his own abusive practices towards his partner.

The dilemmas raised by the principle of accountability can at times appear overwhelming when we consider the complexity of reactions and responses of different extended family members, as in the context of **intervention with Kevin**. How might we access and take into account:

- *The experiences of outrage and betrayal of Susie's parents?*
- *The pleas by other family members for forgiveness and forgetting?*
- *The experiences of Kevin's partner, May, who felt pulled in conflicting directions where:*
  - *some family members wanted her to separate whilst others wanted her to support Kevin?*
  - *she felt disgust and betrayal at Kevin's abusive actions?*
  - *she was worried about Kevin's well-being?*
  - *she was worried about her own future and security?*

- *The experiences and understandings of the priest who had spoken in terms of God's forgiveness?*

How might these conflicting experiences, hopes and expectations impact upon Susie?

Accountable practice requires that we try to understand and appreciate the experiences of others and their potential impact upon those who are in the most vulnerable circumstances. It can be extremely difficult to understand and balance the wishes and hopes of children with the expectations of others and judgements about the 'best interests' of a child. Children, such as Susie, are likely to feel enormous pressures with conflicting loyalties and feelings of responsibility for the distress experienced by family members. However, we must strive to connect with significant family members, counsellors and others whose beliefs, actions and understandings can assist an appreciation of impacts and influences upon Susie's feelings and needs. We are required to hold our work with Kevin and other family members accountable to these understandings of Susie's needs.

It is likely that there may be a common ethical interest in Susie's well-being that can be recognised by all significant persons and which might unite all with a common restorative purpose which is accountable and respectful to the child's experiences and needs. Kevin might be assisted to recognise and appreciate the complex and destructive impact of his abusive actions, to accept full responsibility for his actions and to actively challenge patterns of reliance upon others who may inadvertently attempt to excuse him from or carry these responsibilities on his behalf.

In a similar manner, **intervention with Barry** must be informed by understanding and appreciation of the experiences and needs of his partner, Eve, and son Colin. His journey towards addressing self-doubt and mistaken shame must be complemented with an increasing understanding of the immediate effects of his actions upon family members. Barry could broaden his understanding of the effects of his abusive behaviour from a general sense of '(self)hatred' and 'disgust' at 'hurting' and 'frightening' Eve and Colin, to more specific and deeper connections between particular actions and family members' experiences of his judgement and criticism.

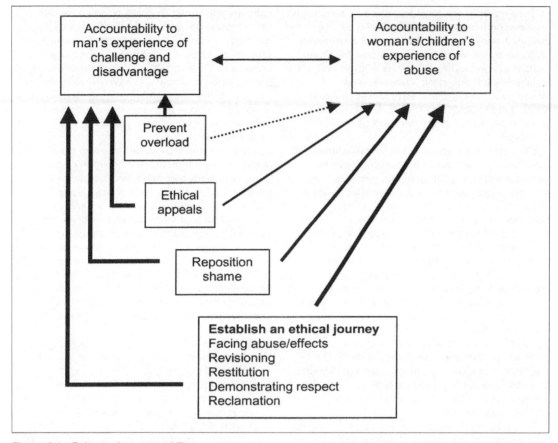

Figure 6.1 Balances in accountability

Balances in accountability

Invitational practice is initially focused upon the man's immediate experience, the prevention of restraining patterns responsibility overload and under-estimation and his ethical preferences. Figure 6.1 below illustrates the gradual shift in focus from the man's concerns towards reaching towards and appreciating the experience of those hurt by his abuse.

The thickness of the arrows reflects an increasing level of focus on the experiences of women and children as the man develops readiness and commitment to face up to and become accountable for his abusive actions. The experience of others might appear almost invisible in the first stages of engagement. The counsellor strives to hold these experiences in a privileged space whilst inviting the man to develop readiness to consider them. Gradually a balance of accountability can be established through this interplay of considering fit between the man's stated ethics, programme goals and the feelings and needs of others who have been abused.

Enhancing our parallel journeys

Accountability practices are enhanced by the development and maintenance of ongoing liaison and collaboration with community groups, agencies and organisations that provide support for people who have been subjected to abuse. Our *parallel journeys* are enhanced in this endeavour, as we attempt to collaboratively negotiate the traditionally adversarial politics which have resulted in mutual mistrust and suspicion and kept services for abusing and abused persons separate and often competing for resources.

Our capacities for consideration and reflection on the experiences of abused persons can be extended with practices that subvert adversarial dialogue by providing structures that promote mutual understanding of common goals and collaboration (Hall, 1994; Tamasese and Waldegrave, 1993). These structures can assist *reaching out towards the world of the other* and promote respect of differences in our *parallel journeys*.

The structures often entail the establishment of *listening circles* where a group of counsellors working with men, for example, might be assisted to imagine and consider a specific aspect of the experiences of women or children subjected to abuse. The counsellors are encouraged to extend their thinking by confining themselves to this task and considering all the possibilities they can imagine, before expressing their realisations for the consideration and critique of a *listening circle* of counsellors who work with women and children. The counsellors for women and children will then reflect upon what they have heard but in the presence of the counsellors for men who form a second *listening circle* where they can attend to and study the feedback provided. The men's counsellors might then respond in the listening presence of a further *listening circle* of the advocates for women and children and vice-versa.

Such structures, which employ *listening circles*, help to prevent adversarial dialogue and defensive argument by encouraging listening to the experiences of others, understanding and active reflection on what has been heard. Counsellors working with men can listen deeply and creatively take account of the experiences of those who have been abused and their needs. Advocates for people who have been abused can offer helpful consultation and critique in a context which is collaborative and respectful rather than adversarial; a political context which extends the *parallel journey* and mirrors the processes and goals of effective intervention.

The effective use of these structured exercises first requires some preparation to establish *readiness* of both groups, whereby concepts of common goals about stopping violence, building respectful relationships and respecting differences are identified and supported. Such preparation runs parallel to intervention with men to assist their readiness to address abusive behaviour and consider the experiences of others. Adversarial processes and practices are subverted in initial discussion which focuses upon ethical discovery and clarification through *listening for intent*. Ethics and strivings which both groups may hold in common can be named and honoured. These might include working towards the cessation of abusive behaviour, collaboration, respect of difference and accountability. These initial discussions form an ethical foundation for effective investment by all parties in the *listening circle* exercises.

After this initial preparation, a typical *listening circle* exercise might assist a group of counsellors, who work with men who have abused, to imagine and wonder about women's and children's experiences of the nature and impact of specific aspects of intervention practice with men. They might consider a concept such as *restitution* and discuss their realisations in the presence of a *listening circle* of advocates for women and children who have been subjected to abuse. This process can be facilitated with a set of structured questions designed to explore how the concept and practices of *restitution* might be experienced:

1. *What hopes might women and children have in relation to men making restitution for their abusive behaviour?*
2. *What concerns might women and children experience about men's attempts to make restitution for their abusive behaviour?*
3. *How might you ensure that you hold your work with men accountable to the experiences of women and children, when issues of restitution are being considered?*
4. *How might you ensure that attempts at restitution do not lead to women and children feeling:*
   – further traumatised?
   – obligated to accept the man's attempts, relinquish feelings of outrage or betrayal or pardon the man and his behaviour?
   – obligated to forgive or reconcile with the man?
5. *What experiences in this work have opened your eyes to the need to take further steps to develop accountability practices?*

Having listened to these considerations and realisations, the advocates for women and children might then be invited to reflect, in the presence of a *listening circle* of the counsellors who work with men:

1. *What is your experience in hearing people who work with those who have abused consider how they might hold their work accountable to those who have been subjected to abuse?*

2. *What questions or dilemmas did it raise?*
3. *What possibilities might it open up if workers were committed to hold their work accountable in this way?*
4. *How might men's workers ensure that they maintain genuine accountability with practice that goes beyond good intentions?*
5. *How might it contribute to the lives of those who have been subjected to abuse, to know that workers are striving to hold their work accountable?*

This paradigm can be employed to address a wide range of issues such as:

● *What hopes or concerns might women and children have about men attending a group programme to address abusive behaviour?*
● *What possibilities or dilemmas might arise when men's programme workers approach women partners in their attempts to establish accountable practice?*

Listening circle exercises can be extremely helpful in furthering the *parallel journeys* of men and women workers in men's intervention programmes. An invitation for men to engage in parallel processes with their male clients by considering the experiences of women colleagues in the context of accountable practice might be assisted by the structures which this paradigm provides:

● *What kinds of inspiration and excitement might women experience in co-leading a men's group (or other form of intervention with men)?*
● *What kinds of challenges might women experience in co-leading a men's group (or other form of intervention with men)?*
● *How might it add to the effectiveness of this work for men to consider women's experiences, in this context?*

As men and women reflect and listen to each other's experiences, characteristic gendered restraints to listening and understanding each other's experiences can be named and considered. In this context, men might listen to and consider the reflections of women as they discuss the effects of a common history of subjugation to the gaze and judgement of men or dominant narratives which expect accommodation and regard critique and challenge to men as unreasonable 'nagging'.

Women might similarly listen to and consider men's reflections about their struggles to address inevitable complicity with dominant cultural interests and tendencies towards defensiveness or passive accommodation. In this non-adversarial context, men and women can witness each other naming and challenging their own restraining gendered ideas and practices and commit to enhancing non-hierarchical but accountable partnerships. These processes, of course, run parallel to those which might characterise our client's journeys towards establishing respectful and non-violent relationships.

A similar paradigm can promote and enhance our *parallel journeys* in the context of any power differentials which have led to specific communities or cultures becoming disadvantaged and marginalised through the hegemony of dominant cultural interests. After initial preparation, members of a dominant culture might be invited to consider and reflect upon specific aspects of the experiences of a *listening circle* of indigenous people, disadvantaged youth or another marginalised group.

Becoming accountable means striving to hold the experiences, views and needs of abused persons in a safe and respectful balance with the man's ethical strivings whilst upholding restorative goals of our programmes. I am continually challenged by the complexity of this endeavour with its requirement to remain interested in the differences that emerge without resorting to judgemental and colonising practices. Efforts to privilege accountability require an openness to the critique and judgement of others. At times I can feel exposed, disappointed and frustrated when attempts to establish accountability to individuals or communities who have been abused, disadvantaged and marginalised appear to go unnoticed or taken for granted. The failure to consult sufficiently and to take account of an individual's experience produces inevitable and necessary feelings of shame which must be faced and processed. Accountable practice requires ongoing reflection with the support of colleagues in order to address the many challenges, disappointments and frustrations which inevitably arise. We must embrace the contradictions that arise in our own parallel journeys in order to experience the excitement and discovery of new possibilities.

Practical dilemmas arise when we hear conflicting accounts of events, or notice significant differences in hopes for the future, in conversations with men and with their family members. Means for establishing safe and respectful forums for addressing such differences are described in Part Four. However, accountable practice continually tests our own abilities to become interested in and respect differences; to continue to reach out towards the world of the other and maintain ethical integrity.

CHAPTER 7

Principles and Practices for Group Intervention

Group intervention programmes have traditionally been regarded as fundamental for effective intervention for men who have abused, resulting in a hegemonic dogma with claims that men's groups constitute 'best practice', regardless of specific differences in needs and requirements of men (Gondolf, 2001; Pence and Paymar, 1993). The group format has been preferred as offering opportunities for men to encourage and learn from each other and as a forum for challenge and confrontation of minimisation and justification of abusive behaviour. Group intervention programmes are also thought to be economic in that they address the needs of a number of men within a given time period. As a result of this dogma, individual and couple modalities for intervention have tended to be neglected as men are encouraged or mandated to participate in 'one size fits all' group programmes with little preparation. Insufficient attention is paid to the singularities and differences of individual men or their readiness to address abusive behaviour, and the way that they relate to other men within the group.

A men's group constitutes a microcosm of broader men's cultures and will tend to reproduce aspects of dominant masculine interests. Men who have enacted abusive behaviour are prone to the captive effects of dominant cultural interests and will tend to order themselves within hierarchies of 'winners' and 'losers', within the group, particularly when anxious and unsure about their fit within a novel environment. Group facilitators can find themselves feeling somewhat overwhelmed and becoming increasingly authoritative, confrontative and controlling in attempts to establish a respectful group culture. Facilitators can inadvertently reproduce power relations and practices which replicate the context for abuse within the group. Often a group member will be marginalised within the power hierarchies of the group and will assume the identity and role of 'loser'. Group members such as Rob (see page 15) can become increasingly uncooperative, combative and dissatisfied within the group, as they attempt to protest their position or status.

They are first responded to with well-intended advice and confrontation about their actions and statements. Unhelpful power hierarchies become entrenched as this somewhat patronising concern gives way to frustration, ridicule and eventually contempt. The man is regarded as someone who 'just doesn't get it' and is increasingly marginalised within the group. This reproduction of dominant cultural interests is likely to subvert well-intended efforts by group facilitators and participants to address abusive behaviour, as a culture which unwittingly supports violence becomes reproduced within the group.

In Invitational practice, group intervention is regarded as a helpful mode of intervention along with individual, couple, family and community strategies. The effective use of group intervention is determined with the following considerations:

- *What aspects of intervention are best suited to a group format?*
- *What aspects of intervention might be problematic in a group format?*
- *How might a group format enhance the restorative project?*
- *How might we determine a man's readiness to participate in a group programme in ways that might enhance his ethical journey?*
- *How might a respectful group culture which values a duty of care be developed and maintained?*
- *How might we establish complementarity and interconnectedness between group intervention and couple, family and community intervention?*

I have not found group intervention to offer any advantage with respect to time economy, because group work still needs to be complemented with a range of individual, couple, family and community strategies. The men's group does not provide a substitute for these modes of intervention. However, group intervention programmes can offer a useful collaborative context for men to challenge their own abusive practices along with broader restraining, gendered ideas regarding the nature of men's conversations, privacy and concepts of masculinity. A men's group forum can help to subvert dominant ideas about privacy and secrecy that support abusive behaviour. The notions of *'being strong (by not publicly showing your feelings)'*; *'not letting your guard down'* and *'going it alone'* are undermined in a collaborative environment which provides a unique opportunity for men to stand together and support one another in challenging the cultural ideology which informs abusive practice.

Group intervention offers opportunities for men to take bold steps forward in their own restorative projects. An effective group forum generates possibilities for bold ethical initiatives in demonstrating compassion and love, in *reaching out towards the world of the other* and in developing and expressing a richer and deeper sense of remorse. Given that restorative practice is about understanding, appreciating and respecting the experiences of others, the group provides a wonderful opportunity for the actualisation and practice of this ethic.

Establishing readiness

Invitational practice places priority on ensuring that the man has established readiness and a sense of commitment in order to undertake an ethical journey. In establishing readiness, we first endeavour to ensure that he has an ethical experience in initial individual interviews; an experience which might be different to that in any other conversations about his abusive behaviour. The interview is structured in ways which might open up opportunities that reach beyond expressions of minimisation and justification of violence in order to enable ethical possibilities to be realised and expressed. Similar care must be taken to ensure that the man is ready to participate in a group programme so that the group might also offer different experiences with different possibilities compared to any previous encounters with men.

Readiness to attend a group programme first requires the establishment of readiness to embark on the ethical journey. This readiness is established and assessed in individual interviews which attend to ethical possibilities and addresses abusive behaviour, in accordance with the paradigm detailed in Part Two. An ethical foundation which might constitute readiness requires recognition by the man that:

- *At least some of his abusive behaviour is problematic.*

- *This behaviour is harmful to others.*
- *This behaviour does not accord with his own ethics.*
- *It is his responsibility to address and cease this behaviour.*
- *He has the capacity to take action to address this behaviour.*

This concept of readiness entails a degree of realisation about the destructiveness of abusive behaviour to self and others, some initial remorse, a sense of responsibility and some feeling of agency. The man decides to embark upon this journey because he is beginning to realise that these facing up steps accord with his ethics. His decision is influenced, but not solely so, by an accommodating response to external pressures or a moral imperative determined by the intervention programme or external authorities.

When a man demonstrates such readiness and expresses some commitment to address his abusive behaviour, he may be invited to consider his readiness to participate in a men's group. Whilst participation in an intervention programme may be mandated by a statutory authority, attending a men's group should never be a requirement of the programme.

A readiness assessment for a men's group should take into account each individual's history of his experience of power relations, marginalisation and sense of belonging and fit in various communities and cultures. These factors, which sometimes relate to differences of race or social class can help determine the likelihood of an individual man becoming marginalised within a specific group. When we take considerable care to ensure both readiness and fit, we can often prevent the development of power relations within the group which undermine a respectful culture and the maintenance of a duty of care.

As in individual counselling, considerable care must be taken to invite ethical participation in the development of respectful and accountable relationships and a culture open to new possibilities being realised. Our assessments should be attuned to recognition of the man's ethics and readiness to address his abusive actions. We must take care not to subject the man to a barrage of assessment instruments and processes which might undermine his ethical discovery and sense of agency by reproducing a political context which fosters a sense of accommodation or reaction to perceived programme imperatives.

Initial conversations about readiness to participate in a men's group might first invite consideration of the nature of group programmes:

- *What can a men's group offer in the restorative project?*
- *What might it mean to join a men's group?*

The men's group is described as an effective forum for addressing and ceasing violence and abusive behaviour. It is a forum which can be a step in preparation towards restitutive practices which might include family meetings and meetings with other community members or community groups.

A men's group provides unique opportunities for understanding and appreciating a wide range of differences in other men's ways of addressing abusive practices and the ideas and beliefs that support them. Dominant ideas about being a man encourage individualism, competitiveness and mistrust of other men. This suggests that a man should be able to sort out problems on his own and should keep up his guard with other men. We then learn to be critical and judgmental of other men's ideas. These ways of thinking support violence. We can learn to become closed off from, mistrusting and judgmental of others, our partners, and even ourselves. This tends to be the case even though we are wanting connection with others and belonging. In fact, we can learn a great deal from pooling our experiences and witnessing other's discoveries in dealing with common problems. The man might be invited to consider these concepts and dilemmas and to consider the potential benefits for collaborative approaches to problem solving:

How have you noticed these ideas and how they operate?

How do you reckon you are challenging them in your conversations with me?

Have you had the opportunity to talk with other men about a common problem before?

What difference does it make when people join together to solve a problem?

Have you discovered the strength in unity?

What might you stand to gain by learning about listening to other men and understanding and respecting different points of view?

How might this help you in your journey?

As the benefits of a group forum are considered, the man may be invited to consider the challenges that he is likely to face in attending the men's group:

What might you be up against in attending the group?

What would you need to find in yourself to take this step?

What might you stand to gain or to lose in taking such a step?

This might entail conversation about fears of the judgement of other men, violation of privacy and shame associated with public exposure which are considered in the context of restraining gendered expectations that limit ethical possibilities. The common experiences of fear, risk and shame experienced by all men are highlighted along with the need to mobilise necessary ethical resources such as courage and determination:

Attending the men's group means taking a stand and facing your fears. It will require considerable courage and determination. It is not for everyone.
– What tells you that it might help you in your journey?
– Would you like to talk to a man who has completed a group programme to check it out further?
– What tells you that you are ready to try it?

Invitational group structure and process

Traditionally, men's groups have offered a structured psycho-educational curriculum which has addressed the nature and effects of violence and abusive behaviour along with strategies for men to increase their awareness of factors and experiences which contribute to abusive actions and to disrupt familiar patterns of controlling and abusive behaviour. The curriculum is generally developed with an understanding of male violence and abuse as a consequence of patriarchal cultural interests which promote strategies for seeking power and control over women. Group processes have been employed to encourage men to support respectful behaviour and to confront expressions of disrespectful behaviour, including minimisation and justification of abusive behaviour. Group facilitators have tended to introduce a set curriculum and structure input, group exercises and discussion around pre-determined topics which have been designed to educate and produce behaviour change (Pence and Paymar, 1993).

The Invitational model for men's groups is concerned with the broad range of power relations in which men participate. Whilst individual men attend the group to address abuses of power within specific relationships in their families and communities, the men's group provides a forum in which the power relations between participants and facilitators, between group members and between facilitators can be opened to critique and intervention. Group intervention places special emphasis upon practices which can enable this critique and offers considerable possibilities in the restorative project with its focus on accountability, *reaching towards the world of the other* and the development of respectful relationships and communities.

Men's groups reproduce microcosms of men's cultures and opportunities for the establishment of communities of men who can imagine and experience new ways of becoming together; new possibilities for relating which might subvert dominant cultural interests. These possibilities require ongoing critique of power relations and practices by all group members and especially by group facilitators who strive to assist the development of a culture of respect of singularity and difference and a mutually felt duty of care within the group. The group structures and practices are informed by this striving and subsequent ethical developments rather than by a set curriculum. Group facilitators strive to co-create novel group environments which subvert dominant cultural interests and patterns of relating and open up ethical possibilities for all group members.

The group is regarded as a developmental project which is informed by the ethical preferences of participants and facilitators whilst remaining accountable to the experiences of others affected by abuse. Group facilitators remain responsible for inviting and assisting ethical realisation and expression along with promoting ongoing critique of power relations and practices. Facilitators must openly attend to their own *parallel journeys* and engage in reflection and critique of their own power practices whilst maintaining the broader responsibilities regarding group participants. This requires group facilitators to embrace the familiar paradox of maintaining positions of

leadership without reproducing violence. A set curriculum can limit ethical realisation and initiative and often tends to reproduce a colonising context in which participants are subjected to set knowledges which underestimate their own ethical capacities. A set curriculum is unlikely to respect the individual experiences and needs of all group members. Each Invitational group programme is unique in that it is re-imagined, re-designed and re-created on an ongoing basis. The development of each new group programme reflects the ethical interests of group participants who, together with the facilitators, co-create the group itinerary. This developmental process constitutes a vital part of effective participation and of the production of new and alternative kinds of communities of men.

Invitational group practice privileges the establishment of a duty of care with mutual support of ethical expression, over the culture of correction and confrontation which is encouraged in some traditional group programmes. Group intervention practices should aim to subvert dominant masculine practices which promote hierarchical ordering through adversarial practices that elevate criticism and correction of others as desirable ways of relating. Invitational group practice supports critique within a context of fairness, equity and respect of difference. An effective group culture is likely to be characterised by self-confrontation through ethical realisation with expressions of respect and realisation by group members, rather than confrontation of others.

However, Invitational group processes are guided by a loose structure with a common flow of themes. Whilst these themes may be introduced sequentially, they constitute a cumulative flow with each theme being continuously developed in its complementary role towards realising the restorative project:

1. **Naming ethics.**
   Initial group meetings are primarily concerned with the establishment of a common ethical focus which enables the clarification and naming of specific individual and group ethical strivings and preferences. In this context, an itinerary is developed which might aid each man in his specific journey and the group as a whole in actualising its strivings.
2. **Naming abusive practices.**
   Once an ethical focus is established, men are invited to examine and name abusive practices

which might restrain or undermine realisation of their ethical strivings. The concept of *facing up* becomes increasingly highlighted along with the political nature of abusive behaviour. Possibilities regarding the discovery of *ethics in the face of adversity* become emphasised and enhanced.

3. **Addressing dangerous (cultural) ideas**. Abusive practices become understood in the context of a broader critique of dominant cultural interests. The concept of misguided attempts to build relationships based upon unhelpful cultural blueprints is developed and men are invited to discover, name and challenge dangerous ideas which block ethical realisation and inform abusive practices.

4. **Understanding the potential impact of abusive behaviour.** The concept and practices associated with *reaching towards the world of the other* are developed and extended in the group as men are invited to study the known and potential effects of abusive behaviour upon significant others and communities. These realisations become increasingly privileged as men are invited to assist one another in opening *windows to shame* and discovering new ethical possibilities and a sense of integrity as a result.

5. **Making restitution.** The concept of restitution is developed in the context of an accountable restorative project which considers making amends and reparation to individuals, communities and culture.

6. **Demonstrating respect of difference.** As levels of realisation increase and practices of restitution are developed, men are invited to consider active ways to demonstrate respect of difference; ways which challenge dominant cultural interests such as those reflected in concepts of *domestic love* and patriarchal practices. These might involve alternative practices of non-ownership, tolerance and cooperation.

Some useful group exercises are also described in Chapters 9 and 10.

Establishing a duty of care

A respectful group culture which can enable new possibilities for a community of men requires a duty of care whereby each man strives to *reach towards the world of the other*; to respect the singularity and difference of the other and to find expression for this respect within the group. This community ethic begins to be developed in the initial group exercises which concern the discovery and naming of individual ethical strivings and preferences. The initial welcome and orientation to the group might include an exercise which is likely to enable expression of ethical commitment along with opportunity for others to witness and be moved by this expression. The following structures for enquiry can be presented to the whole group or to men in smaller sub-groups.

Why do I want to stop abusive behaviour?

When I began to make a genuine commitment to stop abusive behaviour?

What I realised at this time?

What opened my eyes to what I was doing?

What is important to me?

What kinds of relationships have I really wanted with a partner and children?

What am I really wanting to offer or give in these relationships?

What kinds of ways am I wanting to relate to others in these relationships?

Where has my abusive behaviour been leading these relationships?

What have my partner and children been losing that might be important to them?

What have I been losing that is important to me?

These exercises invite men to consider and express their ethical strivings and realisations in a public forum and to listen to other men's expressions. Men might then be invited to reflect upon their experiences in these exercises:

What does it mean to be here?

What did it take to attend tonight? What were you up against?

What was it like to speak out in this group?

What was it like listening to others speak out?

How was this different to other settings where men get together?

What qualities are you needing to find in yourself?

What qualities are you noticing in others?

How are these qualities important to you?

How are you standing up for yourself and what you believe in?

How are you standing up for others?

In this context of personal and public reflection, men are assisted to name restraining factors and valued ethical qualities such as honesty, courage and determination in the face of adversity. Men in the group are beginning to take steps towards *facing up* in a collaborative forum which is becoming respectful of these steps. These reflections will generally enable readiness to consider and discuss the concept of duty of care:

What might make this group of men one which makes a difference?

Through the initial structured exercises, men in the group will have already experienced some aspects of duty of care which values listening and trying to understand the experiences of others, emotional expression, respectful affirmation and collaboration. These qualities can be contrasted with culturally dominant blueprints for relating as men which prescribe competitiveness, emotional guardedness, defensiveness, judgement, criticism and individualism. Men are invited to consider the advantages of developing a broader repertoire of ways of relating and imagine the ethical implications for their journeys. Each man is invited to consider his own readiness to embark upon such a journey in the group:

Which qualities might you want to develop in this group?

How might a duty of care broaden your range of possibilities?

How might it assist you in relating to the ways you are wanting to become?

How might it help you to develop as the person you are wanting to become?

What tells you that you are ready to participate in this group?

What are our responsibilities as group facilitators?

It can be helpful for group facilitators to acknowledge the inevitability and pervasiveness of dominant practices of relating which tend to undermine a duty of care. The pioneering efforts of group participants are acknowledged. Group facilitators are not exempt from the influence of dominant cultural practices and face the same challenges that are faced by group participants. Facilitators can share their own experiences within groups of men which illustrate different outcomes and possibilities and which help to promote collaboration and challenge the restraining notion of *us and them* in the group. Facilitators strive for accountability and transparency in their relationships with group members by discussing the nature of their parallel journeys and engaging in public reflection and discussion about group processes and personal reactions, including uncertainties and concerns.

The responsibilities of facilitators are further discussed and clarified as assisting men to realise their own ethical strivings and not in terms of holding men accountable to any fixed code of conduct. Men are encouraged to speak out about what is important for them and to protest unfairness in these initial discussions. The group is regarded as a safe environment group to experiment with ethical realisation and expression.

In striving to promote duty of care within the group, facilitators structure their enquiry in ways that invite ethical reflection and expression along with respect of difference. Facilitators may, at times, interrupt comments and conversation which becomes judgemental, disrespectful or patronising in the process of making these enquiries. These enquiries tend to invite:

Personal reflection and interest in difference rather than judgemental reaction:
How did Jeff's realisation and comments move you Jack?
What did they trigger in your thinking?
What did that remind you of in your life?
What did you gain from hearing Jeff's realisations?
How does that fit with what you are striving for?
What did you think was important for Jeff when he spoke out?
What do you reckon he was up against in taking these steps?
What do you imagine it required of him?
How might this fit with his hopes and what he is striving for?

Openness with emotional expression:
How did Jeff's realisation and comments affect you?
How did they grab you?

What did they get you thinking?
How did they make you feel?
What words go with this feeling?
What is the feeling try to say?

Protest against injustice rather than passive accommodation:
How will you know it is safe to speak out if anything seems unfair?
How might you ensure that you listen and are spectful when someone else speaks their mind?
What might our job be as group facilitators to make sure this can happen in the group?

Equity in participation by all group members:
How might you reach out to ensure that everyone gets a go in this group?
What might our job be as group facilitators to make sure that all of you have an opportunity to participate?

Establishing commitment to a restorative project

As group members clarify their ethical preferences and strivings in the initial group meetings, they are invited to establish an itinerary for further group meetings. This itinerary is informed by common ethical strivings and the aims of the restorative project; stopping abusive behaviour, restitution for harm done and reclamation of integrity.

A facing up itinerary may be detailed and documented in a collaborative process with all group members and the facilitators (see Chapter 9). The itinerary is continually evaluated throughout the duration of the group and steps that each man takes towards facing up are examined in terms of their appropriateness and helpfulness in actualising ethical strivings in the light of the restorative goals. Each man is invited to reflect upon any step taken:

What tells me that this is the right path for me?

How does it fit with the man I am wanting to become?

How will this help me to stop abusing?

How will it help make restitution for what I have done to others?

How will it help me to contribute respectfully to relationships?

How will it help me to feel self-respect and integrity?

CHAPTER 8

Overview – A Restorative Project

Invitational practice is informed by the restorative project and follows a paradigm which is continually revisited throughout all the stages of intervention. We endeavour to open space for and appeal to the man's (and our own) ethical strivings and invite interest in the contradictions and differences which emerge between the man's intent and his actions, and between his strivings and those of family and community members. In this context of ethical realisation, the man can experience remorse as he reaches out towards the world of the other. He can consider the nature and development of these contradictions and critique unhelpful and misguided efforts to achieve his strivings, along with the cultural blueprints and prescriptions which inform them. This enables challenge to complicit patterns of experience and behaviour and promotes acts of resistance which may in turn support ethical strivings.

Invitational practice thereby invites investment in an ongoing process of ethical clarification, interest in contradiction, realisation and resistance to influences which restrain the actualisation of preferred ways of becoming. An interest in difference opens up ethical possibilities and new ways of living and relating.

The following schematic table provides an overview of this paradigm which summarises the stages of intervention by relating invitational concepts to ethical preoccupations and considerations. Tables 1 and 2 summarise the invitational practices and their complementary ethical preoccupations when attending to ethical possibilities (see Chapter 4). Table 3 concerns invitational practices and ethical preoccupations which relate to establishing readiness to face and address abusive behaviour (see Chapter 5). Tables 1 to 4 represent an invitational paradigm which enables a commitment to the ethical journey and opens up the possibility to establish an ongoing itinerary which concerns ceasing abusive behaviour and reaching out towards the worlds of the other. This aspect of the restorative journey is summarised in Table 5, and described in detail throughout Part Three (see chapters 9–13).

A paradigm for restorative practice

		Ethical pre-occupations (common to man and worker)
Invitational practices		How am I wanting to live?
Restorative goals	Cessation of abuse	How am I wanting to be with others?
	Restitution	What kind of person am I becoming?
	Reclamation of integrity	
1. Opening ethical space		
Curiosity about restraint		
		What am I feeling right now?
Declare a just purpose		What is important for me right now?
Attend to the man's immediate experience		What am I passionately trying to say or do?
Prevent responsibility overload		What might render my ethical preferences invisible?
	Decline attributions of blame	
	Legitimise protest	
2. Appeals to ethics		
Listening for intent		What have I been striving for in this relationship?
Prevent under-estimation		What kind of man/partner/parent have I wanted to become?
Listening for intent		How have I wanted to be in this relationship?
Ethical clarification		
Developmental influences		What has influenced my strivings?
Connections through difference		How have I tried to develop and maintain them over time?
Ethics in the face of adversity		
3. Address abusive behaviour		
Address contradiction – windows to shame		
Allow contradictions to emerge		How have my actions been undermining my intent?
Contrast intent and actions		
Seek permission to enquire about incidents		How does it affect me to take a close look at these actions?
Promote sober conversation		How can Ido this in a way that is safe and enabling?
Provoke windows to shame		What does it mean that I feel shame?
Reposition shame		Where does this experience take me?
Integrity through facing shame		How does it fit with the person I want to be?

A paradigm for restorative practice Continued

4. Readiness for a journey

Broaden the focus on abusive behaviour

How has this contradiction become a pattern in my life?
What practices are stopping from me developing the relationships I have wanted?

Map the effects of abuse

Where are these practices taking my relationships?
Where are they taking me?
How do I really want to be in these relationships?

Affirm ethical preferences

Am I ready to commit to a facing up journey?

Establish commitment

How important is it that I:
    Stop hurting those I care about?
    Make restitution for harm I have caused?
    Reclaim self-respect and integrity?
    Become the person I want to be in relationships?

5. Establish an itinerary
Reaching towards the world of the other

How might I become accountable for my actions?
What might it mean to become interested in difference?

How will it help me to take a closer look?

Facing up – seeing it like it is
  Naming abusive practices
  Naming the effects of abuse

How will this help me to:
    Stop hurting those I care about?
    Make restitution for harm I have caused?
    Reclaim self-respect and integrity?
    Become the person I want to be in relationships?

Revisioning – mapping and resisting pathways to abusive behaviour

How have I come to act against what I have been striving for?

Misguided blueprints for:
  – becoming somebody
  – building relationships
  – love

What has been stopping me from:
  becoming the person I want to be?
  building the relationships I am wanting with others?

Dangerous ideas

How do these ideas lead me away from what I really want?
How am I resisting these unhelpful ideas and practices?

Making restitution

How might I make restitution for the harm I have caused?

Demonstrating respect

How might I become pro-active in resisting dangerous habits and ideas?
How might I test myself in challenging situations?
How am I becoming the person I want to be?
What am I discovering about myself/others/about love?

Part Three

An Itinerary for the Journey

CHAPTER 9

Preparing an Itinerary for Facing Up

Having established a sense of readiness and commitment to embark further upon an ethical journey, the man can be assisted to prepare an itinerary for facing up to his abusive actions and developing ethical and respectful ways of relating. The itinerary provides a structure to guide and evaluate new developments in previously uncharted territory and becomes a project for consideration in both individual and group intervention settings.

The itinerary constitutes a structure to guide facing up which is informed by the man's ethical strivings and preferences and the restorative project goals which concern stopping abusive behaviour, making restitution for harm done to others and reclamation of a sense of self-respect and integrity. When a man has demonstrated a sense of readiness for the journey, his ethical strivings will generally be consistent with the restorative goals and he may be invited to consider their relevance and importance for his journey:

How important is it to you to stop all abusive behaviour?

How important is it to you to try to make amends for the harm you have caused others?

How important is it to you to earn genuine self-respect; to know you have faced your past actions with integrity?

How much do these goals fit what you are striving for?

How much do they fit with the man you are wanting to become?

The man might then be invited to engage in a collaborative discussion to determine and document a facing up itinerary which addresses the question:

What will this journey require?

He will be invited to consider his own initiatives in the context of a suggested framework for facing up:

What steps have you already begun to take in this direction?

What tells you that you are on the right track with these steps?

The man may be informed that a facing up journey requires taking more bold steps and possibly more courage than has been needed ever before. These steps include:

- **Studying and naming abusive behaviour.**
  Taking a closer look at the details of what you have done already. Seeing it and calling it like it really is.
  – *Leaving no stone unturned. It will probably mean seeing and recalling things clearly that have been too hard to look at and that cause more shame than you have faced already.*
  – *If you don't put this under the microscope – if you miss some of the details – where would this leave you?*
  – *Where would it leave you if you wound up skimming the surface and didn't see what others have had to see?*

- **Understanding the pathways towards abuse.**
  Understanding how you got yourself into the position where you have acted against what you really believe in.
  – *How important is it to know by looking backwards what led you off the path you have really striven for?*
  – *How important is it to be able to know and see clearly the warning signs that you didn't heed before?*
  – *If you don't come to understand exactly how you came to act in such hurtful ways and to go so much against your better judgement and standards, how can you be confident about not repeating your past in the future?*

- **Understanding the potential effects of abuse upon others.**
  Studying the possible effects of your abuse upon everyone who may have been influenced. This is the most painful and challenging part of the journey – it means taking giant steps to consider ways you may have hurt others that you probably would never have imagined.

– *How much have others had to live with the burden of the effects of your abusive actions?*
– *How important do you think it is that you try to understand these effects?*
– *Whose job is it to carry this burden?*
– *If you had not studied in detail the possible ways that you may have caused harm to others, what would any attempt at restitution mean?*
– *What would it mean to others?*
– *What would it mean for your journey?*

- **Making restitution for the harm caused to others.**
  Attempting to make amends for the harm you have caused others and your community.
  – *How important is it to try to make some restitution?*
  – *What would it mean if you didn't try or if you left it for others to carry the burden of your actions?*

- **Demonstrating respectful behaviour.**
  Finding respectful ways that fit with what you believe in to contribute to relationships with others. Becoming true to yourself and your principles. Treating others with respect and fairness.
  – *How vital is it to discover how to turn your realisations into actions?*
  – *How much do actions speak louder than words?*

- **Testing yourself.**
  Learning how to face challenging life circumstances in respectful ways.
  – *How important is it to prove to yourself that you can face a challenge rather than try to live life avoiding it?*

These itineraries might also include practices which challenge restraining patterns of reliance upon others such as:

- **Standing on your own two feet.**
  Facing your own responsibilities rather than leaving them to others.
  – *Who has had to worry about the possibility and effects of abuse?*
  – *Who has had to carry the burden of this?*
  – *Whose job is it to carry this burden?*

- **Standing your ground.**
  Resisting dangerous ideas which support abusive behaviour
  – *How important is it to take a stand for yourself and to refuse to be pushed around by (restraining idea or misguided practice)?*
  – *How important is it to (challenge restraining idea or misguided practice) rather than your partner and children?*

CHAPTER 10

Naming Practices – The Nature and Effects of Abuse

A thing does not exist until it is named.

Naming abusive behaviour

Invitational practice eschews popular confrontational approaches which insist that a man recognises and labels his abusive behaviour as *abuse* at the beginning of his intervention programme (Pence and Paymar, 1993). Such an approach constitutes a form of colonisation with an inherent abuse of power that commonly produces reactive responses of minimisation and justification, or alternatively, accommodation to the counsellor's perceived wishes. Colonising approaches seldom produce ethical realisation or open up respectful possibilities.

Men are invited to name abusive practices in a gradual progression towards increasingly precise and accurate descriptions as they demonstrate readiness to understand and embrace the nature and implications of a more veridical account.

This progression is evident in the intervention with Jack where abusive behaviour was not initially named as such and early enquiries referred to, *'the incident with Sue'*, then, *'when Sue was hurt'* and later, *'when you hurt Sue'*. Invitations to name more specifically were made as Jack demonstrated readiness to respond with non-reactive consideration to the nature of each enquiry and labelling of his actions. Jack must eventually understand and appreciate the political nature of his actions so that he can label them as *abusive*. However, an enquiry which refers to, *'your abuse of Sue'*, in these initial stages of intervention, might well produce a reactive response in which Jack perceives a threat of shaming, and in efforts to defend himself might then minimise his actions or dispute such a label.

Naming abusive practices accurately requires sufficient ethical realisation and readiness to understand and face the implications, particularly the sense of disgrace, in applying such labels. As Jack began to consider his actions as inconsistent with, and undermining of, his ethical intent, in that he was *'acting against his better judgement'* in *'ways that hurt the ones you*

love', he became ready to label his behaviour more appropriately and accurately. He became open to both recognise and acknowledge that he was hurting Sue and Paul in ways that were *physical* and with *words*. Readiness to label abusive actions as such generally develops with increasing realisation about the level of harm done to others and a developing capacity to face and reposition shame.

An Invitational concept could then be introduced, which is termed *seeing (and calling) it like it really is*.

Jack was invited to recall and name his abusive actions in increasing detail throughout the course of his intervention. Abusive behaviours need to be appreciated in their contexts of power, coercion and entrapment before they can be labelled accurately in any meaningful way. As Jack began to recognise and explore differentials in power between himself and family members along with the levels of intimidation and fear experienced by Sue and Paul, he could be invited to label his actions in a more accurate and accountable manner:

> *Have you been able to see your interrogations of Sue as abuse before?*
>
> *What difference does it make to use words like 'interrogation' and 'abuse' to describe your actions?*
>
> *What is it that makes your questioning an interrogation?*
>
> *What makes this abuse?*
>
> *How important is it to call it like it really is?*
>
> *What difference does it make to call it abuse?*
>
> *How does (seeing it like it is) fit with what you believe in and the man you want to become?*

Each step towards naming abusive behaviour provides an opportunity for reflection and consideration of its implications for the man's ethical journey. This process of *talking about talking about it*, slows down the facing up process and ensures that each step is evaluated in terms of its meaning and ethical implications for the restorative project. Such reflections upon ethical meaning and readiness privilege the man's journey and strivings and prevent the process of enquiry from becoming one of interrogation and colonisation.

At a later point, Jack began shamefully to describe a particular occasion when he had sexually coerced Sue. He appeared ready to take a bolder step towards naming his actions and was asked:

> *What do you call what you did to Sue that evening?*

Jack averted his eyes and stammered, 'I guess it's rape'. He was then invited to consider the meaning and ethical implications of labelling it more accurately:

> *What makes it rape?*
>
> *What difference does it make when you call it rape?*
>
> *What does it do to you to call it what it really is?*
>
> *Have you been able to look this closely before?*
>
> *What is it taking?*
>
> *How important is it for you to see it and call it like it really is?*
>
> *Where is this taking you?*
>
> *What tells you that this is the right path for you to be taking?*

In both individual and group intervention, men are often invited to document their abusive actions in a written or audio/visual form. These assignments are sometimes guided by structured written guidelines which pose detailed and provocative questions. The process of documenting abusive behaviour facilitates a degree of self-confrontation which can allow more detailed and accurate descriptions to be realised and examined:

> *What difference does it make to see it in black and white?*
>
> *Have you ever looked at it so closely before?*
>
> *What are you seeing more clearly that you never really saw before?*
>
> *What difference is it making to see it like it really is, rather than like you wish it was?*
>
> *How does it affect you?*
>
> *How will this help you?*
>
> *How does it fit with your journey – with your true colours?*

Men who have experienced disadvantage in their own lives might be invited to consider these facing up steps in the context of *ethics in the face of adversity* so these bold steps are never taken for granted:

> *How are you managing to face your abusive actions so clearly when you have been through so much injustice yourself?*
>
> *What is it taking to stay focused on what you have done, rather than get caught up on what was done to you?*
>
> *Do you think anyone ever took the trouble to think about what they put you through?*
>
> *What does it say about you that you are facing what you have done under these circumstances?*
>
> *What does it say about you that you don't gloss over or try to justify what you have done?*

In the early stages of group intervention, men are often invited to document their abusive actions by marking relevant items and estimating their frequency on a checklist which includes a broad range of commonly practiced abusive actions. Following some debriefing, in which the meanings and ethical implications of open and honest participation in this exercise is explored, the same men might be invited to complete the checklist again, but this time by imagining how their partners might mark the man's practice of each item. Differences in naming abuse and violence commonly arise in this exercise and provide an opportunity for men to reach out and consider their partner's likely experience in bold and novel ways. More accountable ways of thinking about a partner's or a child's experience can be discovered by examining differences in naming abusive behaviour. Eventually a man might feel ready to try to understand his partner's actual experience and may become interested in her account of abusive behaviour and its effects. He might become open to appreciate her filling out the checklist in reality.

When men have sexually abused, great care is taken to facilitate a manageable progression towards accurate and accountable labelling of thinking and actions. At first, many men are not ready to hold names like *sexual assault, rape, molestation* and *sexual abuse*. These terms bring with them an enormous sense of disgrace and provoke pervasive patterns of avoidance of responsibility. Even media reports and judicial sentencing remarks often confuse language of intimacy with language of abuse. Abusive actions are sometimes inadvertently described as *fondling* and *having sex with* or as *inappropriate sexual relationships* rather than as *assaults* and *abuses*. The political nature of power differentials and their effects often become overlooked or misunderstood in these discourses and in the experiences of men who have sexually abused. Men who have sexually abused readily become labelled as *abusers, perpetrators, rapists* and *paedophiles*. Their reactions to such terms of identity often provoke avoidance and lead away from labelling behaviour in an accountable manner.

As men are invited to consider these power differentials and the nature and levels of exploitation along with the potential effects of sexual abuse, appropriate and accountable names and labels for behaviour may be introduced. For example, Kevin may be invited to consider the nature of the differential in power and privilege in his relationship with Susie, along with levels of confidence and trust that his whole extended family placed in him in his role as a grandfather with enquiries like:

How old was Susie – how old were you?

What was your role and responsibility with Susie?

How much trust and confidence did her parents place in you?

How much did she trust and look up to you?

What did she understand, and what did you understand, about what you were doing?

In this context, Kevin may be invited to name *set-ups, tricks, lies* and *deception* in his initiatives, along with other strategies for exploitation:

Whose idea was it?

How did you introduce it?

What did you say to Susie?

Was that fair or was it a set-up or trick?

What makes it a set-up or trick?

What difference does it make when you call it a set-up or trick?

What lies did you tell Susie about what you were doing?

What lies did you tell yourself about what you were doing?

What is it that makes them lies?

As Kevin begins to acknowledge his agency and planning in exploiting Susie, the political nature of sexual abuse becomes increasingly apparent and an onus to label this behaviour accurately becomes increasingly and inevitably unavoidable:

What do you call what you did to Susie?

What makes it sexual abuse?

How hard is it to use this term?

What difference does it make?

Men who have sexually abused are invited to document their accounts, once they have demonstrated some understanding of the political nature of abuse and exploitation. These accounts are then likely to facilitate self-confrontation and greater realisation about the nature and effects of abuse. This sense of readiness and written guidelines (Jenkins, 1990) to assist meaningful documentation prevent a superficial account which might avoid responsibility or a prurient exercise of indulgence in abusive fantasy.

Vince had sexually abused his step-daughter and attempted to document an account of his abusive actions as a facing up exercise. He wrote this account in the form of a letter to the young woman. Such a letter is never sent but written in this form as a means of shaping the account in a more personal manner which might serve to highlight and counter the objectification which is characteristic in sexual abuse. The following excerpt is from Vince's account:

Towards the end of the time we all lived at . . . I started becoming aroused by my physical contact with you. I started encouraging this contact by touching, cuddling, physical affection, holding hands with you more and more to indulge myself in this sexual pleasure. Because neither you or anyone else was aware of what I was doing, I felt safe and secure.

The written account tends to highlight strengths and weaknesses in a man's aptitude and readiness to label his abusive actions accurately and appropriately. Vince put considerable effort into trying to document an accurate account in which he faced responsibility for his actions and their effects. However, despite his well-intended effort, this excerpt seems unsatisfactory in its wording:

– Vince appears to attribute his *'arousal'* to interaction with his step-daughter.

– he uses language such as, *'aroused'*, *'indulge myself'* and *'sexual pleasure'* in a context which evokes a sense of eroticism or sexual intimacy.
– despite the acknowledgement that he *'encouraged physical contact'*, the tenor of Vince's account is passive rather than active in describing his actions and attributions.

Vince's intent and his effort were acknowledged as he was interviewed about his intended meanings with enquiries like these:

Did your urges arise from something your step-daughter was thinking and doing or something that you were thinking and doing?

Do you regard your actions and their effects as erotic or as abusive?

A documented account is regarded as a work in progress which will require ongoing revision offering tremendous opportunities for realisation and learning. Vince was invited to discuss his current experience and attributions and his choice of language, in the light of his intentions in documenting this account. In this way, he could be assisted to critique and re-write his account with particular vigilance for language which might unwittingly evoke attributions of responsibility to the step-daughter, a sense of intimacy or eroticism or a passive tenor. Vince's critique led to the following changes:

I started to use and exploit you by looking at you in a sexual way. I was setting up opportunities to use contact (touching, holding hands, hugging) with you to think exploitative sexual thoughts that had nothing to do with you or your feelings. I did it secretly so you wouldn't know what was going on.

Naming the effects of abuse

A deep understanding of the known and potential effects of abusive behaviour upon individuals, families, communities and culture remains at the core of the restorative project. The cessation of abusive behaviour and meaningful restitution hinge on such understanding and appreciation which then provides an authentic and accountable means for reclaiming an earned or deserved sense of integrity. As the man struggles to understand the experience of others he has harmed, he attempts to shoulder the burden previously left for others to carry. An

intense focus upon the impact of abuse enables profound ethical engagement with the man through the development of an accountable sense of remorse and the opening up of interest in *reaching towards the world of the other*. These possibilities can inform respect of difference and a generous concept of love.

Naming the effects is not a discrete project which is introduced as an 'empathy module' at a certain time in a group or individual programme. This kind of understanding cannot be taught. It is realised, discovered and actualised by men in a gradual but ongoing developmental manner right from the beginning of intervention. As the man takes ethical steps to broaden the focus and name his abusive practices, increasing levels of realisation of the potential effects of abuse are inevitable. Invitational practices open possibilities for these realisations and enable the necessary facing and repositioning of the shame which accompanies them. We try to create safe passage for the man to process and incorporate the meanings and implications of these steps into his ethical journey.

It is vital that a man is ready to develop his understanding of the effects of his abusive behaviour and that he understands how this will benefit him in his ethical journey. Over-zealous attempts to confront him with dramatic evidence of these effects will tend only to promote avoidance or perhaps an intellectual accommodation to what is seen as expected, but with little affective connection between heart and head. As abusive practices are named, realisation developed and shame faced, this reaching out aspect of facing up is boldly labelled using terms such as:

- *Seeing it like it is.*
- *Looking at it with eyes wide open.*
- *Looking shame squarely in the eye.*
- *Putting yourself in other person's shoes.*

The man is continually invited to consider the place that studying the impact of his abusive behaviour might have in his journey:

What are you seeing that is opening your eyes?
Have you looked this closely before?
Why do you need to take such painful steps?
How will this befit you and your family?
How will this help you to stop abuse once and for all?

Who has had to look at it, think about it, and worry about it in the past?

What difference does it make if you study it rather than leave it to others to worry about?

What difference does it make when you think more about others than yourself?

Will this make you stronger or weaker?

How important is it to try to understand fully what you have put (others) through?

How important is it to leave no stone unturned?

How important is this for (others)?

What would an apology mean without deepest understanding?

In the past were you more focused on gaining understanding or forgiveness?

What difference is it making as you reach out more to understand (others') feelings?

What are you realising about your past expectations and forgiveness?

How will reaching out help you to become the person you want to be?

Could you live differently with (others) without taking these steps?

Could you live with yourself without taking these steps?

These processes are illustrated in Chapter 5 where Jack was invited to hold a memory with images of his son, Paul, *'terrified'* of his father and *'cowering with fear'*. Jack was invited to 'take a close look' and to consider Paul's likely experience, to examine *'the look in his eyes'* and to wonder about the ethical implications of facing shame in such a bold manner. This window to shame offered an opportunity for Jack *to see (his abuse) like it really is*, to connect with the humanity of his son, and gain a deeper realisation of what he may have been putting Paul through as well as the extent of the violation of his own ethical strivings. Opening this window to shame provided one of Jack's first strong connections with remorse and the effects of his abusive behaviour which enabled a shift in focus from initial preoccupations with Sue's *'unreasonable'* and *'provocative'* actions.

Invitational theory and practice assumes that Jack is not deficient in empathy or compassion. These qualities are not regarded as fixed traits but highly context-specific. Placed in a relevant

context, Jack was able to consider the experiences of Sue and Paul and feel intense remorse. He continued to face his abusive actions, making gradual realisations about their effects upon both Sue and Paul. These realisations became particularly intense and ethically motivating on occasions when he opened other windows to shame.

One such window opened later on his therapeutic intervention, at a time when Jack had begun to reconnect with Sue. Jack was demonstrating respect for Sue and she was beginning to feel safe and entitled to *'be her own person'* in their relationship. At one point, when Jack was feeling close to Sue, he attempted to reinitiate their sexual relationship. Sue did not feel able to respond and declined his invitation. Jack then felt hurt and became critical of her. His response was characterised by a re-emergence of self-centred notions, that he had previously been challenging; *'What more do I have to do? She should trust me by now.'* Sue began to feel guilty and thought that she should want to be intimate with him. However, she also felt angry about Jack's *'pushy'* behaviour.

Such a re-emergence of self-centred feelings and ideas should not lead us to discount the work that Jack had already done. It provided a further opportunity to invite him to re-connect with his ethical preferences and imagine more about Sue's experience.

In such circumstances it is vital that we make place for protest and complaint. I invited Jack to speak out about his experience of hurt and his worries about Sue and their relationship. In this context, I could invite Jack to revisit his ethical strivings and preferences, in particular his recent efforts to challenge *'possessive'* thinking and action and his interest in and realisations about the effects of this behaviour upon Sue. Jack affirmed the importance of these directions and was invited to examine his protest and check for possibilities where his hurt feelings and worries might become hijacked by *'possessive'* thinking; a familiar pattern of past experience.

I then invited Jack to consider what his sexual initiative might have meant to Sue, and why he thought Sue might not be ready to start having sex again. When I asked Jack about his knowledge of Sue's experience of sex and trust, Jack's eyes averted. He stammered and looked ashamed. Here was another window to shame. I enquired:

You look like there is something you don't feel proud about?

What are you realising?

Jack's eyes became tearful as he described an incident that had taken place after a previous occasion when he had physically abused Sue. He *'felt bad'* about his actions and tried to *'make up'* by initiating sex. Sue felt outraged and told him to *'fuck off'*. He responded by sexually assaulting her. I enquired:

What are you seeing?

Jack responded;

'Sue frozen with fear and hatred'.

At this moment, Jack was feeling intense disgrace as he faced a haunting image of Sue feeling violated, humiliated and paralysed. Jack recalled his own experience of childhood sexual assault and added that Sue had also been sexually assaulted as a child by her older brother and that this abuse had had a huge impact on how safe she felt about sex. Jack had previously tended to avoid thinking about this incident and the sense of disgrace he was now experiencing. I needed to help reposition his shame so that it could become enabling rather than disabling. I enquired further:

Have you spoken out about this before?

What does it do to you to look at it so closely?

What does it do to you to see it like it really is?

How does it affect you to speak out about it like this?

Jack named his actions as 'rape' and explained the politics about why this label was accurate and appropriate (see page 110). I commented on his preparedness to *call it what it really is*:

You are looking with your eyes wide open at what you did to Sue.

What difference is this making?

Have you been able to look this closely before?

What is it taking to keep your eyes open?

In reflecting on the fact that he had added to Sue's experiences of sexual assault, Jack replied that he had *'never felt so low'*. He recalled the devastating impact of his own experience of being sexually assaulted by his uncle and lamented that he had *'put this on to Sue'*. Jack appeared to be experiencing a point of remorse, as described by Gaita; an awakening realisation about Sue's humanity and a painful realisation about the extent of violation of Sue and of his own ethics.

In attempting to help Jack reposition his shame and provide safe passage for him to experience it, I enquired:

What would it say about you if you could think about what you did as rape, and if you could see Sue frozen with fear and hatred, but didn't feel ashamed?

What does it say about you that you are thinking and feeling, and that you are not running away?

Jack was gradually assisted to connect his realisations and sense of shame with his ethics:

How important is it for you to see it and call it like it really is?

Where is this taking you?

What tells you that this is the right path for you to be taking?

What do you respect most; facing it or running away from it?

What path fits with the person you are becoming?

How will this help you?

What is it taking?

Will it make you stronger or weaker as a person?

How could you allow this experience to make you stronger rather than bring you down?

How does it fit with the man, partner and father you want to be?

Do you think your Dad ever stopped and thought like this?

What difference would it have made if he had?

Over time, I invited Jack to consider:

You have made apologies before, but have you ever looked this closely at what you have done?

What would an apology mean without this level of realisation?

Jack was invited to consider these realisations in the context of patterns of reliance upon Sue and Paul to face his responsibilities concerning the impact of his abusive behaviour:

Who has carried the hurt and humiliation of this incident, in the past?

Who needs to carry it? Whose job is it?

How will you do this?

Will it make you stronger or weaker as a person?

Are you ready to take this further?

Opportunities to open windows to shame often present in unexpected and paradoxical ways in both individual and group intervention. Jack developed profound realisations about the potential effects of his abuse of Sue in one men's group meeting:

'I never really stopped to think how I let Sue down again and again.'

'I used to apologise to get her to forgive me.'

'If I was Sue I wouldn't trust one bit.'

. . . only to arrive at the next men's group meeting in an agitated state, preoccupied with self-centred complaints:

'I feel really depressed'

'I watched (television documentary about rape in marriage) – all these women going on and on about what it did to them.'

'I've been coming to the group for seven weeks and I'm getting nowhere.'

'I think it's a waste of time.'

'I don't think Sue is ever going to want me back.'

'It's always me (who has to change).'

Jack's recent presentation appears to stand in stark contrast to his previous ethical stance. He appears to have reverted to past attitudes of impatience and minimisation.

- *Is Jack simply showing his 'true colours' over time or could he be struggling with a partially open window to shame?*

We should remain open to opportunities for facing shame in seemingly unlikely places. If Jack has previously held ethical positions about his actions, particularly if he has recently taken bold new steps in realisation about the effects of his abuse, he may have experienced a shocking encounter with shame and be struggling to deal with its implications.

We might revisit Jack's recent ethical realisations, and how he has managed to position shame, as he has tried to find a place for them in his journey. The group might be invited to reflect upon the challenges that facing shame provokes when we take bold new steps. From a position that honours Jack's ethical strivings, we might enquire about the effects of watching the television show on rape in marriage:

Recently, you have been trying pretty hard to put yourself in Sue's shoes.

I am wondering whether you have realised something huge – where you've shocked yourself?

Is it to do with that TV show?

Is it something that you have tried to forget; that you have not wanted to look at; but you have started to see it like it is?

If we remain mindful and respectful of Jack's stated intent, to *'make up'* to Sue, he might revisit his rape and open more fully the window to shame. We might wonder about his initial statement expressing doubt that Sue would *'ever . . . want me back'*. Rather than dismiss this as only a self-centred statement of desperation, we might enquire whether Jack has realised something about the effect of his rape upon Sue:

What are you realising about the effects of rape on Sue?

What are you realising about yourself in raping Sue?

What might Sue be up against in coming to terms with what you did?

How might this affect her ability to get close to you?

Jack could then connect with a realisation that his actions were *'unforgivable'* and an understanding that Sue would never forget what he did to her and might never again feel desire to be close to him. His presentation in the group takes on a different colour in the light of a deeper realisation about the potential effects of sexual assault. Exploration of these possibilities might enable Jack to *stand his ground*, with the support of the group, in facing and finding place for these realisations in his ethical journey.

As Jack demonstrated a readiness to look more closely at Sue's and Paul's experiences, to *open his eyes wider – to see it like it really is*, he was invited to participate in structured individual and group exercises designed to examine the effects of abuse. One such exercise is called *Imagining yourself in the shoes of the other* and is based on the Narrative Therapy practice of Internalised Other Questioning (Epston, 1993; Nyland and Corsiglia, 1998).

Jack first needed to demonstrate that he was ready to take a new bold step towards understanding Sue's or Paul's experience more fully:

– that he is interested in and wants to understand their experience.
– that he realises how this might benefit him in his journey.
– that he recognises how he can use this knowledge to strengthen his resolve.
– that it is his job to carry the burden and responsibility of his actions.

He was then interviewed about Sue's experience, but from the perspective where he was asked to imagine himself as Sue and respond to questions as he imagined Sue might were she asked the same questions. This exercise requires a man to think, feel and respond as he imagines his partner or child might think, feel and respond and generally enables him to reach out and connect more closely and with stronger affect, with the potential experience of the other.

If this exercise is conducted in a group setting, the group can actively participate in the exercise, and witness and respond to the man's realisations. Jack might be invited to choose one or two group members he thinks have worked hard to achieve significant realisations about their partner's or children's experiences, to sit beside him and coach him if he needs assistance during the interview. He might also select a group member he thinks would have confidence in him and who could provide encouragement if he feels he is struggling with the exercise. In this way, a circle of support is established within the group.

The interview is conducted as though Sue was really present. It is commenced with a welcome of Sue, an explanation of her presence in the group and enquiries about her experience of being in the group:

Welcome Sue. Thank you for coming to help us understand more deeply the effects of abusive behaviour upon women and children.

First I am wondering what it might be like to be the only woman in this group of 10 men?

What concerns might you have in being here?

What did it take to walk in here tonight?

Do you think Jack can understand and respect this courage?

I have found that many men thoughtfully address these initial enquiries and consider women's likely experience of men's gaze and critical judgement along with the courage required to speak out in a men's forum.

Care must be taken to ensure Sue's safety and privacy are respected in the exercise. An exercise such as this raises significant dilemmas which are ongoing concerns in all group programmes. How do we ensure that Jack does not talk about matters which might be private to Sue and which she may not want discussed in front of others?

Sue, it is vital that you feel safe to speak your mind here and that you do not feel obliged to have to answer questions that you do not wish to answer. It is vital that your safety and your privacy is looked after. I will try to be mindful of this and regularly check this out.

If I do ask a personal question that you do not want to answer in front of this group of men, how will you let me know so that I don't violate your privacy?

What tells you that Jack understands how important your privacy is?

The interview is continued with contextual enquiries about Sue's initial hopes and the development of the relationship and the family, the nature and history of the development of violence and abuse, the effects of abuse and a history of resistance. Typical forms of enquiry might include:

What were your original hopes and dreams for a relationship and family?

What was important to you?

How have you tried to achieve these hopes?

How much did you love, respect and trust Jack?

How much do you think Jack understands this?

When did you first realise that something was wrong?

What were the initial signs that you and Paul were not being treated with respect?

What did you initially think was happening?

What did you try to do to make things better?

How much do you think Jack understands this?

How did Jack's abusive behaviour develop over time?

How did Jack hurt you with his words and his actions?

What incident sticks in your mind?

How frightening was this?

What were you most scared about?

Was there anything you could do to make it safe?

What hurt you most of all?

What did you wind up having to do to try to feel safe?

What did you feel you had to do to keep the lid on Jack's violence?

What did it feel like having to do this?

How has it affected you?

How has it affected your feelings for Jack and about trust and respect?

How important is it for Jack to understand what he has put you through?

Why is this so important to you?

How much do you think he wants to understand this?

What signs have you seen?

How did it affect you when Jack made apologies?

What did they mean?

What worries you about his attempts to make amends now?

What do you think he realises about the effects on trust?

When did you first try to stand your ground?

How did Jack react to this?

What has made it hard to seek help? What have you been up against?

How have you tried to work for your family and resist violence at the same time?

How hard is this to do?

What has Jack taken for granted? What has he not been able to see?

How important is it for you to stand your ground? Why is this so important?

Have you tried to do this recently?

How does Jack see your resistance?

How much has he been able to understand and appreciate this?

What kind of partner do you think he is wanting?

This exercise tends to open up possibilities for profound realisation and strong affective responses. Most men experience intense feelings of shame and grief as they reach towards a deeper understanding of the possible impact of their abusive actions. Jack and members of the inner circle might be interviewed about the nature and implications of Jack's realisations and the importance of his affective responses for his ethical journey. The experience is also rich and moving for men witnessing the interview in the group. They are invited to respond to Jack's initiative, but with a specific emphasis on their own personal experiences:

How did Jack's realisations and feelings (as Sue) move you?

What did they trigger in your thinking and in your feelings?

What did they remind you of in your life?

What did they open up for you?

What did you start to see and feel more clearly?

In individual intervention, the practice of *imagining yourself in the shoes of the other* can be made a richer and more intense experience by including enquiries which focus upon particularly salient, but most likely private, events which have impacted on Sue. These might include Sue's experience of Jack's rape and the meaning of this in the light of the past sexual assault by her brother. However, enquiries about matters and experiences which relate to events such as sexual abuse could provoke privacy concerns by Sue through public exposure or the possibility of judgement and prurient interest by a group of men. These and other practices which explore the effects of abusive behaviour in a group setting require considerable caution, vigilance and protective intervention by facilitators to ensure that the privacy of abused persons is safeguarded.

As men demonstrate increasing readiness to take bolder steps towards understanding the potential effects of abuse, they may become interested in reading or viewing published accounts and videotapes of the experiences of survivors of abuse. A man might be invited to document an account of the nature and effects of his abusive actions as he imagines the person he has abused might tell it. In assisting him to critique and make place for this account in his journey, he is reminded that he cannot know his partner's or children's actual experience, he can only listen, research and imagine. The importance of *reaching towards the world of the other* is emphasised as an ethical paradigm for respectful connection; it involves consideration of the experiences of others, first by imagining possibilities and then by checking out the accuracy of these speculations by listening to feedback. The step involving imagination requires the man to first reach out and to do his own thinking, which engages his own ethics, rather than go to the abused person and perhaps further impose upon them. Such reaching out engages a capacity for initiative, imagination, empathy and compassion which promotes the development of discretion, shame, and challenges long standing and restraining patterns of reliance.

Tom had begun to move away from self centred ideas; *'I couldn't let him get away with it'*, and reach out towards his son, Peter's, experience, to see him as, *'only a little guy'*; *'cringing and trembling on the sand'* after *'I beat him up'*. Tom felt intense remorse as he began to consider how frightened Peter was of his father and how much his son was losing respect and a sense of belonging and connection with his father. He expressed a commitment to strive for respect and connection in his relationship with Peter which entailed:

– stopping and thinking about Peter's feelings.
– facing up to ways he has hurt and let Peter down.
– leading by example.

Tom was invited to consider how he might continue the movement away from judgmental criticism towards an interest in Peter's ideas, viewpoint and feelings:

Are you interested in discovering who Peter is or in telling him who you want him to be?

Would you want to understand or judge Peter?

What difference might it make to become interested in:
– what Peter thinks?
– what is important for Peter?
– what hopes and dreams Peter might have?

He became increasingly curious and concerned about the effects of his misguided and abusive behaviour upon Peter and how this might have affected his son's view of, and feelings about, him. Tom began to ask about Peter's experience and participation in counselling. At one point, during a discussion of several significant incidents of abuse, he appeared worried and asked; *'How badly do you think this has affected Peter?'* Peter had recently documented a list of injustices that he wanted his father to understand, as part of a process to address a pervasive responsibility overload which restrained his ability to face his own abusive actions towards his cousin. After revisiting some of the realisations Tom had already reached, I began to assess his interest and readiness in broadening his knowledge:

Would you be interested in reading Peter's document?

What makes you really want to know what Peter thinks and feels?

What might make Peter nervous about you reading what he has written?

What tells you that you are ready to take in rather than judge what you read?

What if you find some of it really hard to face?

How will this help you?

How might it help you in relating to Peter?

How would it fit with the man you want to become?

The issue of readiness remains vital in any bold new step towards understanding the effects of abuse.

Men who have sexually abused are similarly invited to study the effects of their abuse upon individuals, family and community members. The structured processes for naming sexually abusive practices enable a shift away from minimised descriptions which are couched in language of intimacy, eroticism, provocation and human limitation, towards *seeing it like it really is*. Kevin was invited to detail his abusive actions in the context of the nature and politics of his relationship with Susie. In this context, language of exploitation, deception through tricks, bribes and confusing mind-games and entrapment are introduced. Realisations about characteristic effects of sexual abuse which include a sense of worthlessness, culpability and mistaken shame become increasingly inevitable:

Whose idea was it?

How did you impose this idea on Susie?

What were you teaching her or leading her to believe?

How were you training her to think and feel about herself?

What would asking, 'Do you like this?', impose on her?

How would realising she had accepted your bribes make her feel about herself?

How might it feel to realise she had been treated as a thing and an object in your fantasy?

What might it be like to have to look after and worry about your feelings and needs?

What kind of burden might carrying this secret impose on Susie?

Men who might have minimised or justified the use of pornography or certain offensive sexual behaviours such as public exposure as relatively harmless or non-problematic are invited to examine their actions in a political context:

How does pornography treat women and men as sexual objects?

What effects could this have on women's sense of safety and well-being?

How might exposure to pornography support sexual abuse?

What impact might an incident of public exposure have on a woman's life?

How certain might she feel about your intent?

How might this impact on the sense of safety for all women?

How might it contribute to women's fear of male abuse?

How does this affect your community?

These processes of naming abuse and its effects can be broadened with exercises in *imagining yourself in the shoes of the other* and documentation practices. However, this work is best done in individual rather than group intervention, given the likelihood of violating the privacy of those subjected to the abuse.

CHAPTER 11

Revisioning Practices – Mapping and Resisting Pathways Towards Abusive Behaviour

I'm not bad, I'm just drawn that way.
(Jessica Rabbit, animated star in
Who Killed Roger Rabbit?)

As men begin to study, name and document their abusive actions and the known and potential effects of these actions, a political understanding of the nature of abuse is gradually developed. Abusive behaviour is placed in a context and details of the nature of patterns of thinking, feeling and action which lead towards abuse become increasingly apparent. Given the ethical and political perspectives, which are privileged in Invitational practice, the man becomes increasingly preoccupied with concerns and dilemmas about restraint:

- *What has been stopping me from developing the kinds of relationships I have really wanted?*
- *What has been stopping me from relating to others in the ways I am really wanting?*
- *How have I come to act in ways which contradict and undermine what I have been striving for?*
- *What has been preventing me from becoming the person I really want to be?*

These preoccupations concern the capture of desire and are likely to motivate resistance. Abusive behaviour becomes understood as misguided complicity with dominant cultural interests. The man is not responsible for these interests or the political structures and processes which constitute them. However, he can take responsibility for his participation in practices which they prescribe; he can develop a political understanding and mobilise his capacity for resistance. These political preoccupations stand in stark contrast to notions of causality;

- *What is causing my abusive behaviour?*

Preoccupations with causality seek explanations which generally place responsibility for action outside of the capacity or influence of the man and undermine a sense of agency and resistance.
Familiar and repetitive patterns of restraining experience and behaviour become identified as

pathways towards abusive behaviour. The concept of a pathway concerns *how* rather than *why* I have come to engage in abusive behaviour. These pathways have a developmental history that can be studied and mapped. With the shift away from preoccupations with pathological drives and desires and towards dominant cultural interests, particularly concepts of masculinity, the influence of popular but misguided blueprints or recipes can be mapped. These blueprints generally prescribe means for:

- *Becoming somebody;* that is becoming successful or competent.
- Building relationships with others.
- Demonstrating love.

They reflect hierarchical power relations which emphasise qualities such as performance, competitiveness, conquest, acquisitiveness and possessiveness. These blueprints become shaped by, and reflected in, sets of *dangerous ideas* which inform abusive practices. These ideas are dangerous, not in any moral sense but because they serve to counter and undermine ethical strivings for a respectful sense of self and a respectful means of relating and loving.

Invitational practice aims at assisting the *externalisation* of dangerous ideas, making these ideas and their history visible and accessible to challenge and resistance (White, 2008). Theories of restraint and processes of externalisation enable bypassing attributions of blame by exposing unwitting patterns of complicity with dominant cultural interests and promoting resistance to the influence of dangerous ideas.

Barry, for example, might identify how *judgement* and *criticism* are restraining his ethical strivings for connected relationships with his partner and son where they feel supported, respected and accepted. He may recognise a history of these practices and their influence in shaping the nature of his efforts to become somebody and to build relationships. In this context, he may realise familiar patterns of thinking and reacting and document recurring ideas which inform these practices which might include:

Never making a mistake.

Always having to be right.

Having to win.

Having the last word in an argument.

Always being in control.

Barry might be invited to externalise these ideas and practices in order to evaluate their influence and their effects, in relation to his ethical strivings. He may conclude that they constitute *dangerous ideas* which inform misguided and unhelpful practices of criticism, judgement and correction:

How might these ideas be leading you away from what you are really wanting for yourself and for your relationships?

How do these ideas try to hijack your hopes and dreams?

How do they masquerade as truths, in order to rob you of what is really important to you and your family?

To what extent are they dangerous to you and your family?

He might examine a personal and cultural history of practices associated with criticism and judgement and consider their pervasiveness in dominant masculine culture:

How did these ideas first enter your life?

How were they supported in your family, sporting teams, workplaces etc?

How are they supported in relationships amongst men?

After having studied the influence of these dangerous ideas and practices, Barry might consider the concept of resistance:

In what ways have you stood up to or defied these dangerous ideas in the past?

How might you challenge misguided and dangerous ideas and practices rather than the people you love?

In developing a context for externalisation, men are invited to consider the self-centred nature of abusive behaviour and its relevance to the restorative project. All forms of abuse require self-centred or selfish thinking, whereby the abusing person puts his thoughts, feelings and ideas first and fails to consider, or value, the thoughts, feelings and needs of the other. A theory of restraint would propose that, unless the abusing person is primarily interested in causing harm, then his abusive actions only make sense if:

– he becomes caught up in escalating and self-intoxicating preoccupations which override awareness of the feelings and needs of others; *exaggerated entitlement.*
– he is unused to considering the feelings and needs of others; *abdication of responsibility.*

These explanatory possibilities suggest directions forward in the restorative project with its focus on *reaching towards the world of the other* in a context of accountability. We might logically invite the man to address and study the nature of patterns of self-intoxication and consider the value of becoming practiced at reaching out to consider the experiences of others, or a shift from selfish to other-ish thinking and practice. This constitutes a logical direction which is the antithesis of a self-centred pathway towards abuse.

Practices of externalisation initially require attending to patterns of self-intoxication with dangerous ideas through continued and passionate rehearsal and repetition. The concept of *self-intoxication* places the locus of responsibility for abusive actions with the man by implying a certain agency in the 'build up' towards acts of abuse. This concept encourages a shift from popular notions which suggest that he is passively reacting to provocation by others who 'push his buttons'. In a sense, the man 'gets himself drunk' through excessive indulgence in thoughts and ideas which he may not have invented himself but nevertheless actively 'imbibes'. When we invite a man to engage in sober reflection by examining details of his thinking, feelings and practices which lead up to acts of abusive behaviour (see Chapter 5) we may assist him to notice and understand familiar patterns of self-intoxication:

How were you working yourself up?

What ideas were you intoxicating yourself with?

What familiar things were you telling yourself?

The man is invited to study patterns of self-intoxication and to notice recurring thoughts, expressions and motifs and then determine their links with dangerous ideas and practices.

As Jack studied his own patterns of self-intoxication leading towards acts of abuse of Sue and Paul, he began to recognise familiar motifs in his thinking:

> 'She doesn't care about me.'
>
> 'She doesn't care about the family.'
>
> 'She thinks more about other people.'
>
> 'I need to teach her a lesson.'

Jack could connect his engagement with these familiar motifs with anxiety, jealousy and worry about the secure future of his relationship with Sue, with feeling hurt and with acts of violence that included the interrogation of Sue, attempts to restrict her freedom and verbal and physical assaults. Jack came to regard his engagement and escalating self-intoxication with these feelings, motifs and actions as expressions of *possessiveness*. By externalising *possessiveness*, Jack was able to study its many expressions and the history of its influence in his life. Possessiveness and its associated practices could be placed in a cultural context in terms of its dominant influence upon popular ideas about love and relationships. Jack could begin to understand his unwitting yet active investment in dangerous ideas and practices which constitute possessiveness. Jack was able to consider and evaluate the relevance of 'old-fashioned' blueprints for masculine competence, for becoming somebody and for building a connected relationship and whether or not these recipes might have 'passed their use-by dates', in relation to his ethical strivings. This required consideration of ideas which included:

Concepts of domestic love:

> It is natural to feel jealous if you love her.
>
> If she loves me she wouldn't want to spend time with anyone else.
>
> We only need each other.

Concepts of male ownership, conquest and defence of property:

> You can't trust anyone – you have to be vigilant.
>
> Men are always on the prowl.

> Women are vulnerable and need protection.
>
> Women are not safe or can't be relied on, out in the world.
>
> You can never let your guard down.

Jack was invited to challenge possessiveness and its associated ideas and practices rather than continue to challenge his partner, Sue:

> What does possessiveness get you thinking and doing, in the name of love?
>
> Where does this idea come from?
>
> How is it influential in our culture?
>
> How has it gained influence in your life?
>
> How does it masquerade as love?
>
> How does it operate? What are its tactics?
>
> How does it try to pull the wool over your eyes?
>
> What feeds it and keeps it going?
>
> How does it try to remain under cover in your life?
>
> When have you disobeyed it or defied it?
>
> How did you manage to do this?
>
> What difference did it make to challenge possessiveness rather than your partner, Sue?
>
> What did you prove to yourself?
>
> How does this fit with the kind of man you are becoming?

The process of externalising and challenging dangerous ideas and practices is called *revisioning* in Invitational practice. As the man engages in sober reflection upon patterns of self-intoxication, he can examine, challenge and revise dangerous ideas which support unhelpful and misguided blueprints for participation in relationships and for masculine competence or becoming somebody. The concept and process of challenging dangerous ideas enables a sense of agency as the man begins to stand apart from, and challenge, thinking and practices which support violence rather than challenging his partner or family members. This in turn disrupts a pattern of experience of insufficiency and failure which inexorably leads to *loser* identity conclusions; *'I cant help it'; 'I lost it'; 'I'm useless'; 'what's the point'.*

Revisioning practices generally involve a fluid progression of externalisation of concepts and practices. Jack's initial contact was characterised by self-intoxication with worry and panic fed by thoughts such as:

'She should be here trying to sort things out.'

'She doesn't care about the family.'

'How will she know that I wont hurt her again if I don't see her?'

'She will think I don't care.'

This sense of panic tended to produce desperate actions whereby Jack would initially try to locate Sue to convince her to reunite. These desperate actions included telephoning Sue's family and friends and driving his car in search of her. Jack would sit at home and drink whilst escalating these intoxicating preoccupations. With sober reflection, he began to recognise and was invited to externalise a sense of *desperation*:

How big does this panic and desperation get?

What does it get you thinking and feeling?

Where does it try to lead you?

What happens when you go along with it?

What message does it give Sue?

How does it make you feel about yourself?

Does it have you consider Sue's views and feelings or try to force your own views?

Does it have you challenge and control your own actions or try to challenge Sue's actions?

How does it try to convince you that it's OK to disrespect Sue's feelings?

How does it try to get you to act against your better judgement?

Are there times when you have stood up to it?

How did you manage this?

What were you up against?

What did you prove to yourself?

What difference might it make to stand up for yourself in this way?

What difference might it make if you stopped trying to force contact and got your own house in order?

When Jack considered this last enquiry, he became somewhat agitated and expressed concerns; 'She might think I don't care anymore'; 'How will she know that I've changed?' Jack was invited back into sober reflection:

Is that you or desperation talking?

What speaks loudest, your actions or your words?

What fits best with your journey?

What fits best with the man you want to become?

Who is standing by you?

Who is on the side of desperation?

What side is alcohol on?

As Jack demonstrated his capacity to resist *desperation*, the focus for externalisation could be sharpened to encompass the concept of *possessiveness* and associated ideas and practices.

Through externalisation of the concepts, *judgement* and *criticism*, and associated dangerous and self-intoxicating ideas, Barry began to understand the nature, history of influence and cultural context, and to resist abusive practices that undermined his ethical strivings. As he examined practices of criticism and judgement of others, he became increasingly aware of their association with related practices of *self-criticism* and *self-doubt* and associated ideas about 'never (being) good enough'. Barry also began to externalise the concept of *self-doubt* in the service of his ethical journey towards respectful ways of relating to his partner and son.

Men such as Tom who have acted abusively in the name of parental discipline might be invited to examine the development of abusive practices in a context of dominant cultural interests which are reflected in ideas such as:

A father should always be in control of children.

A father should always be right or always have the last word.

You must maintain discipline, even if the child fears you.

A child should do as I say (regardless of what I do).

Breaches of rules must always be punished.

You can't walk away from a confrontation.

Any lapse should be regarded as a sign of weakness.

Children should always respect (obey and defer to) their father.

If they fear you, they will respect you.

Any lapse should be regarded as a personal slight or rejection.

Fathers are responsible for discipline (punishment).

Mothers are responsible for nurture.

The process of revisioning allows misguided and unhelpful practices to be externalised and contrasted with preferred ways of parenting. For example:

Getting more into criticism or encouragement.

Always instructing or learning to listen.

Reacting or taking it personally or putting yourself in the child's shoes.

Seeking obedience or seeking respect.

Seeking respect in fear or admiration.

Having to win or learning to win some-lose some.

Leading by coercion or by example.

Preaching or practicing what you preach.

Loving to show or showing love.

Trying to control others or self-control.

Externalisation exercises can be helpful in a men's group where popular concepts and dangerous ideas can be subjected to collaborative examination and critique. Group members may discover and name influential concepts such as:

Having to win

Possessiveness

Getting even

Provocation

It takes two

Arguments and conflict cause violence

Losing it

Men are invited to expose these dangerous concepts and associated ideas and practices and their influence in dominant blueprints for masculine competence, relationships and love. Structured interviews and collaborative discussions may be informed by enquiries like the following:

How has this idea operated in your life?

What does it get you thinking?

How does it affect you and others?

What other names does it go by?

What are its tactics?

What does it hide behind?

What does it try to set itself up as?

What kind of front does it use?

What special quality does it masquerade as?

How does it get away with it?

How does it interfere with your relationships?

How does it try to hijack love, respect, justice and culture?

What does it blind you to in your partner and children?

How does it lead you away from your own beliefs and values?

Where does it come from?

Who and what supports it? What keeps it alive and well?

What parts of society and culture has it set itself up in?

How has it tried to hijack masculinity?

How does it try to pose as truth?

Where and when is it strongest or weakest?

When have you been able to see it coming?

How have you been able to see it for what it is?

How did you see through it?

When have you been able to defy it?

What were you up against?

How did you manage to stand up for yourself?

How does this fit with the man you are becoming?

How might you be standing up for other men or for mankind?

Self-intoxicating preoccupations and practices which culminate in sexual abuse are similarly externalised in a context of dominant cultural interests that are reflected in common but dangerous ideas. It is no surprise that males perpetrate most sexual abuse given that dominant ideas about male heterosexual interest tend to be linked with:

- *Exaggerated entitlement.*
  Concepts of sexual conquest, performance and ownership of partners are stressed in blueprints for becoming somebody:
  Making sexual conquests.
  Being highly experienced.
  Being competitive with other men.
  Being able to win over and seduce.
  Being always ready and able to perform.
  Having a right of sexual access to a partner.
- *Abdication of responsibility.*
  Blueprints for relating tend to diminish a sense of male responsibility in sexual initiative:

Normalising practices which sexually objectify women.
Promotion of sexual opportunities with low interpersonal demand.
Females arouse males and are therefore responsible for the consequences.
Females are responsible for setting limits whereas a male's job is to test these limits.

When a man's desire becomes captured by these interests, his thinking and action may become increasingly complicit with such dangerous ideas. These ideas and associated practices are then regarded as characteristic of all men and therefore universal truths. He may be invited to identify self-intoxicating preoccupations which involve sexual objectification of others and the sexualisation of much of his daily experience. Sexualised thinking occupies and takes over ways of viewing others, ways of relating and even strategies for stress relief and dealing with boredom. These ideas and their self-intoxicating influence may become further entrenched through the use of pornography and masturbation fantasy. Misguided strategies for seeking a sense of competence and status, for becoming somebody, produce detached and self-centred patterns of relating which can increasingly prescribe practices of sexual objectification, disrespect and abuse.

Dominant interests concerning entitlement, conquest and objectification can become reflected in the (ab)use of a child as a status object. This often becomes apparent when men who have abused children are invited to consider their specific choices; *What led up to your choice of (this child) as a target?* The power differential enables an undemanding and seemingly uncomplicated sense of conquest, performance and ownership, where the man may feel an unchallenged sense of status and competence. He increasingly intoxicates himself with these ideas as he creates a fantasy world and imposes it on a child who is often regarded as a willing partner who shares responsibility. His actions become misrepresented as caring, loving and harmless.

As the exploitative nature of abuse is recognised and patterns of self-intoxicating preoccupation are identified, the man's descriptions tend to shift from the self-indulgent:

We had a special relationship.

I didn't hurt him.

She seemed to like it too.

. . . towards facing up to corrupt and destructive strategies for conquest and status:

I took advantage because she was vulnerable and easy to set up.

He was only little and had no idea what was going on but I knew what I was doing.

I knew there was no threat. I could do what I wanted and get away with it.

It was a selfish and shameful way to feel good at his expense.

I was only thinking about what I wanted and I didn't care about her feelings.

I used to tell myself that I was giving her pleasure when I was just using her.

I tried to teach her that it was love and that she wanted it too. I kept telling this lie to her.

I used to kid myself that I was teaching her about sex.

I taught her to worry about my feelings and what I was doing.

I tricked him into it by pretending it was a game.

Then I told him what would happen if he told anyone. I trapped him.

I set up a fantasy world and put it on to her so I didn't have to deal with the real world.

I copped out from my own responsibilities and hid behind her.

Many men begin to realise the pervasiveness of self-intoxicating sexualised preoccupations which can extend beyond a particular set of abusive actions to include persistent forms of sexualised interaction with friends and family members which border on harassment or cause offence, use of pornography, visiting prostitutes and sex industry entertainment, voyeurism, public exposure and other violations of relationship boundaries and privacy. For these men, self-intoxicating sexualised fantasy becomes increasingly central in dealing with most aspects of life and in their recipes for *becoming somebody.* Encounters with others provide little interpersonal demand and relationships are often characterised by patterns of avoidance of responsibility and excessive reliance upon others to face these responsibilities. These practices produce seeming caricatures of over-compliance with dominant cultural interests.

Kevin examined the ways he exploited Susie by tricking and misleading her in pretending that his actions were part of legitimate games and then making her promise to keep them secret with offers of bribes.

He began to question his initial assertions:

> *'I didn't do things that would hurt her.'*
> *'If she didn't want to, I wouldn't do it.'*

. . . as another aspect of a fantasy world which he imposed upon Susie. Kevin could recognise that these were dangerous ideas which constituted part of the pattern of self-intoxication leading him to justify his actions. He actively developed this fantasy world with lies and deceptions in order to conclude that, *'Susie wanted this special relationship'*. Kevin recognised that he deluded himself in this fantasy world; it was easy to feel 'big' and important alongside a small and '*innocent*' child who he had entrapped with a confusing set of corrupt interactions. He examined the implications of asking Susie questions, *'Do you like this?; Do you want to do it?'*, with their implicit invitation for her to feel a sense of culpability and him to avoid responsibility for his actions. These tactics for imposing his fantasy world upon Susie, trapping

her and thereby coercing her participation, became increasingly visible and were named accordingly as systematic and selfish means of exploitation which he justified in the names of intimacy and *becoming somebody*.

Kevin began to recognise patterns whereby he had avoided responsibility for his actions and relied on others to face his challenges or take care of his feelings. He acknowledged how he had put Susie in an untenable position where, *'she had to worry about my feelings'* and then hid behind her vulnerability. He began to realise other ways he tended to rely upon May and other family members, rather than face his own problems. He could recognise that he was still inviting this kind of 'protection' from his parish priest, from family members who minimised his actions, and from May when he talked to her about suicide. These realisations firmed his resolve *'to stand on my own two feet'* and take responsibility for his actions and their effects on Susie and all family members; *'to come out of the fantasy world and face up to life in the real world'*.

When men who have abused begin to address and resist the restraining influence of self-intoxicating preoccupations along with practices for objectification of and reliance upon others, possibilities for *reaching out towards the world of the other* are opened up. Invitations to hold and explore these opportunities are considered in Chapters 12 and 13.

CHAPTER 12

Restitution Practices

The concept of restitution is an expression of accountability which entails *reaching out towards the world of the other* and requires that the man has taken substantial steps with significant realisations in:

- Naming abusive practices.
- Understanding the political nature of abuse.
- Understanding and naming the potential effects of abuse.
- Facing shame – experiencing an ethical sense of remorse.
- Recognising and resisting patterns of self-intoxicating experience and dangerous ideas which inform abusive behaviour.
- Challenging restraining patterns of avoidance of responsibility and reliance upon others.

Restitution is informed by the ethic of remorse and a generous concept of love. Accordingly, it is proffered with 'no strings attached' and no expectations of relinquishment, pardoning or reconnection from the other. Meaningful and accountable acts of restitution are based on the realisation that abusive acts have the potential for permanent destruction of trust, respect and a sense of safety, and the man has no entitlement to expect forgiveness or anything in return. Acts of restitution can assist those who have been abused and may be proffered in this spirit. However, the nature and process of restitution remains a vital aspect of the man's ethical responsibility towards restoration and reclamation of integrity; a responsibility which has implications beyond the possibility of healing specific harm done to the abused persons.

Acts of restitution often entail expressions of realisation about the nature and effects of abusive actions which are then made accessible to those who have been harmed by the abuse. However, many abuse survivors will not want to witness such expressions. In this context, restorative action might involve respecting the privacy of others by maintaining a commitment to keep away from them. The man should, however, strive regardless to make these realisations and be prepared to express them should this ever be required.

Acts of restitution have a restorative focus in that they attempt to compensate or make reparation for harm done to individuals, families and communities. There can be many forms of reparation from a commitment to future ethical behaviour to financial or material compensation. Such restitution is sometimes determined in Restorative Justice forums (Braithwaite, 2002; Daly, 2003). When men recognise that their actions have caused damage to their communities or broader culture, they may choose to contribute something restorative to that community or culture. This can be in the form of community work or participation in organisations concerned with community service. A range of formal and informal possibilities exist for men to engage in community action to address and challenge abusive practices or to assist others to address abusive behaviour.

A man may be invited to engage in documenting *statements of realisation* to help prepare to make an ethical account of his realisations about his abuse and its effects. Realisations are expressed in a written, audiotape or video format, in the form of a set of letters or messages addressed to individuals harmed or affected by the abusive behaviour. These statements serve to assist the development of readiness to make meaningful and accountable restitution and are not sent to the addressee, unless specifically requested. The statement of realisation constitutes a developmental restorative project which enables the man to receive feedback and to critique his own levels of understanding and realisation along with the congruence between his expressions and his actions. Consequently, each statement is a work in progress which is critiqued and revised on an ongoing basis.

The following statement of realisation is a compilation of excerpts from a number of letters by different men which will be used to illustrate the process of critique and revision.

Dear Mary,
I now realise what I have put you through and I feel terrible about it. I abused my own wife and frightened my

son out of his wits. I am the person you were supposed to
be able to trust and who was supposed to care for you and
protect you and instead I treated you like garbage with
violence and put-downs.

I am disgusted with myself for the way I treated you and
Tim, the violence, the jealousy, the put-downs, the blaming. I have made you live in fear and have lost your love
and respect through the way I treated you.

I have been thinking a lot about why I treated you the
way I did. You are the only person I have ever cared about
and I have always wanted to make our family the best. I
realise my Dad treated me like shit along with just about
everyone else I ever met. I had to look out for myself all of
my life with people putting me down and using me up. I
never had anyone to stand by me or show me how to treat
the people I love. I've never told you about this but I was
interfered with by my Uncle when I was a kid and I think
this really screwed me up. I think I have never learned to
show love and caring in a proper way to anyone in our
family. I am determined to make up for this.

I have let you down and cannot forgive myself for this.
I will carry sorrow and regret in my heart for the rest of
my life.

I have been thinking about this a lot and I am benefiting
from seeing a counsellor who is helping me to understand
things more clearly. I am facing up to myself and the ways
I have treated you for the first time in my life and I can't
tell you just how ashamed of myself I feel about it.

I am never going to treat you like this again and I am
going to be a proper father to Tim so I don't do to him
what my father did to me. I think we can make it work if
you'll just give me another chance. We can put this behind
us and have the family we have always dreamed of.

I love you. Michael.

A man writing such a statement would generally
have made considerable effort to provide a
well-intended account of his actions and their
effects. However, the account appears to fluctuate
between descriptions which seem self-indulgent
and realisations which profoundly strive to reach
out towards the world of the other.

- *How might we assist this man to critique his
  statement in ways which can enable reaching out
  towards the world of the other and further an ethical
  and accountable restorative project?*
- *How might we enquire in ways that maximise
  accountability to the experiences of family members
  along with a sense of agency and integrity for the
  man?*

After having the man read his statement out loud,
we might first invite him to describe an ethical
context for his statement along with his
experiences in writing it:

*How did it affect you trying to put your realisations
into writing?*

What parts were hardest to write or to read out?

How has it affected you to begin this task?

*What else did you realise as you started to write it
or as you read it out loud?*

*What was the main point that you wanted to
highlight?*

Where do you think you achieved that best?

What parts are you less satisfied with?

The man might emphasise his realisations about
the levels of betrayal of his partner and son and
his determination to take responsibility for this.
He may acknowledge having reached deeper
levels of realisation in writing about his betrayals
of trust, love and respect in the first two
paragraphs. His preparedness to reach out
further and to face deeper levels of shame can be
honoured and implications for his ethical journey
can be explored. The man's agency and intent can
be acknowledged and honoured throughout the
critique.

We might then invite the man to enhance, add
to or revise aspects of the text in ways that might
prevent possible misunderstandings or better
fulfil his ethical intent. These enquiries might
focus upon clear statements of intent, apparent
requests for forgiveness and use of language of
mutuality rather than responsibility:

*What is the reason you have chosen to write this
statement to (partner)?*

*Is it about seeking forgiveness or is it about owing
her something?*

*Why do you believe that it is important for you to do
this?*

*How might you include this in the initial part of the
statement?*

*What in the last paragraph might seem to contradict
this intention?*

Is that what you meant?

*Do you think you are entitled to ask for 'another
chance'?*

*What might your use of the term 'we' suggest in a
statement where you are wanting to take
responsibility for **your** actions?*

*How might your sign off, 'I love you', be interpreted
by (partner)?*

How then might you make it clear that you realise you are not entitled to forgiveness?

How might you edit and revise your statement so that you take responsibility for your actions rather than requesting things from (partner)?

The man might be invited to consider other uses of language that might inadvertently undermine his intent or convey unintended meanings:

In the first line, do you think you have realised ***everything*** *you have put (partner) through or is there likely to be more to understand?*

Are you striving to understand, beginning to understand or have you reached full understanding?

In the fifth paragraph, you write that you 'can't tell (partner)' how ashamed you feel:
– What might it mean if you did tell how ashamed and why?
– How might you 'tell' this?

Invitations may be offered for the man to extend and broaden particular realisations:

You write about betrayal of trust in the first paragraph:
– What opened your eyes to this realisation?
– Why was this so important and so devastating?
– What specific ways did you betray (partner and son)?
– How might you spell this out in more detail?

You write of self-disgust in the second paragraph:
– How specifically did you treat them?
– How did you make them live in fear? Fear of what?
– How did this affect your son?
– What opened your eyes to this?
– What is it that is shameful about your actions?
– What might these details add to your statement?

In paragraph five you write of a commitment to be 'a proper father' to your son;
– What have you realised about the effects of your actions upon your son?
– What specifically are you committing to do differently?
– What opened your eyes to the need to do this?

In the third paragraph you write about, 'why I treated you the way I did' and refer to your own past challenges and injustices;
– What message of realisation do you want to get across here?
– What parts of this paragraph could be interpreted as seeking sympathy or excusing your actions?

– Would you want any of this to be interpreted as excusing your behaviour?
– Do you want to offer realisations or reasons?
– What difference would it make to explain exactly 'how' you treated (partner and son) rather than 'why?'
– How could you explain your actions making it clear that you make no excuses for what you did?

The man might reflect upon this feedback and enquiry and rewrite parts of his statement so that it more clearly and accurately represents his realisations and ethical position. For example, the third paragraph might be re-presented as follows:

I have been thinking a lot about how I treated you and why I treated you the way I did. I cared about you and wanted our family to be the best but I didn't show this in the way I treated you and Tim. I only thought about what I wanted and didn't think about your feelings or what you wanted. There are no excuses for how I treated you and Tim. I was selfish and tried to control you, not love or respect you. I tried to make you do what I wanted and completely disregarded your feelings. I never took responsibility for what I did and left it for you and Tim to have to deal with my behaviour. I talked a lot about love but never walked the talk.

The following statement of realisation was revised to its current form by Felix, who had physically, emotionally and sexually abused his ex-partner over many years. He did not reunite with his partner but did maintain a relationship with their children. Whilst the statement was not written with the intent to share it with his ex-partner, she did ask to see it at a much later stage when discussion of Felix's realisations helped form the basis of a respectful collaborative parenting relationship.

I am writing down these things I feel I must face up to, mostly because I have been running away from them for so long, but also because I owe it to you and (9-year-old son) and (7-year-old daughter) to be honest about what I have done to you.

The truth is I abused you and my son and my daughter for 11 years, the whole time that we were together, but I've only started to call it abuse about six months ago. I'm ashamed to say that I've spent the last 11 years of my life trying to find excuses for myself and blaming everyone else but the person who is responsible, me. I carried on criticising and blaming you, people at work and even my son and daughter. I saw myself as the one who was hard done by. I was right and every one else was wrong. I was too cowardly to face up to what I was doing to the ones I love. Yes, I do love you, but I certainly haven't shown you much love.

I first agreed to go to a counsellor, not because I thought I had a problem, but because I thought it would help to get back together. I now realise that I do have a problem with violence and abuse and I have decided to face it for the first time in my life. When I start to look at how I've treated you, I don't like what I see. I am starting to think about what I have put you and the kids through, for the first time, and I feel totally disgusted with myself. I realise I've got a long way to go to change myself and I've only just started to think about the hurt and suffering that I have caused you all. I now know that this is what I've got to understand and stop thinking about myself all the time.

I realise it wasn't just the violence. I thought that was the only problem for a while and I'm ashamed to say I blamed you and the kids for that. I kept thinking and saying you were pushing me and treating me wrong, but I was wanting to control you and make you responsible for my problems. I bullied you and the kids, mostly with words and put downs. I was always criticising you, always finding fault, always having to be right.

When we first got together I would get upset and sulk whenever you disagreed with me or wanted to do something different. Like when you wanted to go out or visit your mum and dad. I would keep it up and make you feel bad, so you always had to back down and agree with me. I couldn't handle you having your own mind. If you disagreed, I would think you were doing it just to get at me. I was so insecure, I tried to bring you down and hold you back to make me feel OK. I couldn't see that you were trying to love me and you didn't want to hurt me. I didn't care about your feelings. You were trying to help me and put up with me. I just used you and treated you like your feelings don't matter.

I tried to put you off seeing your friends and your family because I wanted to control you by keeping you just to myself. I was really rude and shitty to them all and I put you down in front of them. This is all about control and very selfish. I would be nice to you when you did what I wanted, but treated you like shit when you didn't. I got really jealous of your friends. I remember the first time I hit you after you were talking to a friend on the phone. I slapped you pretty hard across your face. You cried and I made you promise not to phone her. You must have been so confused and frightened about what I was on about. You must have felt so hurt that I didn't trust you and that I could treat you like this. Now I think about what it must have felt like for you, to be slapped and put down by your own husband. To have me walk all over your feelings and treat you like I owned you. But that was only the beginning. I started to criticise things you did and I would put you down and call you really horrible names when I didn't get my own way. I picked on the things I knew would hurt you, like how you looked and sex. I badgered you into having sex when you didn't want to, and the worst thing of all was that I forced it on you just before you left. I blamed you at the time, but I know this was rape.

The last five years I got more and more violent. I don't know how many times I threatened to hit you. I even threatened to run you over with the car when you talked about leaving one time. I punched you in the face, I grabbed you and shook you, I pushed you and kicked you. I smashed things in front of you and the kids. I was bullying you with force. I took advantage of the fact I was much bigger than you and there was no way you could fight back. You must have been terrified. The night we went out for our anniversary, I beat you up so badly that you were bruised for weeks.*

Each time I would say I was sorry and try to make it up to you. You must have got so sick of hearing me say I was sorry, only to be wondering how long it would be before I abused you again. I did feel sorry but I think I was more sorry for myself and scared of losing you. I hated what I did to you, but not enough to stop it. I turned it around so that I blamed you and expected you to put it right. I never took a good look at myself. I never stopped to think about how I was making you feel.

I am only just beginning to realise how betrayed you must feel. You tried to make our marriage work and I just took advantage of your efforts. You must have been living in terror in your own house, waiting for me to put you down or explode and beat you up. I am only beginning to realise how much I have abused and betrayed your trust and love. I have thought a lot about how my Dad made me feel and I realise that I have put you through one hundred times worse. You were trapped. I wouldn't let you get away. I followed you and harassed you after you left and wouldn't let you be. I made your life hell.

I couldn't handle you speaking your own mind. I had to win. I had to bring you down. I had to control you. It has taken me a long time to grow up and see this. I have been worrying about myself but I now realise that the costs for you and the kids have been much greater. I was supposed to be a husband and a father who would stand by and support you, someone you could trust and respect but I only hurt and betrayed you all. I undermined you all and put you down so that you would feel bad about yourselves.

You were trying to keep the family together and to make it work. I kept making hollow promises and dashing your hopes. I can understand why you left me. I didn't give you a chance and I let our children down so badly. I can never forgive myself for that. I betrayed any trust you had in me and gave you a life of misery.

When I think about what I put our son and daughter through it makes me feel sick with shame. I have made my own kids frightened of their Dad and have killed their trust and any respect for me. I think of the terrible things I said about you in front of them. I didn't stop to think about their feelings when I was abusing you. What a terrible example to set for our children. I have caused them so much worry and hurt about what I was going to do to their mum, about what I was going to do to them and about splitting up their family.

I know you've asked why I treated you this way, many times. I've thought of lots of reasons but I know they are only excuses and justifications. The truth is I have been very selfish. I've thought only of myself and what I want and never taken the trouble to think about your or the kid's feelings and what is important for you. I tried to control you for my own selfish reasons. I tried to make you take on my ways of doing things because I couldn't handle you being yourself and living your own life. I thought I could bully you into submission. I killed off your love and respect and trust of me in trying to control you.

I am not writing this as an apology because I realise that I have made too many false apologies in the past and saying sorry can mean nothing any more. It wont undo the past or change the terrible hurts I have done to you all. I know I must think more about what I have done and how it has affected you all because I only thought of myself in the past. I am determined never to abuse anyone ever again. There are no excuses for what I did to you. I am disgusted with myself but I don't intend to wallow in self-pity. I will make sure I understand as much as I can about the hurt I have caused you and I know the best thing I can do is to stay away from you and let you live your own life. I know I have got a lot of changing to do and I won't do it by harassing you. I cant undo what I have done but I can stop being so selfish and think of the people I have abused and betrayed for a change. I can make sure I never treat anyone like this again.

Felix was beginning to understand the need to extend himself through consideration of others' experiences and acknowledgement of his realisations, in order to be able to 'move on' in life. This desire had personal and spiritual meanings for Felix and concerned restitution. However, it was not based on an attempt to reclaim a relationship with his ex-partner or to seek absolution from her. Felix was becoming increasingly focused on restoration through studying the impact of his actions upon others, especially his children, in order to prevent further abuse and maintain respect for others.

Restitution meetings are sometimes facilitated between men who have abused and individuals or communities who have been harmed by the abuse. These forums require considerable preparation with all participants, to ensure the man's readiness to make an accountable expression of his realisations and the readiness of others to actively critique what they hear and experience at the meeting. The man must demonstrate readiness to listen to the experiences of others; an interest in reaching out and wanting to understand what he has put them through, rather than a need for forgiveness and absolution.

Individuals harmed by the abuse might be encouraged to maintain high expectations, to trust their own reactions and judgements and to feel entitled to be firm critics of all they experience at the meeting. When individuals want to confront a man about his abusive actions and their effects, I encourage them to wait until he might be ready to listen to and understand what they have to say. Too often an abused person's experiences and feelings can be ignored, misunderstood or discounted and dismissed because the person addressed is unready to listen and appreciate their significance. We should facilitate such feelings and experiences to become listened to, understood and honoured; never disputed and disrespected.

As Tom became increasingly interested in understanding Peter's experience, he was open to reading his son's account of experiences of injustice and invited to consider how he might respond. Tom prepared for a meeting with Peter whereby he might offer some restitution to his son. This meeting was particularly moving for all present as Tom appeared to broaden and extend his realisations in the presence of his partner and son. He faced Peter and acknowledged the veracity of the incidents his son had documented. Tom surprised his family when he apologised, actually the first time either Judith or Peter had heard an apology from Tom, and then acknowledged. *'I'm your Dad; I'm supposed to protect you and look after you, not bully you and hurt you'*. Tom turned to Judith and admitted his shame at realising how she had tried to protect Peter *'from his own Dad'*. He then spoke of his realisations about Peter's likely experience of witnessing his father abusing his mother and what he had put them both through. As Tom expressed his commitment to treating Judith and Peter with respect, his son spontaneously acknowledged, for the first time, his realisation about what he had put his family through with his abuse of Susie and his initial reluctance to address it. The restitution meeting thereby offered an opportunity to address a *responsibility overload* and to open up new possibilities for Peter to face his own abusive actions.

CHAPTER 13

Practices for Demonstrating Respect

If you judge someone, you have no time to love them.
(Mother Teresa)

The restorative project invites an increasing investment in *reaching out towards the world of the other* whereby realisations and ethical commitments become demonstrated and actualised in relationships. The premise that *actions speak louder than words* is central to the ethical journey, as the man seeks new ways to actualise his preferences towards respectful and ethical practices:

- *How are you becoming the person you have wanted to be?*
- *How are you demonstrating this to yourself?*
- *How are you contributing in your relationships?*
- *What are you offering to others?*
- *How are you showing love, respect etc?*

Opportunities to extend realisations and develop new, respectful practices often arise out of the conflicts and dilemmas experienced between men and their partners and other family members, in their struggles to understand and respond to differences that are becoming increasingly apparent over the course of intervention.

This was evident with Jack and Sue, when Jack had been participating in individual and group intervention for three months. The group facilitators had noted that Jack was taking significant steps in acknowledging responsibility for and ceasing much of his previous possessive, intimidating and coercive behaviour towards Sue. He was acknowledging Sue's entitlement to develop her own independent interests, activities and friends and seldom challenged her initiatives in this regard. Jack was taking a more active role in sharing parenting responsibilities.

Sue's counsellor had observed that Sue was expressing a greater sense of entitlement to speak her mind, *'be her own person'* and be treated respectfully and to develop her own interests and friends. Sue and Jack were now seeing one another on a regular and ongoing basis, after a period of separation for six weeks with very little contact.

Jack remained committed to stopping abusive behaviour, but had recently presented on several occasions in an anxious and agitated state, with an apparently escalating sense of injustice. In these conversations he would at times make statements and assertions such as:

Sue doesn't acknowledge or respond to the changes I'm making.

I'm working my butt off but she's not making an effort for our family.

I know I can't expect her to forgive me, but she has to put it behind her sometime.

She seems to raise the goal posts each time we are together.

She goes off at me for the slightest thing.

We don't make love anymore.

I think it's because she was sexually abused by her brother – she thinks all men are bastards; she needs help too; she has problems too.

Sue was now more assertive and refusing to tolerate abuse in her life. She acknowledged Jack's efforts and that he had made *'huge changes'*:

'We have had some really good times together in the last couple of weeks. We have talked like we never have before. I have started to see (again) some of the reasons why I got married to Jack. He has stopped his violence and is listening to me now.'

Sue also expressed concerns:

'I can't trust him, though, and I can't tell him because he's trying so hard'; 'Sometimes I feel so angry when I think back'; 'He expects me to just forget what happened'; 'I can't forget'; 'I can't get too close to him – I really let him have it then.'

'I feel such a cold bitch when he's trying so hard'; 'but I've got to stand my ground or I'll go under'; 'Sometimes I don't think I'll ever be able to forgive him.'

The complexity of both partner's experiences is evident in the contradictions in their expressions and actions. On one hand, Sue was feeling safer and expressing a greater sense of entitlement. She was in fact speaking out more, having raised her expectations about Jack's behaviour and was no longer prepared to tolerate abuse of any kind. Sue appeared to be feeling and expressing grief, indeed outrage, at Jack's past abusive behaviour. We might wonder about her recent steps towards entitlement and towards experiencing some recent intimacy and connection with Jack:

- *To what extent is Sue feeling safer with and more respected by Jack?*
- *To what extent is Sue becoming bolder in 'being her own person?'*

On the other hand, Sue has expressed a sense of obligation to offer support and perhaps forgiveness to Jack and has at times struggled to 'stand (her) ground' when spending time with him. Sue might be invited to wonder about her ability to take bold steps which resist previous patterns of reliance in this relationship:

- *How is Sue becoming able to stand her ground in the face of Jack's (and cultural) expectations?*
- *How is Sue becoming able to acknowledge Jack's efforts and to move closer to Jack, whilst still standing her ground?*
- *How is Sue becoming able to critique the practices associated with forgiveness and maintain her refusal to forget?*

Jack had demonstrated genuine ethical developments and remained committed to addressing and preventing abusive behaviour, yet he appeared to be reverting to previous patterns of blame and reliance on Sue with expectations that she offer greater acknowledgement, encouragement, trust, intimacy and forgiveness. What was happening?

- *Had there been genuine ethical developments or was Jack only concerned about getting back with Sue?*
- *Was Jack showing his true colours under pressure or over time, or could there be more to him than this?*

Dilemmas such as these are not unusual when men who have abused become excited and enthusiastic about genuine ethical realisations and developments, particularly when expectations about time frames for these developments become apparent. A sense of

impatience can become evident when the concept of time is considered:

- *How long should an intervention programme take?*
- *When should my partner trust my changes?*
- *When should we get back together?*

These preoccupations are informed by cultural expectations, which concern notions of atonement, forgiveness and time, which can blind a man to ethical possibilities and opportunities which may be right in front of him and readily accessible. If we become interested in this complexity which counterpoints ethical realisation and impatience, these possibilities can be explored and developed.

Jack was enthusiastic and excited, but becoming increasingly impatient. What opportunities were there for Jack to understand and appreciate more about Sue's experience and the impact of his own ethical actions, that he might have failed to notice?

- *Had he noticed evidence that Sue might be feeling safer?*
- *Had he realised that Sue might have moved closer to him?*
- *Had he recognised opportunities to understand what was important to Sue?*

After first listening to and acknowledging Jack's protest, along with his fears and worries about the future, he was invited to revisit his ethical preferences regarding the kind of person he was wanting to become and how he wanted to contribute in a relationship. He restated his commitment to principles of equity and partnership and an interest in understanding Sue's ideas and feelings and respecting her entitlement to have and express them. He reaffirmed his commitment to a relationship based on mutual desire rather than obligation or duty.

If Jack began to notice and attend to evidence of Sue's experience of safety, he might challenge restraining ideas that problematise Sue's assertiveness as 'go(ing) off at me' or 'rais(ing) the goal posts'. He could then discover new ways to demonstrate interest in, and respect of, Sue's initiatives. I invited Jack to consider the opportunities before him:

Do you think Sue is feeling safer to speak her mind to you?

How have you noticed this?

Why do you think this could be?

What might it tell you about the efforts you are making to stop violence?

How might these steps be vital for Sue and the person she is becoming?

How does this fit with the way you want to be in this relationship?

What might have stopped you from noticing the importance of Sue speaking her mind and standing her ground?

How might you demonstrate respect for these steps that Sue is taking?

What difference might this make in how you relate to Sue?

How might this fit with the man you are becoming?

Jack was also invited to consider Sue's initiatives towards intimacy and connection:

How has Sue been interested in getting closer to you more recently?

Do you think she is taking these steps out of interest or duty?

How might your efforts be contributing to Sue showing this interest?

What concerns might she have in taking these steps?

What might be stopping you from appreciating and savouring this interest?

How might impatience and urgency be getting in the way?

How might you show appreciation of Sue's interest?

How might you demonstrate understanding of Sue's likely concerns?

What difference might this make in how you relate to Sue?

How might this fit with the man you are becoming?

As Jack began to examine Sue's initiatives from a broader ethical perspective, he could be invited to question urgent expectations and consider opportunities to develop greater understanding of her experience:

What opportunities are you noticing for understanding more about Sue?

What difference has this made in the past?

How has it helped you in your journey?

What are you realising might make it difficult for Sue to feel desire for sexual intimacy with you now?

How might Sue have experienced your past apologies and promises of change?

How often were they hollow promises?

How would you be feeling if you were Sue?

Would you feel trust now?

Why is it important for Sue to question what you are doing and to feel mistrust?

How might you show that you understand and respect Sue's doubt and mistrust?

How might you demonstrate that you are not seeking forgiveness and forgetting?

How might you demonstrate that you can respect Sue's pace?

What difference might this make in how you relate to Sue?

How might this fit with the man you are becoming?

How might you maintain your enthusiasm and hopes without letting them be hijacked by impatience?

How have you stood up to impatience in the past?

What difference has it made?

How might this offer new opportunities for you?

How might you demonstrate that you can handle Sue being her own person?

How might you prove to yourself that you don't want to own Sue?

Jack could recognise further opportunities to challenge possessiveness and stop it hijacking his fears and worries about the future. In addition, to this he began to consider a new proactive ethical task; how to demonstrate *non-ownership*. This led to initiatives which extended beyond ceasing possessive actions, which included acknowledging to Sue his understanding and respect of her feelings of mistrust and offering to care for Paul so that Sue could attend independent activities.

The man is encouraged to seek out and initiate new opportunities to practice *reaching out towards the world of the other*. Such initiatives can extend and develop from realisations made when externalising dangerous ideas and practices. Respectful preferences and strivings are clarified and scrutinised regarding their implications for new action. Demonstrating respect requires a readiness to turn realisations into actions in the service of becoming ethical, rather than seeking forgiveness and reconnection. Consequently, the man is asked how he might *prove to himself*, as opposed to demonstrate to his partner or family members. He is invited to actualise the person that he wants to become and how he wants to conduct himself in relationships, as opposed to becoming preoccupied with his hopes for the relationship itself. The ethical journey entails *testing yourself* in relation to ethical preferences rather than testing the relationship; responding to challenging circumstances with respectful and ethical actions. Restraining patterns of reliance are disrupted with ethical and accountable actions.

The following examples of invitational enquiry concern several common restraining ideas and practices, with a shift from realisation about the influence of dangerous ideas to demonstrating respectful action.

Criticism and judgement (in the name of truth)

Where has this been taking your relationship?

What has criticism stopped you from understanding about your partner / your kids?

Where has it been taking you?
– earning respect or fear?
– gaining love as desire or obligation?

How do you want to be in this relationship?

How do you want to show loving?

What kinds of love do you want to offer?
– critical or supportive?
– denigrating or elevating?
– discouraging or encouraging?
– putting down or building up?
– judgemental or tolerant?
– minding or understanding your partner's business?
– minding your partner's business or getting your own house in order?

How are you standing up for this kind of love?

How are you beginning to show these kinds of love?

How are you starting to show that:
– you don't want to own her or control her?
– you can handle her being her own person?
– you can handle her having her own ideas and making her own decisions?
– you can handle her disagreeing with you?
– you are interested in her ideas and decisions?

– you are interested in listening and understanding rather than judging and criticising?
– you are interested in the differences she brings?
– you can respect differences rather than try to change them?
– you don't need her to say what she thinks you want to hear?
– you won't hurt her or put her down if she speaks her mind?
– you don't need her to walk on eggshells around you?
– you mind your own business rather than try to mind her business?

How might you test yourself further in defying criticism and judgement?

What situations might provide further challenge?

Possessiveness (in the name of love)

Where has this been taking your relationship?

What has possessiveness blinded you to in your partner?

How has possessiveness and jealousy been hijacking love?

Where is it leading you?

How do you want to be in this relationship?

How do you want to show loving?

What kinds of love do you want to offer?
– accepting or limiting your partner?
– working for partnership or ownership?
– controlling your fears or your partner?

How are you standing up for this kind of love?

How are you beginning to show these kinds of love?

How are you starting to show that:
– you don't want to own her or control her?
– you can respect her space and privacy?
– you don't need to check up on her?
– you support her separate interests and friends?
– you are interested in understanding who she is?

How might you test yourself further in defying possessiveness?

What situations might provide further challenge?

Vengeance and getting even (in the name of justice)

Where has this been taking your relationship?

How has it undermined love?

Where is it leading you?

How do you want to be in this relationship?

How do you want to show loving?

What kinds of love do you want to offer?
– seeking partnership or having to win?
– tolerant or vengeful?
– feeling genuine or false pride?
– cooperative or competitive?
– accepting or intimidating?
– earning respect or fear?

How are you standing up for this kind of love?

How are you beginning to show this kind of love?

How are you starting to show that:
– you can stand up for yourself without having to get even?
– you can stand up to your own hurt feelings?
– you don't need to hurt back when you feel hurt yourself?
– offering love is more important than restoring hurt pride?
– you call the shots not your hurt feelings?

How might you test yourself further in defying getting even?

What situations might provide further challenge?

Provocation (in the name of human limitation)

Where has this idea been taking your relationship?

How has it undermined love?

Where is it leading you?

How do you want to be in this relationship?

How do you want to show loving?

What kinds of love do you want to offer?
– mindful or reactive, when challenged?
– tolerant of intolerant of differences?

How are you standing up for this kind of love?

How are you beginning to show this kind of love?

How are you starting to prove to yourself that:
– you won't hurt her if she speaks her mind?
– you don't need her to walk on eggshells around you?
– you can stand on your own two feet?
– you can handle being separate?
– you don't need her to watch your behaviour for you?
– you can watch your own behaviour?
– you can take responsible action for yourself ?
– you don't need to rely or lean on her?
– you take full responsibility for your abuse?
– you are understanding the effects of your abuse upon her?

– you are not trying to convince her:
– to forgive and forget?
– to trust you?
– to get over the effects of your abuse?
– that you have changed?
– to get back together?

How might you test yourself further in defying provocation?

What situations might provide further challenge?

Both Tom and Barry were invited to consider proactive means to demonstrate respectful parenting with their children. They were challenging and resisting restraining ideas and practices concerning *judgement* and *criticism* which had informed abusive behaviour and undermined their strivings to become respectful fathers. They both realised they had been preoccupied with discipline and control, vigilant for 'errors' in others' behaviour and somewhat obsessed with the need to 'correct' the behaviour of their children.

Tom and Barry were practising 'stepping back' from *judgement* and *criticism*. This meant declining opportunities to criticise and correct, and reflecting on ideas which subverted the need to win or have the last word. They had begun to notice strength, rather than weakness, in 'walking away' and were refusing to regard expressions of difference by their children as personal insults which required correction.

Both were invited to consider how they might add to these developments in stopping judgmental practices by finding proactive ways to 'step forward' with respectful initiatives:

How might you demonstrate that you are interested in the different ways your son thinks?

How might you demonstrate that you are interested in what your son likes to do?

How are you wanting to show love to your son?

How might you find new ways to show support, belonging, affection, admiration?

How might you seek out and recognise opportunities to show this kind of love?

What difference might this make in how you relate to your son?

How might this fit with the father you are wanting to become?

In a similar manner, Kevin became open to proactive possibilities as he demonstrated an increasing interest in challenging long-standing and restraining patterns of reliance upon his partner May and other extended family members. As he realised more about the extent of his betrayal of all members of his family, he considered new ways to face and take on responsibility for his actions.

How might you demonstrate that you don't need others in the family to try to lighten your load?
– that you don't need them to make excuses for you or play down the nature of what you did to Susie?
– that you are capable and you want to carry the full load yourself?
How might you demonstrate to May that she doesn't need to look after your feelings?
– that you don't need her to disguise her outrage and betrayal?
– that you can shoulder your own responsibilities?

Kevin decided to approach extended family members to make clear his need to shoulder the full burden of responsibility and to encourage them to understand the effects of his actions upon Susie's family and offer them the support and protection that they might require from the family. He stopped *'acting pathetically'* around May, assured her that he would take care of himself and began to initiate conversations about his understanding of the nature of his betrayal of her and the whole family. He made it clear that he could handle her expressions of outrage and betrayal and that he supported her entitlement to show her true feelings.

Part Four

Broadening the Journey: A Relationship and Family and Community Context

People ask me how I stay in touch. I stay in touch by talking to strangers ... In the time left I want to be a stranger in my own land.

(Michael Leunig, 2006)

Restorative practice inevitably holds a broader focus within relationships, family and community focus, especially when men who have abused begin to establish respectful relationships with family and community members. Invitational practice increasingly becomes situated in a relational context which privileges safety, respect and accountability, as processes for demonstrating respect and restitution are developed in meetings with family and community members.

Tom's meetings with his partner, Judith and son, Peter, (see page 13), became increasingly vital in his ethical journey. These forums enabled him to understand more about their experiences, reach out and feel a deeper sense of remorse and offer meaningful restitution. Once Tom, Judith and Peter were ready to participate in structured family meetings, they could be assisted to experience ways of relating which involved listening, acknowledgement and expressions of realisation, in ways that had never happened before.

Kevin's meetings with his partner, May, and members of his extended family (see page 136), enabled him to express his determination to face the responsibility for his actions and a position which privileged his granddaughter's, and her family's, feelings and needs. He publicly refused

to rely upon the goodwill of extended family members who inadvertently excused or under estimated the seriousness and potential impact of his abusive actions and declared a need for the family to unite in support of Susie and her family. These meetings had a substantial impact in his journey towards facing up and hastened the beginnings of reconciliation between extended family members who had become estranged and adversarial.

When disadvantaged and marginalised communities begin to recognise widespread abusive practices, with enormous effects upon its members in vulnerable circumstances, ethical conversations at a community level, are generally required. A group of men in a community might be assisted to participate in a forum which explores community values and what is important for men in this community. I have found that a shared ethical concern about the effects of violence upon children in the community often becomes expressed and clarified in this context. I have been privileged to witness such ethical realisations brought forward in school, church and indigenous communities where abuse has had destructive effects upon all members (Jenkins, 2006).

This section will detail and illustrate invitational practice in the context of couple and relationship forums. The focus in Chapter 15 is placed on addressing abusive behaviour in a couple relationship. Chapter 16 addresses mutual violence in couple relationships.

CHAPTER 14

A Context for Relationship Counselling

Over the past two decades, intervention concerned with violence and abuse with men and women has mostly been conducted in separate forums, with a focus on advocacy, housing and welfare priorities for women and a separate focus on intervention programmes for men that are designed to assist them to take responsibility to stop violence.

In this context, relationship counselling has tended to be shunned and neglected. The relationship counselling approaches of the 1980s, which were based on systems theory, tended to neglect the political context of abusive behaviour and were roundly criticised by feminist researchers. The use of couple counselling approaches has remained controversial with concerns about their potential to compromise the safety of women and inadvertently support a patriarchal status quo. Apolitical counselling for couples has the potential to overlook or minimise the political disadvantage of women, through the inference of psychological and interactional explanation and practice, whereby violence is regarded as a symptom of relationship dysfunction or poor communication skills.

As a result, relationship counselling tended to lose favour and has even come to be regarded as dangerous and irresponsible (Bograd and Mederos, 1999; Bograd, 1984; Hansen, 1993). However, intervention practice which fails to take account of the relationship can contribute to misunderstanding and confusion and may undermine respectful relationship goals.

Relationship counselling can be conducted in a manner which takes account of the political context of abuse and which is safe and respectful to women, whilst holding men accountable for their actions (Goldner, 1992, 1999; Jenkins, 1990, 2007; Jory and Anderson, 1999, 2000; Jory, Anderson and Greer, 1997). This requires careful consideration of when and how to establish a safe, respectful and accountable context for relationship counselling; one which is sensitive to the politics of violence and abuse and its place in the maintenance of patriarchal culture. In fact, it can be problematic not to address issues of safety, the nature and effects of violence and abuse, and

the prevention of future violence and abuse in a couple context.

Many programmes, which are informed by dominant contemporary theory and practice, cease intervention after the completion of individual or group programmes, conducted in separate forums, for men and women. However, in situations of abuse, many couples choose to remain in a relationship and may continue to live together. Others may choose to reunite after a period of separation. Relationship counselling can be particularly helpful in complementing and enhancing individual and group counselling programmes.

Those who are interested in maintaining a relationship and developing a safe and respectful partnership and those who wish to negotiate a respectful separation in which the effects of past relationship violence upon children can be addressed, may well benefit from relationship counselling.

Separate, individual goals which include safety and entitlement to be free of violence and coercion, along with acceptance of responsibility and accountability for the perpetration of violence and controlling behaviour, can be expressed and developed within a relationship context. In fact, it becomes increasingly important to provide a forum where the nature of violence and its effects, along with ethical preferences for partnership practices which ensure safety, respect and tolerance of differences, can be publicly named and witnessed. In these forums, each partner can openly and publicly reflect upon and receive feedback regarding their own, individual responsibilities and respectful developments within the relationship.

Assessing readiness for engagement with couples

Dora, aged 37 years, and Geoff, aged 33 years, requested counselling to address longstanding conflict in their relationship, *'before we kill each other'*. Geoff experienced Dora as mistrusting, *'possessive'* and *'always harassing me'* and '*undermining closeness and intimacy*'. Dora felt that Geoff was uncaring, '*secretive*' and '*only interested in his job and sex*'. Each was highly judgmental and blaming, believing that the other acted in wilfully hurtful ways to disappoint and let them down. Both Geoff and Dora expressed righteous indignation about the other's recalcitrant attitudes and appeared to alternate between feelings of intoxicating rage and resigned exasperation.

Both had engaged in physical violence and offensive and insulting putdowns. Dora had punched, kicked, and on one recent occasion assaulted Geoff with a cricket stump in the presence of their children. Geoff had pushed and shoved Dora and had pinned her down on the floor, also in the children's presence.

Dora felt offended, when previously attempting to seek counselling, because the counsellor had regarded her as a victim of domestic abuse and had been reluctant to see her together with Geoff. Dora acknowledged that Geoff's size and strength gave him a physical advantage, but asserted that she did not feel afraid of him. She felt patronised by the previous counsellor and was determined to '*sort things out together*'.

Lee, aged 30, telephoned to request couple counselling for himself and his partner of four years, Simon, aged 35. Lee tearfully disclosed how, '*an argument turned ugly*' and Simon '*got physical and trashed the house*' and then '*he beat me*'. Lee declared, '*I've had enough*', and acknowledged previous threats and abuse by Simon. Lee disclosed that he is '*frightened to be in the same room*' with Simon, and had been staying at a friend's place. Lee had experienced threats and physical assaults by Simon over the four years of their relationship. He associated this violence with Simon becoming '*insanely jealous*', '*paranoid*' and frequently suspecting that Lee wanted to have relationships with other men.

Both Dora and Lee have requested couple counselling, in circumstances where there has been significant violence within their relationships. It is vital that we first assess the readiness of both partners to participate in couple counselling that is likely to be both safe and respectful to all concerned. This assessment of readiness may initially be conducted by telephone, prior to any face-to-face contact.

Readiness relates to the following parameters:

1. **Is the context one of abuse or reciprocal violence?**
   Couple counselling is generally not appropriate for first contact in situations of abuse where:

   – there is a significant imbalance in power and privilege.
   – the person subjected to violence experiences high levels of fear, intimidation or a sense of entrapment.
   – the person subjected to violence feels forced to accommodate to the needs and demands of the person enacting violence.

2. **Does each person feel sufficiently safe to participate in couple counselling?**
   An initial couple meeting may be safe, respectful and helpful when:

   – the person subjected to violence feels safe about the prospect of speaking out about their hopes, expectations and experience of the violence, in the presence of their partner.
   – the person enacting violence demonstrates a preparedness to listen to their partner speak about hopes, expectations and experience of violence.

   Safety is enhanced when both partners:

   – want a safe, violence-free relationship.
   – regard violence as unacceptable conduct.
   – regard a person who has enacted violence as responsible for their violence.

3. **Is there an expressed commitment to a concept of partnership which privileges equity of entitlement?**
   Does the person who has been subjected to violence believe that they are entitled to:

   – feel safe and free of violence in the relationship?
   – speak freely and act independently without feeling compelled to defer to or accommodate to the expectations of the other?
   – does the person who has enacted violence express support for their partner's entitlements?

4. **Is there an expressed commitment to partnership regarding relationship and family responsibilities?**

Does the person who has enacted violence or abusive behaviour:

– acknowledge a responsibility to address their own violence?
– acknowledge a responsibility for self-reliance; to study the nature and development of patterns of violence and not rely upon the other person to anticipate violence or 'keep the peace?'

Are both persons committed to a concept of sharing responsibility for developing and maintaining a respectful emotional climate in the relationship and family?

5. **Is there an expressed commitment to a concept of partnership with a balance between a sense of togetherness and belonging and a sense of separateness and independence, in the relationship?**
Does each person:

– acknowledge a responsibility to actively contribute to a mutual sense of belonging in the relationship?
– respect the other's entitlement to separate activities, interests and friends?

The first two criteria are pivotal in determining readiness. Dora's and Geoff's relationship was characterised by high levels of violence and coercion. However, initial enquiries suggested a context for reciprocal violence where there was a characteristic sense of even-handedness with an absence of any one-sided feeling of intimidation, forced accommodation or entrapment. Whilst there appeared to be substantial evidence of disrespect for the other's feelings and needs, neither partner felt fearful to express their views in the presence of the other. Whilst Dora and Geoff tended to blame each other for their violence, they were appalled by many of their actions and held expectations that supported concepts of equity and partnership regarding entitlement, shared responsibilities and independence. In this context an initial couple meeting might be arranged where conversation about safety and respect would enable the appropriateness of such a forum to be ensured.

The initial telephone conversation with Lee suggested a high likelihood that this was a context for abuse rather than reciprocal violence and that Lee did not feel sufficiently safe to talk about his hopes, expectations and his experience of violence, in the presence of his partner, without fear of recrimination. Lee did not feel that Simon would respect his entitlement to safely express his own needs and requirements without having to accommodate to Simon's wishes and had experienced little evidence that Simon accepted responsibility for his own violence. Simon did not appear to respect Lee's entitlement to separate activities, interests or friends. Lee had requested couple counselling. A couple forum appeared unlikely to provide a safe and respectful environment which might enable goals of safety, respect, equity or partnership, in this context.

CHAPTER 15

Invitational Practice in Situations of Abuse

In situations of abuse, separate initial meetings with the abusing person can provide the privacy and safety needed to assist him to become ready to later participate safely and respectfully in a couple meeting. A separate forum is generally conducive to a man becoming open in reflecting on his ethics and his actions and considering new possibilities, because it frees him from the distractions of habitual and restraining patterns of interaction with his partner and lessens fears of judgement and loss of face. Most importantly, his partner is not exposed to threats or intimidation during this process, nor is she placed in a position where she might be expected or feel obligated to continue to support him with his own personal responsibilities.

In such forums, Jack had begun to clarify ethical preferences, face up to the nature and effects of his abusive behaviour and challenge patterns of possessive and controlling thinking and action which had informed this behaviour.

Separate forums with Sue provided a safe environment in which she could consider her own relationship preferences and establish a sense of entitlement:

– to be safe and treated with respect in her relationships.
– to hold and express her own views, ideas and preferences.
– to have these ideas, views and preferences respected.
– to freely associate with family and friends.

In a separate and private forum, Sue could speak openly about violence and its effects, without feeling a requirement to tone down or moderate her concerns. She could be assisted to identify, address and challenge restraining ideas and relationship blueprints which promote a sense of obligation or requirement to accommodate to Jack's wishes, in order to prevent violence or establish harmony in the relationship and family. Sue came to recognise that her experience was not unique, in the light of dominant cultural interests which prescribe that women sacrifice their own needs and 'be for others'.

In this way, Sue could also be assisted to develop readiness to participate in couple counselling, if wanted, at a suitable time in the future.

Preparation for couple counselling

Couple counselling can only be helpful in a context which privileges safety, equity and partnership. It is vital that the very first couple counselling meeting provides a forum in which both partners feel safe and respected in each other's presence. The responsibility of the counsellor is to prepare each person and facilitate a context for meeting which minimises the likelihood of intimidation and fear; one which promotes openness, limits escalations of exaggerated entitlement by the person who has abused and precludes a sense of obligation and accommodation by the person who has been subjected to abuse.

We can act to ensure the likelihood of a safe and respectful context by:

– carefully assessing, monitoring and discussing the readiness of each partner to participate in couple work.
– commencing couple work only once such readiness is satisfactorily demonstrated.
– carefully establishing a structure for safety and respect in initial meetings; one which errs on the side of caution.

A structure is developed which begins with a sequence of separate, then joint, information forums which progress towards couple counselling meetings, in which safe and respectful interaction is privileged and possibilities for disrespectful behaviour are limited.

Individual information forums

It is desirable for individual, therapeutic intervention with each partner to be conducted by separate counsellors. The experience and needs of children, who are inevitably affected by abusive behaviour and by the steps taken to address it, are also best monitored and addressed by a separate counsellor. This helps to ensure safe and respectful relationship boundaries and privacy which better enables the articulation of individual needs, priorities and fears.

These counsellors meet together at intervals, with each partner, to ensure a level of accountability and connection between the nature and impact of the individual work. In this way, similarities and differences between each partner's (and the children's) experiences and accounts of behaviour and interactions can be understood. Intervention practices can be informed by each partner's individual and relationship preferences along with the steps they are taking in trying to realise them. Information forums enable a sense of collaboration towards common, safe and respectful objectives for all family members.

Accordingly, Jack's counsellor began to meet with Sue and her counsellor. In these meetings, Sue's counsellor interviewed Sue about her experience of Jack's abusive behaviour, along with her preferences and needs. Sue was invited to contribute to discussions about ways to ensure that work with Jack would be both sensitive to and respectful of her experience and how it might support her needs for safety and respect.

Principles of safety and accountability were privileged in these forums with counsellors mindful about:

- assisting Sue to ensure that her participation in information meetings did not obligate her to feel responsible to assist Jack to face responsibility for his abusive behaviour. The priority for Jack to take responsibility for his controlling, interrogative and possessive behaviour was maintained at all times.
- informing Sue, in accordance with established limited confidentiality agreements made with Jack, of the nature of Jack's intervention programme and his motivation and commitment to realising therapeutic goals. Sue was assisted to consider realistic criteria to evaluate steps that Jack might take to address and cease abusive behaviour.
- discussing any issues of concern arising from Jack's current behaviour which might impact upon Sue's safety or well-being.

In this context, Sue's experiences, needs and preferences could inform intervention with Jack,

whilst she could gain feedback about the nature of his intervention and commitment, without undue fear of intimidation, retaliation or the pressure of obligation to accommodate or defer to him.

Jack and his counsellor also met with Sue's counsellor. In these meetings Jack was assisted to consider and understand Sue's experiences and needs. Feedback from Sue's counsellor assisted him to reflect upon Sue's entitlement to feel safe and respected, to express her feelings and preferences, to be her own person and to challenge feelings of obligation which might accord with cultural and gendered expectations. Jack began to consider the complementary nature of their journeys; his need to take responsibility for his actions and Sue's need to relinquish feelings of responsibility to 'walk on eggshells', defer or try to placate Jack in trying to prevent abusive behaviour.

Such forums provided a safe and respectful context for Jack to better understand Sue's experience and to address any concerns he may have, whilst maintaining a focus on his own responsibilities. The potential distraction of escalating, disrespectful exchanges with Sue could be avoided.

Couple information forums

Couple information forums provide a further step towards establishing readiness for safe and accountable couple counselling. Couple information meetings may be commenced when each person demonstrates understanding and acceptance of the need to address their own behaviour and their own restraining ideas.

Jack had participated in individual and group intervention for six weeks and had begun to take significant steps towards responsibility for his abusive behaviour towards Sue. He had ceased unwanted contact and attempts to reunite with Sue. He now understood the need for him to address patterns of controlling and possessive behaviour and the 'dangerous ideas' or thinking which informed this behaviour. Jack no longer attributed the cause of his abusive behaviour to Sue being 'unreasonable'. He was beginning to recognise that his own misguided ideas and practices had been stopping him from achieving the kind of relationship he wanted with Sue and Paul. He appeared to understand Sue's need for privacy to reflect upon her needs and hopes for the future and to affirm her own sense of entitlement to a life free of abuse and harassment, without a requirement to accommodate to Jack in order to 'keep the peace'.

Jack had also begun to consider and reflect upon the impact of his abusive and controlling behaviour and the harm he had done to Sue and Paul. His remorse was beginning to shift from self-centred preoccupations and feelings of personal loss towards greater concern for the feelings and experiences of others.

Jack could now be interviewed about his readiness to participate in a couple information meeting with Sue and both counsellors:

> *What tells you that you are ready to meet with Sue?*
>
> *What tells you that you are ready to listen to what Sue has to say about what she thinks is important?*
>
> *What tells you that you are ready to listen to Sue talk about her experience of your abusive behaviour and of being hurt by you?*
>
> *What tells you that you are ready to try to understand; to take on board what Sue is feeling and saying?*
>
> *What if Sue says something that worries you; what if she expresses doubts about the future of your relationship?*
>
> *What tells you that you can listen to what Sue has to say without trying to challenge or question her thoughts or ideas?*
>
> *What tells you that you are ready to hear whatever Sue has to say without harassing her during or following the meeting?*

In this way, Jack was invited to reflect on his readiness to participate in a respectful meeting with Sue and to provide evidence, in his current thinking and recent actions, that might demonstrate such readiness.

Jack was invited to imagine and reflect upon what Sue's experience might be in anticipating and attending such a meeting:

> *What do you think Sue's concerns could be in attending a meeting with you and speaking her mind?*
>
> *What concerns might Sue have about her safety?*
>
> *What concerns might Sue have about your expectations?*

Sue was also interviewed about her readiness for a meeting with Jack:

> *What tells you that now is a good time to tell Jack about your hopes and what you are trying to achieve?*
>
> *What evidence have you seen that suggests that Jack might be interested in listening to these hopes and goals?*
>
> *What tells you that you are ready to speak out and that you don't need to 'tread on egg shells' around Jack?*
>
> *What tells you that you won't feel a need to look after Jack's feelings or say things that you think he might want to hear?*
>
> *What would you need to feel safe in speaking about what is important to you?*

Sue reflected upon her own growing sense of entitlement to speak her mind and be free of harassment and abuse and her refusal to tolerate further abuse in her own or her son's lives. She also recognised that Jack had ceased harassing and pursuing her, her family and her friends with desperate phone calls and entreaties for her to reunite with him. She pointed out that this made her feel safer and more respected. Sue added that she felt safe because the counsellors would be present.

Sue was invited to consider structures and strategies which might address any anticipated problems arising in the proposed meeting, in the event of her feeling unsafe. She declared that, whilst she was nervous, she wanted this meeting and in fact, was looking forward to it as an opportunity to speak her mind, without feeling a requirement to accommodate to Jack's feelings and needs.

Both persons are required to demonstrate readiness before such a meeting is initiated. However, they are encouraged to take their time and not feel any pressure to hastily achieve readiness. Readiness enquiries could help Jack to focus on his responsibility for safety, by heightening the significance of him being prepared to listen to his partner without criticism or judgment, and to appreciate her likely concerns in meeting with him. Sue could become more strongly oriented towards her own sense of entitlement to safety and respect and assessing evidence of Jack's interest in her views and experience. These priorities can help to avoid a premature focus upon possibilities for reconciliation.

Couple information meetings are commenced with an introduction about the structure and purposes of the meeting. This process of *talking about talking about it*, creates a sense of boundaries and limits and provides structures for safety and respect. The levels of caution in assessing readiness and careful explanation underscore the priorities of safety and respect. It is vital that these early meetings provide each person with a new experience of being together, with limited opportunities for old pattern and habits of disrespectful interaction.

> *The purpose of this meeting is to inform each other of the goals you have and the steps you are taking towards putting safety first in your lives and putting a stop to violence and abuse. The priority here is stopping violence and abusive behaviour and establishing safety and respect; this must be ensured before any other relationship issues or hopes about the future of a relationship can be helpfully discussed. Our job as counsellors is to ensure that this priority is upheld and to interrupt and stop any conversation that moves away from it. We are not here to talk about the future of your relationship or any other issues, apart from stopping abuse and safety. Is that O.K. with each of you?*
>
> *Our responsibility is to ensure that this meeting is safe and respectful. We will interview each of you about your goals and the steps you are taking. Whilst each person is being interviewed, it is important that the other takes the opportunity to listen and does not interrupt. After this you will then have an opportunity to ask questions and become clear about what the other has said; to ensure that you have understood what is important for them.*
>
> *The purpose of this meeting is to make sure that you understand each other's goals and the steps each of you are wanting to take. It is an opportunity to understand, not to question or challenge the other person's goals or ideas. If you feel any concerns about what the other person is saying, you will have an opportunity to discuss these with your counsellor in the debriefing period following the meeting.*
>
> *Our job is to look after safety and respect. We will check in with you both regularly about feeling safe and respected and we will interrupt or stop the meeting if any of us have any concerns about this.*

In this way, a structure and process is established to promote and monitor safety and respect in the forum. If there is a need to interrupt or stop the meeting, then public commitments are sought to ensure that disrespectful discussion or contact does not occur after the meeting. Individual debriefing is conducted to acknowledge individual achievements, clarify concerns and ensure ongoing safety and respect.

For example, if Jack began to critique or challenge any of Sue's statements about the steps she is taking towards her goals of entitlement to feel safe and free of abuse, his challenge would be interrupted by his counsellor. If Jack accepted this interruption, he might be invited to reflect on and consider the meaning of such a challenge to Sue, in the light of his own stated goals and preferences, particularly his commitment to listen to and respect Sue. He might be invited to reflect upon the potential impact of such a challenge for Sue's experience of respect and safety in meeting with him. Jack would be invited to reconsider his readiness to participate in such a meeting, acknowledge the need to address this issue and re-commit to listen and understand more about Sue's experience. Sue might be invited to reflect on the meaning of this challenge in terms of feeling safe and respected. The counsellors would then decide whether to continue the meeting or to postpone it until a time when Jack was ready to listen to what is important to her.

Alternatively, the meeting might be interrupted if Sue began to depart from describing steps towards her goals and began to engage in an escalating expression of outrage towards Jack, concerning his past behaviour. Sue might then be invited to reflect upon her readiness to proceed at a measured pace, despite feelings of outrage. Clearly at some point, Jack does need to be ready and willing to hear about the impact of his behaviour upon Sue, appreciate how much this has hurt her and how outraged she might feel. However, at this time, Jack may well be unready and unprepared to listen to and appreciate the nature and intensity of Sue's outrage. It is not likely to be helpful to either person if intensely expressed feelings are not listened to or understood, especially if they lead into an adversarial escalation; an experience all too familiar for this couple.

In any event, counsellors should err on the side of caution by interrupting or stopping any conversation which appears to depart from the meeting agenda and agreed upon structures and processes.

Couple counselling meetings

Counselling in a couple context should promote and enable:

1. Further development of mutual understanding, clarification and interest in each other's efforts to establish a safe relationship which is free of violence and

abuse. This forum allows for further
clarification and commitment to individual
responsibilities, for one partner to cease all
abusive behaviour and the other to refuse to
tolerate any further abuse.

2. A deeper commitment by the person who has
abused to make restitution for harm caused to
family members and others in the community.
A couple setting can enable a stronger sense of
accountability whereby the partner who has
abused can invest in deepening their interest,
understanding and acknowledgement of the
actual and potential effects of their actions
upon others.

3. Subversion of interactional restraints to a
respectful relationship; in particular, the
pattern of reliance upon the person who has
been subjected to abusive behaviour, to take
responsibility to be vigilant, monitor, try to
prevent and deal with the consequences of the
actions of the person who has abused.

4. Creation of a safe and respectful forum in
which conflict can safely be experienced and
addressed without fear of violence and
abusive behaviour.

5. Creation of a relationship context which
fosters respect of difference and diversity.

A couple counselling meeting often provides the
first opportunity for both partners to engage in
mutually respectful conversation about abusive
behaviour and its effects outside of the context of
disrespectful exchanges, crises and pleas for
forgiveness and forgetting in their aftermath.

Clarification of readiness in a couple meeting

Couple counselling may be commenced when:

- there is evidence that both persons are
demonstrating commitment to addressing
individual goals regarding stopping violence
and entitlement to safety and respect.
- couple information meetings are fostering a
sense of safety and respect.
- there is no current evidence of significant
abusive behaviour.

Jack and Sue had been living separately for ten
weeks, with limited contact to allow Jack to
maintain connection with their son, Paul.
However, contact and conversation together had
increased in the last four weeks and had been

experienced by both as respectful. They had
participated in two couple information meetings
which both experienced as safe, respectful and
helpful.

Jack remained keen to reunite with Sue and
Paul. However, he understood the need to accept
and support their separate living arrangement.
He had ceased pressuring Sue for increased
contact and was directing his energy towards
addressing his abusive behaviour and its effects.
Sue was very aware of Jack's hopes but
ambivalent about reunification, having become
more acutely aware of her own feelings of hurt,
betrayal and outrage, in relation to Jack's abusive
behaviour. She wanted Jack to understand her
experience but worried about his possible
reactions to her current feelings, anticipating that
he would be disappointed, hurt and angry. Both
Sue and Jack expressed a desire to meet further to
discuss their individual efforts to address abuse
and its effects.

Through the process of *talking about talking
about it*, structures for maintaining safety and
respect were established at the beginning of the
couple meeting. Having reiterated that safety is
paramount, along with the priority on stopping
abuse before addressing other relationship
concerns, the purposes and meanings of
discussing abusive behaviour and its effects were
discussed and agreed upon. Commitments about
readiness are vital, given that conversation about
the actual nature and effects of abusive behaviour
is likely to take place in these meetings.

*Before we invite you, Sue, and you, Jack, to talk about your
realisations about abusive behaviour, its effects on your
lives and what you are doing about it, each of you needs
to be sure that you are ready to have these conversations
today. Each of you must feel sure that these conversations
will be safe and respectful. First, I want to check that it
will be safe and respectful for you to speak your minds here
today.*

This *talking about talking about it* enquiry might
first be directed towards Jack to assist him to
establish and demonstrate his readiness and
commitment. Sue might then have the
opportunity to assess levels of safety and respect
for herself:

*What tells you, Jack, that it will be safe for Sue to
speak about her true feelings here today?*

*How do you know that you are ready and that you
can handle Sue speaking about your abusive
behaviour and its effects on her life here today?*

What signs have you seen that tell you that you can listen to what Sue has to say, rather than challenge or question her ideas, like in the past?

What if Sue says something that is painful to hear or that you feel hurt about?

What recent evidence have you noticed, that tells you:
– that you can listen to Sue speak her mind?
– that you can listen without reacting?
– that you don't need Sue to keep her thoughts or opinions to herself?
– that you can respect Sue being her own person and speaking her own mind?

What worries or concerns might Sue have in coming here today and speaking her mind about what is important to her?

Can you understand why Sue might have these worries or concerns?

Does it make sense to you that Sue might feel this way?

How important is it for you to understand what Sue thinks and feels:
– about her needs, ideas and goals?
– about the effects of your abusive behaviour?
– about the ways she is making her life safe and free from violence?
How have you wanted to reassure Sue that:
– you want to hear her true feelings?
– you will respect her speaking her mind?
– she is safe whatever she says or does?
– she can be her own person in your presence?
– you don't need her to look after your feelings by keeping her thoughts to yourself?

These enquiries cover similar ground to those made in individual preparation for a couple information meeting. However, in this context, the enquiries and Jack's responses are witnessed by Sue and afford her an opportunity to hear Jack's realisations and evaluate her own safety and readiness to participate in the meeting.

Similar enquiries may then be directed towards Sue to establish her readiness:

What tells you that it may be safe to speak your mind here today?

What tells you that it may be safe to talk about abuse and its effects here today?

What signs have you seen that tell you that Jack might be ready to hear your true feelings and that he doesn't need you to water them down or pretend?

What signs have you seen that tell you that Jack might be ready to talk openly and honestly about his abusive behaviour and its effects?

What tells you that Jack is ready and wants to hear your true feelings and that he won't crack up at you or hurt you when you leave here?

What signs have you seen that tell you that he is interested in what you think?

How important is it to you that Jack does try to understand how his violence and abusive behaviour has affected you and Paul?

After such initial clarification, the abused person might begin to discuss aspects of their experience of the man's violence and abusive behaviour. The counsellors may intervene to check that the abused person is mindfully considering their own safety in raising such issues. Counsellors may then check once again with the man that he still feels ready and able to listen to the abused person's experience, without reacting in ways that might challenge or restrict that person's expressions or experience.

Before long, Sue began to express feelings of hurt and outrage. She declared that she 'could never trust Jack again' and began to express her uncertainty about any future with Jack. Her counsellor interrupted and enquired:

Have you spoken out like this with Jack before?

What tells you it is safe to speak your feelings in this way?

Complementary enquiries were then addressed to Jack:

Have you heard Sue speak honestly about the depth of hurt you caused her before?

Have you listened to her talk about the effects on her trust before?

How does it affect you to hear Sue speak honestly and truthfully?

What tells you that you are ready to listen and understand what she is saying?

What tells you that you can listen and respect Sue even though it hurts you to hear what she is saying?

What do you think it takes for Sue to speak her true feelings?

Would you rather she spoke her mind or just said what she thought you might want to hear?

What does it say about Sue that she is taking such a courageous step?

What does it say about you that you are prepared to listen and want to try to understand what you have put her through?

These *talking about talking about it* enquiries enable both people to step back momentarily and reflect upon the nature and meaning of what is being discussed. Both partners are able to consider their readiness to take steps which may open up new possibilities in conversation. This kind of consideration encourages sober reflection and can prevent familiar patterns of escalating interaction.

Despite strong feelings of hurt, worry and shame, Jack continued to assert his readiness to listen to and try to understand Sue's experience. As he demonstrated this readiness by listening and acknowledging the legitimacy of her experiences, Sue acknowledged that she felt relieved and supported by Jack. Both were able to appreciate this novel form of conversation as respectful and valuable.

Reflecting on individual responsibilities

When Jack and Sue were invited to notice, reflect upon and evaluate these new experiences, they began to recall other recent examples of interaction in which Sue had 'spoken her mind' or acted independently, and Jack had demonstrated a willingness to listen to and respect her ideas and decisions. Both recalled situations, which would previously have been challenging, in which Jack had set his own limits on his reactions and Sue had refused to '*walk on eggshells*' or accommodate him in order to '*keep the peace*'. Both were invited to critique the ways in which they had successfully challenged their own restraining patterns of thinking and habits that had previously interfered with safe and respectful ways of relating.

Such discussions of contact and conversation provide opportunities for reflection on new possibilities for relating and may lead to plans for further connection. In situations where there have been statutory orders that prohibit or limit forms of contact, it may be necessary to negotiate variations to avoid inadvertent criminal breaches.

Jack began to describe a telephone conversation in which Sue had told him that she was planning a night out with some friends. Jack stated that he immediately experienced '*possessive feelings*' upon

hearing about Sue's plans. His '*first thoughts*' were to interrogate Sue about where she was planning to go and with whom. Jack said that he recognised this familiar pattern of '*possessive thinking*' and decided to question his thinking rather than question Sue. Jack decided, '*to keep my mouth shut*'. Instead of interrogating Sue, '*I wished her a good time*'.

The counsellors inquired, '*What led you to do this?*'

Jack responded, '*I saw it straight away – this was possessive thinking*'; '*Once I start, I keep on and on at Sue and drive her away*'; '*I knew right away I had to stop and back off*'.

The counsellors continued to invite Jack to reflect upon and critique the nature and meaning of his decisions and actions:

How did you manage to spot that kind of thinking so quickly?

How strong was the possessive feeling?

What did it take for you to put a stop to it?

What did you prove to yourself in stopping it and wishing Sue a good night?

In this way, Jack could be invited to detail and make visible his ideas, the ethics that inform them and the means by which he enabled respectful thinking and action. He was invited to consider their meaning, in terms of realising his own ethics and preferences:

What difference does it make when you challenge your own unhelpful and dangerous patterns of thinking, rather than challenge Sue and her ideas?

Where is this kind of thinking and action taking you?

How does it fit with the kind of man and partner you want to be?

Jack was also invited to imagine and speculate about Sue's experience when she told him of her plans:

What concerns do you think Sue might have had in telling you about her planned night out?

How important do you think it is for Sue to be able to speak out about what she wants to do and to feel safe in doing so?

Jack thought Sue might be highly anxious about the possibility of him, '*attacking her and criticising* her friends' and *'trying to make her feel bad'*, given her past experience. He imagined that it would have taken considerable courage for Sue to speak out about her plans.

In a similar manner, Sue was invited to consider her decision and actions, in the light of her ethics and preferences:

> *How important is it for you to be able to speak out about your plans and to feel safe in doing so?*
>
> *What concerns did you have in raising this matter with Jack?*
>
> *How big were those concerns?*
>
> *What did it take to speak out in this way?*
>
> *What did you prove to yourself in speaking out?*

In this way, Sue could be invited to reflect upon the steps she is taking to challenge patterns of restraining thinking that previously led her to *'walk on eggshells'* in order to *'keep the peace'*. She could affirm a sense of growing confidence and *'courage'* in feeling less accommodating and obligated, and more *'my own person'*.

Sue was then invited to reflect on what she imagined Jack's reactions might be to this new courage and confidence:

> *What does it mean to you that Jack listened to and tried to respect what was important to you?*
>
> *How much do you think Jack might appreciate or be proud of you for taking these new steps?*

In response, Jack was invited to comment on what it means to him that Sue is taking such steps:

> *What does it mean to you that Sue has spoken out and told you of her plans?*
>
> *Have you found yourself beginning to respect this courage?*
>
> *Would you prefer a partner who says what she thinks or one who pretends and says what she thinks you want to hear?*
>
> *What does it say about the steps you are taking to stop abusive behaviour, that Sue was prepared to take a risk in speaking out?*

In this way, both Jack and Sue were invited to explore the meanings of the steps each are taking, in the light of their stated desires to challenge pervasive and long-standing patterns of restraint

to safety, equity and respect in their relationship and family.

These conversations were extended to assist Jack to anticipate any sense of obligation that Sue might experience, following her acknowledgement of his respectful behaviour:

> *How might the steps you are taking affect your expectations about making further contact with Sue?*
>
> *What concerns might Sue have as a result of her acknowledgement of the steps that you're taking towards respectful behaviour?*
>
> *What kind of thoughts might you need to watch out for, in order to avoid setting unrealistic expectations at this time?*

Jack could anticipate that Sue might be anxious about him wanting further contact and putting this priority before that of ensuring that he fully ceases possessive behaviour. He acknowledged that he did, at times, *'get a bit carried away'* and try to *'go at a pace (which was) faster than what Sue is ready for'*. Jack referred to this phenomenon as, *'the thin edge of the wedge'* and acknowledged that he needed to be vigilant in order to prevent a sense of urgency which might lead to him *'putting pressure on Sue'*. In this way, Jack could strengthen and affirm his commitment to fully address restraining ideas which have informed violence and disrespectful behaviour and to guard against putting contact with Sue before this priority.

These conversations were gradually broadened by inviting Jack to consider, reflect upon, try to understand and appreciate evidence of Sue developing and expressing a sense of entitlement to *'be her own person'*:

> *What signs are you seeing that tell you that Sue is:*
> *– speaking her own mind?*
> *– becoming more her own person?*
> *– making her own decisions?*
> *– refusing to take a back seat in her own life?*
> *– no longer 'walking on eggshells' or trying to 'keep the peace?'*
> *– quitting feeling that she should go along with your needs?*
> *– no longer prepared to take responsibility for your actions?*

Sue was invited to consider and reflect upon evidence that might demonstrate that Jack is taking responsibility for his abusive behaviour:

What signs are you seeing that tell you that Jack is taking responsibility for his abusive behaviour?

What signs have you seen that demonstrate that Jack won't hurt you or threaten you whatever you do or say?

Sue may also be invited to consider evidence which suggests that Jack is addressing restraining ideas concerning feelings of exaggerated entitlement, ownership and possessiveness:

What signs have you seen which tell you that Jack:
– can handle you being your own person?
– respects your right to speak your mind and make your own decisions?
– doesn't want to own or possess you?

These enquiries to Sue may also relate to evidence of Jack becoming more self-reliant:

What signs have you seen which suggest that Jack:
– doesn't need you to put his feelings first?
– doesn't need you to walk on eggshells around him?
– doesn't need you to watch his moods and behaviour for him, or to set limits for him?
– doesn't need you to be the peacekeeper?

Restitution – acknowledging the effects of abuse

Invitational enquiries are increasingly directed towards assisting the man to develop a deeper understanding of the effects of his abusive behaviour and demonstrate this understanding in his words and actions. This stage of couple counselling tends to be the most vital in ensuring the prevention of future abuse and in opening possibilities for resolution of abuse-related trauma and reconnection between partners.

The process of imagining and considering the potential effects of abusive behaviour started early in Jack's separate therapeutic counselling. In couple counselling, Jack has the opportunity to demonstrate this understanding in Sue's presence.

Sue was initially invited to consider the importance of, and current evidence for, such understanding, through *talking about talking about it* style enquiries:

How important is it to you for Jack to understand both how his abuse has affected you and what he has put you through?

What signs have you seen that tell you Jack wants to understand what he has put you and Paul through and that he is not just hoping for a quick fix of forgiveness and forgetting?

What tells you that Jack is beginning to understand how difficult it is and how long it might take for him to earn respect and trust; that he doesn't expect these prematurely?

What tells you that Jack is beginning to understand that some trust may be permanently damaged and perhaps never regained?

What tells you that Jack is beginning to understand how important it is for you to check out safety beyond a shadow of doubt – that he is refusing to let feelings of urgency and impatience get the better of him?

The counsellors then enquired about Jack's understanding of the importance of reflection upon the effects of abusive behaviour and the nature of realisations he had already made:

What would it mean if you tried to face up to your abusive behaviour or if you tried to reconnect with Sue, but didn't take the trouble to try to understand exactly what you have put her through?

Who has had to think most about the effects of abuse in the past?

What difference would it make if you made it your business to study and understand the possible effects of your past actions, rather than leaving it for Sue and Paul to worry about?

What would it mean (did it mean in the past) if you tried to make apologies to Sue but didn't really understand what you had put her through?

What does it take to take a close look at these effects of your actions?

What would it mean if you tried to skip over this step to avoid feelings of shame and discomfort?

What tells you that you are ready and wanting to understand as much as you can about what you put Sue through, despite feelings of shame and grief?

Once Jack affirmed a commitment to this form of restitution, he could begin to share his realisations and listen to feedback from Sue about the veracity of his understandings. It is vital, given past habits of reliance, that Jack first takes the initiative to imagine, share his realisations and listen to feedback, rather than look to Sue to provide this information or do this work for him.

Both partners are invited to challenge the commonly held idea that attempts at restitution by a partner who has abused should lead to an obligation by the abused partner to forgive or pardon. Such expectations that forgiveness and trust must be returned, following efforts at restitution, are informed by dominant Judeo-Christian concepts of forgiveness and produce a sense of coercion towards an obligation to forgive rather than an authentic sense of restitution (Jenkins, Hall and Joy, 2002). These interests tend to distract the person who has abused from responsibility for their own behaviour and promote unhelpful expectations of their partner. It is generally helpful to legitimise the abused person's mistrust, whilst inviting both partners to consider and appreciate the likely effects of a long-standing pattern of coercive and abusive behaviour, accompanied by hollow apologies and broken promises, which may result in trust never being regained. In this context, an expectation of forgiveness is self-centred and unrealistic.

Establishing a relationship focus

A focus on individual responsibilities in a relationship context will usually help clarify each person's commitment to either exploring the possibility of a future together or separating. The person subjected to abuse may recognise that they no longer want the relationship, once free of a sense of obligation. Trust and respect may feel irreparably damaged. Relationship preferences may appear incompatible or it may seem that the relationship was held together by ideas and habits which are no longer valued or wanted. In these circumstances, a respectful separation can be negotiated which attends to children's requirements and needs and provides space to grieve.

Alternatively, both may want to consider reconnection in a new kind of safe and respectful partnership. Conversation that focuses upon the relationship may be appropriate and helpful, when each person demonstrates an ongoing commitment to challenge individual restraining practices. The man is actively committed to the pursuit of a deep understanding of the effects of abusive behaviour and towards restitution to the abused person. In other words, a relationship focus can be enabled when each person is concerned with addressing their own responsibilities, rather than their partner's

unhelpful habits. This is consistent with the priority to address issues of abusive behaviour and safety before addressing relationship issues.

Jack continued to respect Sue's privacy and support her entitlement to pursue her own interests. Sue was feeling increasingly listened to and respected by Jack. She no longer restricted her activities and interests, was asserting her needs and planning daily activities accordingly.

Jack was engaging in deeper reflection about the nature of his abusive actions and the extent to which he had humiliated and hurt Sue. He spoke of, *'opening my eyes'* and *'seeing it like it really is'* and began to face inevitable feelings of shame associated with these realisations. He began to initiate conversations with Sue, in which he acknowledged how his sense of urgency and impatience to reconcile with her had been *'adding insult to injury'*. Jack acknowledged that he had been *'totally insensitive'* in failing to recognise and understand the devastating effects of his abusive behaviour upon trust and respect in their relationship. He acknowledged that his past apologies had been *'hollow'* because he had been more interested in reconciling with Sue than understanding how his behaviour had affected her and stopping his abuse. Jack pointed out that he still struggled at times to contain his impatience and identified times when he *'pressured'* Sue to regain trust, even though he realised that he may have permanently destroyed that trust.

In this context, both partners might be invited to consider the meanings the steps that they are taking have for their relationship. This can help to clarify concepts that reflect relationship preferences and their historical development.

They may well consider how their current ideas and practices fit with relationship preferences and concepts concerning connection and partnership:

- *What sort of relationship have you wanted?*
- *What kind of person have you wanted to be in that relationship?*
- *What have you wanted to offer to your partner?*
- *What have you wanted to offer to your children?*
- *What is it that you have wanted to build together?*

Jack and Sue were invited to reclaim and to reshape their hopes, dreams and visions, many of which they had in common, and were about their relationship and family. With acknowledgement and the honouring of a history of respectful intent, Jack and Sue could each be invited to consider how their hopes and dreams and their relationship had been hijacked or derailed by a range of misguided and unhelpful ideas and practices. Jack was assisted to name several misguided cultural ideas which promote controlling, coercive, possessive and vengeful actions. He considered how these ideas masquerade as relationship truths and blueprints for intimacy and connection:

> *If she really loved me, she would think the way I think.*
>
> *We don't need other people, we only need each other.*
>
> *I only get jealous because I love you so much.*

Jack considered how these ideas had gained influence in the context of his family of origin and in relation to dominant cultural interests, including gendered expectations about love and violence. In this way, Sue was able to witness Jack describing the development of his abusive behaviour through misguided and dangerous ideas which had served to derail well-intended hopes and dreams for a respectful relationship and family.

In a complementary manner, Jack witnessed Sue describing the historical development of a range of ideas and practices which promote a sense of *'duty'* to anticipate Jack's feelings and needs, to accommodate to them by *'treading on eggshells'* and deferring in order to *'keep the peace'*. Sue considered the development of these practices in the context of her family of origin and in relation to a dominant, gendered interest which requires women to sacrifice their own needs to *'be for others'*. She acknowledged how these cultural interests had undermined her resistance to Jack's violence and hijacked her hopes and dreams for a fulfilling relationship.

Such conversations are only possible when both people are committed to challenging their own restraining ideas and practices, rather than challenging each other. This can take place in a context which respects and honours the existence of well-intended hopes, dreams and preferences for the relationship. Each person may then be able to speak openly and non-defensively to name misguided ideas and practices which have undermined respectful relationship goals.

As Jack and Sue felt listened to and respected by each other, they recognised that they were beginning to be able to have conversations about serious problems without needing to blame the other person and without feeling blamed. In this exceptional context, they could be invited to clarify current relationship preferences. This clarification enables relationship preferences and concepts to become more clearly defined and meaningful.

After affirming his position about wanting a relationship in which Sue and Paul both feel safe and are free from any violence or abusive behaviour, the counsellors enquired:

> *Are there any circumstances in which you think you might be entitled to coerce or hurt Sue or Paul?*
>
> *What if Sue acted in a way that you thought was grossly unfair?*
>
> *What kind of circumstances would be the most testing for you?*
>
> *If you began to act in a way that Sue found hurtful, would you want her to put up with it or refuse to put up with it?*

When discussing relationship preferences, a range of concepts tend to arise and require clarification. These commonly include:

Respect of difference. *How important is it for differences to be respected in this relationship?*
- *Should differences be hidden or should they be spoken about?*
- *What would it mean for love, if you tried to suppress differences?*
- *How might you be able to speak about difference without hurting the other person?*

The concept of partnership equality. *What does equality and partnership mean for decision-making in your relationship?*
- *Which responsibilities are important to share?*
- *How will you decide?*
- *How does this concept challenge old ideas?*
- *What ideas and actions support partnership?*
- *What ideas and actions might derail partnership?*
- *How are your ideas about partnership different from those of your parents?*
- *What kind of example are you wanting to set for your children?*

The concept of interdependence which concerns balance between separateness and togetherness. *What kinds of challenges are likely to arise in becoming your own persons with your own interests and in building togetherness?*

– *How important is this balance?*
– *What would it mean for love if you neglect separateness?*
– *What would it mean for love if you neglect togetherness?*
– *How does this concept challenge old ideas?*

The concept of intimacy. *What are you understanding about your partner's style of intimacy and what makes them feel connected to you?*
– *How important is it to understand and respect your partner's style of intimacy?*
– *What challenges might arise in negotiating these differences?*
– *What old ideas does this concept challenge?*

Jack and Sue became acutely aware of the need to consider different styles of intimacy when Jack expressed interest in recommencing a sexual relationship with Sue. He felt hurt when Sue declined his sexual initiative. Sue felt unready to commence a sexual relationship. However, she also felt guilty and worried that perhaps she was being unreasonable and letting Jack down.

First, Jack was invited to consider his sexual initiative and his experience of disappointment, in the context of the history of his abusive behaviour and its effects upon intimacy and trust:

How did you decide that the time might be right for you both to initiate sex?

What do you think that sexual initiative meant to Sue?

Why do you think Sue was not ready to recommence sex?

As Jack reflected on these enquiries and then listened to Sue being interviewed about this event, he recognised that Sue needed to feel a strong sense of closeness, trust and connection in order to feel sexual desire. He acknowledged that Sue was still unsure about the degree to which she could trust him and that this was not unreasonable, given he had '*totally destroyed her trust*' over several years. He then averted his eyes and looked distressed and ashamed. He recalled and acknowledged a situation in the past when he had sexually assaulted Sue in a misguided and abusive attempt to '*make up*' after an incident when he had physically abused her. Jack acknowledged that he had raised this issue previously, in individual counselling, when he had named it as '*rape*' (see Chapter 10). Jack acknowledged that he had

tended to '*use sex to get close*' but that on this occasion, sex had become a means to violate and humiliate Sue. He was then able to reaffirm a commitment to respect Sue's experience and to explore intimacy at a mutually agreed upon and realistic pace.

At a later stage, Sue and Jack were able to consider and appreciate each other's different preferences regarding intimacy and sex. They could then negotiate ways to enable mutual readiness for sexual intimacy and a mutual agreement about entitlement to decline unwanted sexual initiatives.

Throughout relationship counselling, each partner is continually invited to reflect on, and attribute meaning to, new steps taken to challenge restraining habits and ideas and practise respectful behaviour. Each person is invited to reflect in the presence of the other, who is invited to listen, witness, and in turn consider the meanings of these developments for a relationship:

What led you to take this step?

How did you manage to take a step like this in the face of (restraining idea)?

What did it take?

What did you prove to yourself?

What might it offer to your partner?

What might it offer to your children?

What does it say about the person, parent and partner you are becoming?

What implications might it have for your relationship?

What implications might it have for your family?

Challenging interactional restraints

Right from the beginning, both partners are invited to maintain a focus on their own responsibilities, rather than critique their partner's problems, developments and achievements. Persons who have abused have generally become overly reliant upon other family members to be vigilant, and for them to anticipate the abuser's moods, accommodate to their behaviour and attempt to set limits for them, in order to '*keep the peace*'. This interactional restraint is challenged with a focus upon *minding your own business* and methods of interviewing which promote listening and reflection rather than adversarial dialogue. Persons who have abused are invited to directly challenge patterns of reliance upon their partners:

> *Who has paid most attention to or studied the way you build up your feelings?*
>
> *Whose job is this?*
>
> *What would happen if you continued to rely on your partner to anticipate your mood or try to keep the peace?*

Persons who have abused are invited to monitor their own actions and to *test themselves* by practising facing differences and conflict, without resorting to coercive or violent practices. This keeps a focus on self-responsibility for recognising, monitoring and evaluating one's own actions rather than relying on a partner to defuse or prevent conflict. An emphasis on *proving it to yourself, rather than to your partner,* supports the focus on self-monitoring and evaluation, rather than taking action to seek approval or becoming preoccupied with seeking a partner's trust or forgiveness.

Both partners are encouraged to engage in forms of *conflict testing*, to address differences and face conflict, rather than engage in familiar and unhelpful habits of trying to avoid conflict. An invitation to embrace difference and address conflict challenges unhelpful ideas about love which suggests that *a loving relationship is free of difference and free of conflict*. Concepts of an inevitable link between conflict and violence are also challenged in conflict testing. The distinction between conflict and violence may be highlighted as both partners demonstrate that they can experience conflict and feel hurt or disappointed, without engaging in violence.

Jack and Sue attended one couple counselling meeting and announced that they had been successful because, *'we haven't had one argument in a fortnight'*. It became evident that both had been avoiding certain issues that had caused concern. To their surprise, the counsellors expressed disappointment at their 'conflict free' fortnight:

> *Jack, how will you know that you can disagree with Sue without hurting her, if you don't test this ability and practise?*
>
> *Sue, how will you know whether you are really safe to speak your mind; even to be unreasonable at times, if you don't test this out and practice?*

CHAPTER 16

Reciprocal Couple Violence – Respecting Difference

Love is the difficult realisation that something other than oneself is real.

Iris Murdoch

The following invitational practices may be helpful once abusive behaviour and its effects have been sufficiently addressed and there is ample evidence of safety and equity within a relationship. These practices also suit situations of reciprocal couple violence, such as that of Dora and Geoff (see page 141), where there is evidence of equity in the relationship and mutual violence does not constitute abusive behaviour.

In situations of reciprocal couple violence, violence and coercive behaviours are best addressed with a focus upon recognition and respect of difference. The concept of respect of difference invites a shift away from concepts of *domestic* towards *generous* notions of love. Couples such as Dora and Geoff tend to be preoccupied with their perceptions of the other's 'problems'. Each partner's perceptions of the other are critical, judgemental and blaming. The other person is seen as failing to display 'correct' and 'proper' feelings and behaviour, in relation to love and care; *'She doesn't care about me'*; *'He doesn't love me for who I am'*. These differences are then regarded as wilful and hurtful. Differences become disputed in self-righteous displays of ownership towards each other.

Invitational practice with couples such as Dora and Geoff aims to create opportunities where they might become interested, perhaps intrigued, with their differences and the possibilities that these differences might open up. Rather than judge each other's behaviour according to a perceived, universal standard of truth, each partner is invited to consider the kind of person they want to become and how their partner's differences might contribute to this becoming. This situates a sense of identity or becoming within a relationship context (Freedman and Coombs, 2004). Each partner is invited to consider how and in what direction this relational sense of identity, informed by difference, might lead their relationship; what kind of relationship it might become.

The invitational process involves interviewing each partner in the presence of the other, who is invited to listen, witness and reflect upon what they have heard. This process tends to avoid dialogue between partners, in order to subvert long-standing habits of criticism, blame and judgement, as well as interruption and talking over the other.

Naming differences

Each partner is interviewed about their hopes, dreams, visions and preferences for the relationship:

> *How have you wanted this relationship and family to develop?*
>
> *What has been important to you?*
>
> *What qualities have you valued or cherished in this relationship and family?*
>
> *What have you wanted to provide and contribute to this relationship and family?*
>
> *What has been important to you in developing a sense of love and caring, intimacy and belonging, etc?*
>
> *What has led to these things becoming important to you?*
>
> *How have you tried to help to realise these qualities?*
>
> *What would it mean if you stopped trying to achieve these things?*

This interviewing process is concerned with establishing the intent and preferences of each person. The counsellor will interrupt stories of blame and criticism of the other person and shift the focus back to an exploration of intent. The person who is witnessing the interview is encouraged to listen and try to understand what is important to their partner. In witnessing, they are asked to avoid interruption, judgement or criticism of their partner's current behaviour.

As each partner's relationship preferences are clarified, commonalities and differences in intent and practice are recognised and named.

Relationship partners often express preferences which reflect similar aims and intent. However, they may subscribe to different methods and practices in their attempts to achieve these preferred outcomes. Such differences in method and practice often stem from different *styles of loving* (Roughan and Jenkins, 1990), which reflect contrasting but well-intended blueprints for achieving intimacy and connection. Differences in preferences or styles of loving can be understood and named within their cultural, historical and developmental contexts which reflect different experiences within differing families and communities, as well as cultural and gendered expectations.

Geoff expressed a desire and commitment to family with a strong sense of belonging and partnership. He supported a longstanding family tradition which valued men *'putting family first'* by *'working hard'* and being *'good providers'*. He believed that intimacy was best established and maintained in a relationship through a climate of *'trust, peace and harmony'* which could only be achieved by *'working together'* to prevent conflict. This required each person to refrain from complaint, anticipate compromise and *'bite your tongue'*. Sexual intimacy played a vital role in maintaining a connected relationship.

Dora also desired a strong sense of partnership and belonging. She felt this was best achieved through *'spending time together'* and *'sorting out difficulties'* by *'getting things off your chest'*, *'speaking your true feelings'* and *'talking through your problems'*. She felt let down, as a child, by her father who had neglected the family to *'live like a single man'* and believed that *'being together and communication are what counts'*. Dora placed less emphasis on sex but felt that sexual intimacy develops from *'closeness and good communication'*.

Both Dora and Geoff deplored violence and felt embarrassed about past incidents. They both supported a sense of partnership, equity and belonging in a relationship and family but described somewhat different means for achieving these goals. Each felt that their own preferred means reflected universal and self-evident truths and that the other was acting dishonourably and uncaringly in not acting accordingly.

History of dispute

A history of dispute concerning these differences may be delineated and related to a growing sense of disappointment, hurt feelings and resentment:

> *When did you begin to feel concern about these differences?*
>
> *What did these differences come to mean to you?*
>
> *What did you think your partner's intentions were?*
>
> *What did you try to do about it?*

Each is invited to consider their reactions to significant events throughout the relationship and the meanings that each attributed to these events, particularly in relation to concepts of love and caring. The other is invited to listen and then to reflect upon their intentions, as well as the impact of their actions upon their partner. Discrepancies between each person's intent, their actions and perceptions by the other are named and clarified.

It can rapidly become apparent that each person has attempted to act ethically, honourably and with good intent, but from the perspective of different styles of loving and using different methods of showing love and contributing to the relationship or family. The beginnings of escalation can be traced to differences in styles of loving and corresponding misunderstandings of each partner's intent.

Escalation is inevitable as differences become increasingly misinterpreted, polarised and adversarial, with each partner believing that their own methods and styles of loving are universal and correct and that their partner is wilfully undermining the relationship.

Dora asserted that intimacy and connection were enhanced by *'talking about your feelings'* and confrontation in the face of apparent conflict. Yet Geoff's contrasting practices for avoiding a potentially volatile interaction, could also be seen as attempts to achieve the same goals. Both had felt a similar sense of bewilderment, frustration and disappointment. The metaphor of a cartoon snowball gathering momentum as it rolls down a mountain was invoked, as both partners were invited to consider the effects of their well-intended efforts to fight for connection in their relationship, under the mutually mistaken notion that there is one true style of loving that is self evident and which their partner is failing to respect.

Each partner is invited to consider the consequences of this inevitable escalation which tends to consist of increasing feelings of disappointment, being let down and hurt, eventually giving way to resentment and despair. These consequences promote a profound loss of respect and a sense of legitimisation for the use of coercive, hurtful and even vengeful reactions and practices. Inevitably, both experience a loss of self-respect as each partner finds themselves engaging in unethical practices which do not accord with their own preferred ways of relating.

As misperceptions, misunderstandings and misguided actions are delineated, in the context of respectful and honourable intent, the sad inevitability of such escalation becomes increasingly apparent. The questions can be posed:

Is this anybody's fault?

Is anyone really to blame?

Such inquiry may help to transcend habits of judgement and blame and allow both partners to consider how they may have become unwittingly and inexorably recruited into a *'domestic love'* paradigm. Their relationship might be regarded as having been hijacked by unhelpful cultural ideas about the love and the suppression of difference.

Captive effects of domestic love

The concept of *domestic love* may be introduced as a restraining set of ideas and practices which sabotages respectful relationship preferences such as partnership, collaboration, hospitality, reciprocity and interdependence. *Domestic love* is presented as a rigid and inflexible set of ideas and practices which suggests that there is only one universal and self-evident form or style of loving. It requires each person to think, feel and act in the same way and it undervalues valuable differences which bring variety, flexibility, excitement and passion into a relationship. The concept of *domestic love* legitimises violence and coercion to enforce sameness in thinking and action, in the name of love.

Both partners are invited to consider the influence of this concept in their lives and relationship:

How has this idea of domestic love been influential in your life and relationship?

How has this idea been put to you as a truth?

How has it been robbing you of opportunities for diversity in your relationship?

How has it undermined connection and caring in your relationship?

How has it tried to rob you of your dreams and visions for a relationship?

How does it masquerade as a true form of love?

How has it attempted to hijack your relationship?

How has this idea even tried to justify violence in the name of love?

Each person is invited to consider and critique the concept of domestic love within an historical and cultural context of dominant and pervasive popular ideas and their representation in popular culture.

Becoming interested in differences

Both partners are invited to consider and take a position on domestic love in relation to their lives and their relationship. The reclamation of hopes, dreams, visions and respectful relationship preferences requires becoming interested in differences. The metaphor of two people who speak different languages, but want to make connection, may be invoked. There is little point in arguing which language is better or more correct. Equitable connection requires learning to speak each other's language.

Having developed some understanding of dominant cultural influences which go beyond family of origin and having considered a history of misunderstood intent, different styles of loving and the inevitable escalation of blame and judgemental thinking, each partner may be invited to re-position their differences from a disabling to an enabling perspective:

What difference does it make when you stand apart from the ideas and practices of domestic love?

What difference does it make when you take an interest in your partner's different perspectives, different styles of loving and ways of relating?

How does this affect your partner's attitude to your different ideas and ways?

Are you ready to further consider your differences in a different light?

If both partners demonstrate interest and therefore readiness to experiment with difference, in response to this last enquiry, such an experiment might be proposed.

Each partner may then be interviewed in the listening presence of the other. The person witnessing the interview is invited to listen with interested ears, an open mind, and from a perspective of curiosity, rather then from a position of judgement or critique.

Each partner is interviewed in accordance with the following guidelines;

The person you are becoming

What are some of the important ways you have been changing and developing as a person, over the time of your relationship?

How do these developments fit with the kind of person that you have wanted to become?

What kind of changes in yourself have you invested in and appreciated over this time?

How have these developments been important to you?

A relational sense of becoming

Consider a time when you have observed or noticed a difference in your partner's ways of thinking, living and being, that has caught your attention and helped to open up different or new possibilities for you.
– What was the difference that you noticed?
– How did that difference contribute to the changes you have been making?
– How did you recognise that this difference might add to your life?
– How were you able to be open to considering this difference without dismissing it?
– How did this different way help change you in ways that you have valued?
– What have you valued about this development in yourself?

– How did it add richness or add possibilities in your life?
– What new things were you able to discover about yourself?
– What do you think your partner might have appreciated about these developments?
– What do you think your partner has stood to gain?
– What impact has this development had or could it have, on your connection with your partner?
– What impact do you imagine this development could have on your relationship?

The listening partner is then interviewed with specific enquiries about their reactions and experiences in witnessing their partner's observations and reflections on difference.

Interviewing a listening partner

What are you experiencing in listening to your partner talk about a time of appreciating a difference that you brought?

Were you aware that the differences that you brought have contributed to your partner's development as a person?

Did you know that these differences have contributed to a sense of (connection) in your relationship?

How has it felt when your partner has been interested in the differences that you bring?
– What times have you experienced this?
– How did you first become aware of it?
– How has it moved you?
– How has it contributed to your development as a person?
– What has it offered you and your relationship?
– How have these differences contributed to excitement and passion in your relationship?

In the absence of familiar and restraining patterns of adversarial dialogue, a sense of interest in difference can emerge.

Part Five

Collaborative Evaluation on the Journey

CHAPTER 17

Ethical Assessment in Partner Care

Goal attainment assessment

This chapter describes a paradigm with responsibility-based measures for the assessment and evaluation of outcomes in intervention with men who have acted abusively towards their relationship partners. The same kind of methodology has been adapted for evaluation with men and adolescent boys who have engaged in sexually abusive behaviour. The practices employed in *responsibility assessment* (see Table 1) and *goal attainment assessment* (see Table 2), to evaluate client outcomes are complementary to those used in the evaluation of worker competencies, as described in *Competency Standards for Intervention Workers* (Anderson et al., 1997).

Invitational practice is informed by the following restorative goals:

- Cessation of abusive behaviour (violence, coercive and controlling behaviour).
- Acceptance of responsibility for these actions and their impact upon others.
- Restitution for harm done to individuals and the community.
- Development and practice of ethical and respectful ways of relating.
- Restoration of a sense of self-respect and integrity.

Consequently, evaluation methods and strategies should be attuned to measuring the extent of attainment of these outcomes, rather than characterlogical assessment of specific personality or psychological qualities, traits or constructs.

Criteria for the assessment of goal attainment concern patterns of observable behaviour of men; the presence or absence of abusive, coercive and controlling actions and threats along with the extent of ethical and respectful practices. The statements and comments of men reflect patterns of thinking which concern beliefs about personal rights and entitlements, attributions of responsibility for specific actions, understanding of the experience of others, concern for the well-being of others and dominant self-preoccupations.

Goal attainment assessment is focused towards evidence supporting the relinquishment of specific patterns of thinking and behaviour which include:

- **A sense of exaggerated entitlement** to privilege the man's 'rights' over those of his partner:
  - expectations that a partner should adjust her thinking and behaviour to accord with the man's views; e.g. *'she can't see reason'*.
  - expectations of deference or submission from a partner; e.g.*'she shouldn't contradict me'*.

- **A sense of justification for the use of coercion or force:**
  - coercion and force may be justified as 'legitimate' forms of 'correction', 'defence', 'warning' or responses to 'provocation'; e.g. *'she deserved it'*; *'she was asking for it'*; *'she was getting out of control, I had to stop her'*; *'if she wasn't so stupid, I wouldn't have to do it'*.
  - beliefs that coercion and violence are legitimate means of resolving conflict in intimate relationships; e.g. *'you sometimes have to hurt the ones you love'*.
  - violence may be part of a tactical or planned sequence of behaviours designed to influence or control a partner's thinking and behaviour; e.g. *'I had to shake some sense into her'*; *'I needed to teach her a lesson'*.

- **Patterns of self-righteous and self-intoxicating thinking:**
  - **escalating patterns of blame, vengeful and contemptuous thinking directed towards a partner; e.g.** *'how dare you'*; *'you'll pay for that you bitch'*; *'she never thinks of my feelings'*.

- **Objectification of a partner:**
  - *treating a partner as an object by overlooking or negating her feelings and experience. This constitutes a lack of understanding or empathy for her experience which may be temporary at the time of violent actions or may comprise a pervasive pattern; e.g. 'what is it carrying on about'; 'I don't know why she's making such a fuss'.*

- **Patterns of avoidance of responsibility**
  - minimisation of the existence, nature or extent of violence; e.g. *'I'm not violent'*; *'I didn't hurt her'*; *'it was only a tap'*; *'she can't be frightened of me'*.
  - attributions of blame to other people, external events or life circumstances; e.g. *'I was drunk'*; *'I was stressed out'*.
  - minimisation of the ability to set limits on behaviour; e.g. *'I lost it'*; *'I snapped'*; *'I flipped out'*.
  - expectations that a partner will accept blame for the violence; e.g. *'she asked for it'*; *'she pushed me to my limit'*.
  - reliance upon a partner to tolerate or forgive abusive actions; e.g. *'I've said I'm sorry, why can't she let it drop now'*.

These patterns of self-centred and disrespectful thinking are characteristic, in one form or another, of most abusive behaviour. However, overly-entitled thinking and abdication of responsibility may also characterise many aspects of intimate and family relationships as well as relationships in broader social and vocational settings.

Goal attainment measures attempt to establish and document the extent of relinquishment of such thinking and behaviour, along with evidence of thinking and behaviour which actively supports ethical practices which promote fairness, respect, equity and responsible participation in family and social relationships.

Goal attainment rating

This is a solution-focused method of evaluation which enables the rating of levels of responsible and respectful behaviour demonstrated by men who have perpetrated domestic abuse. This method contrasts with traditional methods of assessment of personality traits, psychological constructs or characteristics which are presumed to be associated with violence or propensity to perpetrate violence (Conroy and Murrie, 2007). The rating process encourages a focus on behaviours which can be identified and either challenged or aspired to by the man, as opposed to highlighting qualities which might be regarded as limiting and part of his individual make up, personality or character.

The process of documentation and measurement of responsible and respectful

behaviours creates a context which promotes a sense of agency and direction towards ethical realisation. Problem-focused assessments often inadvertently encourage a preoccupation with labelling problem states or characteristics which in turn fosters a sense of incapacity and personal limitation. Goal Attainment Rating remains focused upon aspirational goals which are developed throughout intervention and centred with the man's ethical strivings.

Goal attainment rating is focused on determining and documenting levels of responsible and respectful thinking and behaviour in a collaborative context. The evaluation process seeks evidence of goal attainment by documenting observations of the man's actions made by partners, family members, intervention workers, independent observers, and by the man himself. This constitutes a collaborative project which is particularly attuned to evidence as experienced and reported by partners and family members. Goal Attainment Rating aspires to be accountable. Consequently, it is well suited to an intervention programme with a strong solution focus on stopping violence and developing responsible and respectful behaviour.

Goal attainment criteria

Goal attainment can be rated for individual men on the following sets of criteria which are defined and expanded in the Goal Attainment Assessment Protocol (see Table 2).

A: Responsibility for abuse

This goal attainment table concerns the evidence for:

- The cessation of physically and emotionally abusive behaviour.
- The establishment of effective plans to prevent further abusive behaviour.
- Acknowledgement of the nature, significance and seriousness of abusive behaviour.
- Acknowledgement of culpability for abusive behaviour.
- Recognition of the potential impact of abusive behaviour.
- The demonstration and practice of responsible and respectful behaviour.
- Facing the consequences of abusive actions.

B: Responsibility and respect in couple relationships

This goal attainment table concerns the evidence for behaviour in a relationship which supports and promotes:

- An equitable balance of power and status.
- Balance in relationship and family responsibilities.
- Balance in effort and activity concerning dependence and independence.

C: Responsibility and respect in family relationships

This goal attainment table concerns the evidence for behaviour in a family relationship which supports and promotes:

- Partnership.
- Shared parenting responsibilities.
- Respectful parenting practices.
- Nurturing and protective parent-child relationship boundaries.

D: Responsibility and respect in broader social contexts

This goal attainment table concerns the evidence for respectful behaviour in broader social and workplace relationships.

The rating of goal attainment

The goal attainment assessment protocol is commonly used in separate, structured interviews with:

- a close informant, usually a partner, advocate or family member.
- the man who has abused.
- programme workers or independent observers.

Each responsibility-based criterion (bold type in Table 2) is defined and expanded by a checklist (plain type) which contains examples of behaviours, attributions and perceptions by family members. The partner or advocate is invited to reflect on, with the aid of the checklist, a level of goal attainment by the man for each of the criteria and then rate this on a five-point scale.

Partners and advocates are encouraged to recall and state examples of observable behavioural evidence which support or refute goal attainment, for all checklist items and criteria.

The man is encouraged, in his interview, to rate his own goal attainment and to furnish examples of behavioural evidence to support his self-assessment on each criteria. He is invited to consider and try to incorporate the intervention worker's observations and reports, when reviewing this evidence.

In assessment interviews, intervention workers document ratings, with supporting evidence, for each of the criteria. Workers add their own observations to the pro-forma. This process may yield several goal attainment ratings by different informants. These ratings can be documented and compared. If sufficiently consistent and reliable, they may be compiled to form a common rating score by the intervention worker. However, in order to maximise accountability to the experiences of those victimised, ratings by partners and family members are given priority when comparing, compiling and evaluating intervention outcomes.

The structured interviews themselves constitute an educative process for partners and for the man himself, as each person attempts to define behavioural criteria for intervention goals and provide observable evidence of goal attainment. Partners and family members are encouraged to seek and critique objective evidence in order to make valid and convincing assessments and judgements. In this way, assumptions and broad generalisations which are based on hope or wishful thinking, as opposed to behavioural evidence, can be exposed and subverted. The process itself tends to highlight and promote ethical and respectful choices and outcomes. Many men find the process to be very helpful, not only in highlighting achievements, but in clarifying aspects of their journey which may have been overlooked and which may require more focus and exploration.

Evaluation methodology

Baseline measures

Goal attainment ratings may be completed at specific stages of intervention, such as the completion of a Stopping Violence Group programme, and at regular follow-up periods. The assessment process enables a means for reflection on the nature of the journey and the evaluation of its outcomes. These assessments also provide a helpful basis for determining readiness and safe and accountable decision-making when planning new directions, such as couple counselling or reconnection.

The focus in assessment is maintained with ongoing goal attainment and achieving levels of competency in ethical actualisation and expression, rather than pre- and post-intervention comparisons. However, it can sometimes be meaningful to relate individual goal attainment ratings to a reference point or baseline measure.

A responsibility assessment (Table 1) can be compiled during the initial meetings with the man whilst he is becoming ready for his ethical journey. This assessment can provide a baseline measurement of the nature and frequency of abusive behaviour and initial levels of responsibility for each man at the early stages of intervention.

Completion of the responsibility assessment enables the determination of responsibility indices which provide baseline measures of levels of responsibility for men entering intervention programmes. Baseline responsibility indices are determined from information obtained in initial interviews with men to assess journey readiness and with women and children to assess safety needs. A responsibility indicator is a factor which is associated with responsible and respectful behaviour. Such factors are related to intervention goals and are regarded as predictive of further responsible and respectful behaviour.

Responsibility indicators can refer to similar parameters as do risk indicators. However, they are better suited to a solution-focused, responsibility-based intervention programme, in that they are attuned to the assessment and promotion of responsible and respectful goal attainment. Hence the process of determining responsibility indices is referred to as *responsibility assessment* as opposed to *risk or dangerousness assessment*.

Responsibility indices consist of ratings of factors which relate to:

- The extent of violence and abusive behaviour.
- Responsibility for abusive behaviour in a current relationship.
- Evidence and allegations of violence or abusive behaviour in other contexts.
- Evidence and allegations of criminal or other irresponsible behaviour.
- Responsible and respectful behaviour in couple relationships.

- Responsible and respectful behaviour in family relationships.
- Responsible and respectful behaviour in broader social contexts.

The responsibility assessment protocol includes a useful standardised measure of the nature and frequency of domestic abuse, the abusive behaviour inventory (ABI) (Table 3) (Shepard and Campbell, 1992). This 30 item instrument consists of two forms, one to be filled out by a partner and one by the man himself. It enables ratings, over a six month period, of the perceived frequency of items of abuse, resulting in a physical abuse score and a psychological abuse score (see Table 3, for ABI forms and scoring information).

A responsibility assessment may yield three responsibility indices:

- **Responsibility index A**, which concerns the extent of and levels of responsibility accepted for recent abusive behaviour.
- **Responsibility index B**, which concerns the presence or absence of criminal actions, irresponsible behaviour or violence outside of the family or relationship context.
- **Responsibility index C**, which concerns levels of respectful and responsible behaviour in relationship, family and broader social contexts.

In order to maximise accountability to the experiences of those who have been victimised, intervention workers must place priority on the perceptions, judgements and ratings of partners and family members when rating responsibility indicators.

These indices may be used to establish high, moderate or low baselines of responsibility for men entering an intervention programme.

Assessment in a group context

Pre-group assessment

Responsibility indices are determined in the initial readiness interviews with the man, to establish his suitability for commencing the intervention programme, and the assessment interviews with the woman and other family members, concerning accountability, levels of safety and other needs. The ABI forms are also completed prior to commencement of the group.

It is desirable that the baseline assessment data provided by the woman or children is obtained by workers who are assisting the woman and children, rather than the man's worker. This helps to establish clear boundaries between the man's responsibilities and those of the woman and children. It minimises any inadvertent collusions with the man's expectations or wishes which may stem from the woman's sense of obligation or lack of personal entitlement.

Pre-group assessment data will generally include the following sets of data:
Responsibility Index A
Responsibility Index B
Responsibility Index C

ABI physical abuse – Partner assessment
ABI psychological abuse – Partner assessment
ABI physical abuse – Man's self-assessment
ABI psychological abuse – Man's self-assessment

Each man is allocated a high, moderate or low baseline responsibility rating for each index (see Table 3 scoring details).

Post-group and follow-up assessments

Goal attainment ratings for men are completed, in separate structured interviews, to provide:

– a self-assessment by each participating man.
– a partner or family member assessment by a partner, family member or advocate who wishes to participate.
– worker assessments by intervention programme workers.

These assessments are conducted at the completion of the group programme, and at one-year follow-up intervals, for at least a three-year period.

The criteria in the protocol for sections A and D, Responsibility for Abuse and Responsibility and Respect in Broader Social Contexts are completed for each man.

The criteria in sections B and C, Responsibility and Respect in Couple Relationships and Maturity and Respect in Family Relationships . . . are completed if the man is having some ongoing contact with the partner or family members or if couple or family reconciliation is under way.

The ABI is also completed by each man and partners (where appropriate) at the completion of the group programme and at one-year follow-up intervals.

Use of assessment instruments

The goal attainment ratings and responsibility indices are not standardised assessment tools. They have been determined in conjunction with intervention practices and goals and therefore have to face validity in this context. These instruments constitute attempts to organise and make consistent the information used for decision-making about safety and responsibility levels in relationships and families. This same information is commonly used to inform courts and other statutory systems when they require assessments of levels of safety and responsibility.

The assessment instruments can also be used to provide structure for subsequent qualitative analyses of a range of matters concerning intervention with men who have abused. Structured interviews with the men may be recorded to enable independent raters to conduct qualitative analyses to explore issues such as:

– attributions by men about factors associated with goal attainment.
– changes in patterns of attribution of responsibility for abusive behaviour.
– the relationship between specific responsibility indices and the cessation of abusive behaviour.
– appropriateness and suitability of aspects of the intervention programme.

Table 1   Responsibility assessment

Name _____   Date _____

1. Limited extent of abusive behaviour (based on ABI scores-partner assessment)	high ABI (4–5)	mod. ABI (2–3)	none ABI (1)
Limited extent of physical abuse	1	2	3
Limited extent of emotional abuse	1	2	3

2. Responsibility for abusive behaviour (current relationship)	low resp.		high resp.
Full acknowledegment of abusive behaviour – detailed account of physical and emotional abuse – no minimisation or understatement – consistent with partner and children's account	1	2	3
Acknowledgement of nature and seriousness of abusive behaviour – labels as 'abuse' – acknowledges power differential – regards it as serious and harmful to others	1	2	3
Acknowledgement of obligation and ability to cease abuse – recognises he has a problem – shows motivation to address problem – regards himself as capable of ceasing abuse	1	2	3
Acknowledgement of culpability – accepts full responsibility for the abuse and impact – no excuses or justifications	1	2	3
Recognises potential impact of abusive behaviour – can detail likely impact upon others	1	2	3
Shows remorse regarding impact upon others – empathy for other's hurts and losses – faces sense of shame – committed to understand impact of abuse	1	2	3
Shows concern and consideration for abused person – respecting other's feelings and requests – realistic expectations of others	1	2	3
Faces consequences of actions – respects statutory consequences and orders	1	2	3

3. No evidence or allegations of other violence or abusive behaviour	low resp. (some)		high resp. (none)
Towards previous intimate relationships or family members	1	2	3
Towards others in work, social, recreational, driving situations etc. in the past 12 months	1	2	3

4. No evidence or allegations of recent criminal or irresponsible behaviour (past 12 months)	low resp. (some)		high resp. (none)
Criminal offences	1	2	3
Alcohol or drug abuse	1	2	3

5. Responsibility and respect in couple relationships (see Goal Attainment Part B)	low resp.		high resp.
Promotes equal power and status	1	2	3
Promotes shared responsibility	1	2	3
Promotes balance between dependence and independence	1	2	3

6. Responsibility and respect in family relationships (see Goal Attainment Part C)	low resp.		high resp.
Shares responsibility/respectful to children	1	2	3

7. Responsibility and respect in broader social contexts (see Goal Attainment Part D)	low resp.		high resp.
Social network, social skills, work relationships, respectful to women	1	2	3

Responsibility Index A (Current abuse – sections 1 and 2)	
Responsibility Index B (Other irresponsible behaviour sections 3 and 4)	
Responsibility Index C (Respectful behaviour – sections 5, 6 and 7)	

Table 2   Goal attainment assessment protocol

1 Very Low Level	2 Low Level	3 Moderate Level	4 High Level	5 Very High Level

A: Responsibility for Abuse

1. Abusive behaviour ceased

There is no current evidence of physically abusive behaviour (over the past weeks/months) No current evidence or allegations of: – physical assault – threats of physical assault or intimidation – damage to property	1	2	3	4	5
There is no current evidence of emotionally abusive or controlling behaviour (over the past weeks/months) No current evidence or allegations of: – put downs or disrespectful actions – attempts to humiliate or discredit partner – attempts to coerce partner or control partner's thinking or actions – attempts to deprive partner of any rights or entitlements	1	2	3	4	5

2. Effective plans to prevent abusive behaviour

The man has developed and is using effective responsibility plans to prevent the development of patterns of abusive behaviour The man is recognising and stopping the 'build up' of patterns of: – self-righteous, blaming and vengeful thinking – 'power tactics' or controlling behaviours The man is recognising and managing feelings of anger, hurt, threat, etc. without behaving abusively The man does not rely on avoiding conflict The man is facing conflict or 'provocation' in intimate relationships without behaving abusively The man does not rely on his partner to take action to stop or prevent abuse The man is taking this responsibility for himself	1	2	3	4	5

3. Acknowledgement of abusive behaviour

The man has acknowledged the full extent of his abusive behaviour The man has detailed and documented a full account of his physically and emotionally abusive actions The man's account is consistent with the woman's account in that there is no evidence of understatement The man has acknowledged, or is prepared to acknowledge, to the woman and family members the full extent of his abusive behaviour	1	2	3	4	5

4. Acknowledgement of the nature, significance and seriousness of the abusive behaviour

The man regards and labels his actions as 'abusive' with significant harmful effects upon others The man understands and labels his actions as: – unjust – an abuse of power – attempts to exert control over his partner	1	2	3	4	5

The man acknowledges the power differential in his relationship with the woman and recognises the woman's experience of fear and entrapment
The man regards the abuse as serious and leading to trauma and harm to his partner and other family members
The man regards the woman's responses of fear, trauma and anger, etc. as appropriate and justified
The man does not attempt to minimise his abusive actions

The man acknowledges that he has both the obligation and the ability to cease his abusive behaviour

    1   2   3   4   5

The man recognises that he has a problem with abusive and controlling behaviour which is *his* responsibility to address
The man shows a high level of self-motivation to address this problem
The man acknowledges that he is capable of choosing to cease his abusive behaviour and does not subscribe to explanations of losing control or personal limitation
The man's goals and plans for stopping abuse are attainable and realistic. Plans are based on active steps towards responsibility, not on hope or wishful thinking
The man acknowledges the likelihood of further abuse if he fails to address this problem

5. Acknowledgement of culpability

The man acknowledges that he is fully responsible for his abusive actions   1   2   3   4   5
The man acknowledges that he is fully responsible for his abusive actions and:
    – does not blame others, external circumstances or factors outside of his own personal control
    – does not attempt to excuse or justify his actions
The man believes that the woman is blameless for the abusive behaviour and:
    – recognises he has no right to abuse her
    – recognises that it is his and not his partner's responsibility to stop or prevent abuse
The man acknowledges his actions have led to the distress and trauma which the woman and other family members have experienced

6. Recognising the impact of abuse

The man understands the potential impact of his abuse upon the woman and family members   1   2   3   4   5
The man is committed to try to understand fully the potential impact of his actions upon the woman and other family members by:
    – trying to 'put himself in the woman's shoes' and to imagine the impact of his actions
    – trying to understand his children's experience of his violence and abusive behaviour
    – actively seeking and researching information on the impact and effects of abuse
    – demonstrating a desire and openness to listen to, understand and accept the woman's account of her experience
The man feels remorse based on an understanding of losses and hurts he has caused to others, not just the losses and hurts he has experienced himself and:
    – is facing the discomfort of his shame in trying to understand the impact of his actions
The man demonstrates understanding and compassion for the woman's and children's experience
    – has detailed and documented a realistic account of what he imagines he has put the woman and children through and their experiences of the abuse
    – has detailed and documented a realistic account of any difficulties that the woman and family members may experience as a consequence of his abuse
The man demonstrates an understanding of the woman's and children's likely feelings and reactions, such as:

• fear	• betrayal	• outrage
• intimidation	• loss of trust	• hurt
• humiliation	• respect	

The man demonstrates an awareness and understanding of the difficulties that the woman is likely to experience with him, such as:

- feeling unsafe
- feeling mistrust
- feeling betrayed
- feeling intimidated
- being unable to forgive and forget
- feeling disrespect
- feeling outraged

The man demonstrates an understanding of the children's experiences (age appropriate)

The man is prepared to make a meaningful statement of realisation and responsibility to the woman and family members which is:

- based on his understanding and realisation about the likely impact of his abuse
- upon the woman and the other family members

The man has realistic expectations of the woman and:

- respects her feelings and regards them as legitimate
- does not expect respect or trust which is unearned
- understands that he may have permanently lost her trust and respect
- does not expect her to forgive and forget
- does not prematurely expect to resume an intimate relationship with her
- does not prematurely expect family reunion
- is prepared to respect her pace in any contact or reconciliation
- respects the woman's needs and requests for personal space, separateness and privacy.

7. Demonstration of responsibility and respect

The man actively demonstrates responsibility for his abusive behaviour	1	2	3	4	5

Separateness
The man understands and respects the woman's requests and needs for privacy and separateness and:

- supports and respects restraint orders and other statutory orders
- supports and cooperates with agreements and requests for separateness by the woman
- respects woman's privacy and personal space
- has ceased all unwanted pursuit of the woman
- understands the need to initiate separateness to establish safety
- demonstrates responsibility
- demonstrates self-reliance
- does not use contact with the children to pursue or harass the woman

Responsibility plan
The man has detailed and documented an active behaviour plan to demonstrate responsibility and respect to the woman and other family members
The man has made clear and unequivocal statements to the woman and all family members, if desired by them:

- that he is fully responsible for the abuse
- about his realisations of the impact of the abuse

The man corrects others who attempt to excuse him from responsibility or attributes responsibility to the woman, other people or external events
The man actively respects the woman's rights and entitlements and:

- is not intrusive or controlling
- respects the woman's entitlement to her own feelings, ideas and actions and privacy

The man pursues contact and family reunion, if appropriate, at a pace that is sensitive to the woman's and family member's experience of the abuse and their wishes and needs

Woman's experience
The woman and family members feel that the man has a good understanding of the impact of the abuse
The woman and family members feel that the man is interested to hear and understand their experience of the impact of his abuse

8. Facing the consequences of actions

The man is prepared to face appropriate consequences for any disrespectful or abusive behaviour	1	2	3	4	5

The man has demonstrated preparedness to face statutory consequences for abusive actions

The man takes responsible action following any instance of disrespectful or controlling behaviour whereby he:
  – acknowledges the behaviour
  – establishes separateness if this is respectful of the woman's requests
  – notifies worker of incidents

The man takes responsible action following any re-occurrence of abusive behaviour, such as:
  – notifies worker
  – supports notification to police
  – supports and respects restraint orders
  – being prepared to face justice consequences

B. Responsibility and Respect in Couple Relationships

Balance of power and status **The man is actively contributing to developing a relationship characterised by equal power and status.**	1	2	3	4	5

The man is respecting the woman's right to have and to express her own views and feelings

The man is respecting the woman's independence and right to self-determination

The man is respecting the woman's privacy and personal space

The man is listening to and respecting the woman's ideas and points of view

The man and the woman are sharing decision-making regarding the relationship

The woman feels respected, listened to and understood by the man

The woman feels safe to express her views and feelings with the man

The woman feels that the man respects her independence and right to self-determination

The woman feels that the man is interested in her ideas and feelings

Balance of responsibility **The man is actively contributing to developing a relationship characterised by sharing responsibilities for couple and family relationships**	1	2	3	4	5

The man initiates and participates in joint activities which promote a sense of togetherness and belonging

The man shares appropriate initiatives in facing, addressing and discussing relationship pressures, problems and areas of conflict

The man initiates and participates in discussion with the woman regarding future plans, projects and priorities for the relationship and family

The man confides in and discusses personal concerns with the woman

The man remembers family events and puts a value on his role in sharing responsibilities in the marriage. He does not rely on the woman to face his responsibilities for him

The man demonstrates considerate, nurturing and caring behaviour with the woman

The man demonstrates assertive skills with the woman, and stands up for what he believes, in ways which are respectful to the woman

Balance of dependence and independence **The man is actively contributing to developing a couple relationship characterised by a balance between dependence and independence**	1	2	3	4	5

The man's lifestyle is characterised by a balance between activities which reflect togetherness and activities which reflect separateness

The man respects and supports the woman's right to a lifestyle which is characterised by a balance between activities which promote togetherness and activities which promote separateness

The man has developed a social network outside the family and does not expect all social needs to be met within the family
The man respects and supports the woman's right to an external social network

C: Responsibility and Respect in Family Relationships

The man is actively contributing to developing responsible and respectful family relationships by facing and handling family responsibilities	1	2	3	4	5

Partnership
The man recognises shared responsibility with the woman to provide appropriate care and support for the children
The man negotiates an active role in sharing in parental responsibilities with the woman and:
  – organises and participates in family activities
  – puts a value on and remembers family events
  – shares parenting responsibilities
  – spends time with, listens to, helps and supports children
The man negotiates respectfully with the woman for mutually acceptable family and parenting goals, methods of discipline, etc.

Supports children
The man is caring, understanding, considerate, affirming and supportive with the children
The man understands and respects the children's feelings and needs
The children experience the man as supportive, understanding and respectful
The children find the man approachable when they need help or have difficulties

Realistic expectations and discipline
The man has realistic expectations regarding each of the children's behaviour appropriate to age and development
The man disciplines the children in respectful and appropriate ways
The man demonstrates an appropriate balance of affirming and supportive behaviour and disciplinary and corrective behaviour with the children

Boundaries
The man acknowledges and respects appropriate parent-child boundaries and:
  – respects their rights, privacy and personal space
  – does not expect children to face age-inappropriate responsibilities
The man does not engage in inappropriate alliances, exclusions, favouritism, taking of sides or taking advantage of other family members

Sets example of responsibility
The man encourages respectful and responsible behaviour and respectfully corrects children's exploitative or abusive behaviour
The man models behaviour with the woman which is respectful, caring, considerate, supportive and characterised by equity, fairness and shared responsibility

D: Responsibility and Respect in Broader Social Contexts

The man is actively developing respectful and responsible relationships outside of the family context	1	2	3	4	5

Social network
The man has developed a social network outside the family
The man is competent and confident in initiating and maintaining relationships

Social skills
The man is respectfully assertive with others
The man trusts and confides in others
The man faces and handles conflict and criticism in respectful and responsible ways

The man shows concern, consideration and understanding of others' feelings
The man is flexible and tolerant of different opinions and ideas of others

Work relationships
The man relates to others respectfully in his work environment
    – handles conflict and pressure respectfully
    – workmates find him approachable
    – appropriate social skills

Respectful to women
The man is respectful and considerate to women

Table 3A   Abusive behaviour inventory – man's form

Here is a list of behaviours that many women report have been used by their partners or former partners. We would like you to estimate how often these behaviours occurred during the **six months** prior to your beginning this programme. Your answers are strictly confidential.

Circle a number on each of the items listed below to show your closest estimate of how often it happened in your relationship with your partner or former partner during the **six months** before you started the programme.

1 = Never   2 = Rarely   3 = Occasionally   4 = Frequently   5 = Very frequently

1. Called her names and/or criticised her	1	2	3	4	5
2. Tried to keep her from doing something she wanted to do, such as going out with friends or going to meetings	1	2	3	4	5
3. Gave her angry stares or looks	1	2	3	4	5
4. Prevented her from having money for her own use	1	2	3	4	5
5. Ended a discussion with her and made the decision yourself	1	2	3	4	5
6. Threatened to hit or throw something at her	1	2	3	4	5
7. Pushed, grabbed or shoved her	1	2	3	4	5
8. Put down her family and friends	1	2	3	4	5
9. Accused her of paying too much attention to someone or something else	1	2	3	4	5
10. Put her on an allowance	1	2	3	4	5
11. Used the children to threaten her, such as told her that she would lose custody or said you would leave town with the children	1	2	3	4	5
12. Became very upset with her because dinner, housework, or laundry was not ready when you wanted it done or done the way you thought it should be	1	2	3	4	5
13. Said things to scare her, such as told her something 'bad' would happen or you threatened to commit suicide	1	2	3	4	5
14. Slapped, hit or punched her	1	2	3	4	5
15. Made her do something humiliating or degrading, as in making her beg for forgiveness or having to ask your permission to use the car or do something	1	2	3	4	5
16. Checked up on her, when you listened to her phone calls, checked the mileage on her car, or called her repeatedly at work	1	2	3	4	5
17. Drove recklessly when she was in the car	1	2	3	4	5
18. Pressured her to have sex in a way that she didn't like or want	1	2	3	4	5
19. Refused to do housework or childcare	1	2	3	4	5
20. Threatened her with a knife, gun, or other weapon	1	2	3	4	5
21. Spanked her	1	2	3	4	5
22. Told her that she was a bad parent	1	2	3	4	5
23. Stopped her or tried to stop her from going to work or school	1	2	3	4	5
24. Threw, hit, kicked, or smashed something	1	2	3	4	5
25. Kicked her	1	2	3	4	5
26. Physically forced her to have sex	1	2	3	4	5
27. Threw her around	1	2	3	4	5
28. Physically attacked the sexual parts of her body	1	2	3	4	5
29. Choked or strangled her	1	2	3	4	5
30. Used a knife, gun, or other weapon against her	1	2	3	4	5

Table 3B   Abusive behaviour inventory – partner form

Here is a list of behaviours that many women report have been used by their partners or former partners. We would like you to estimate how often these behaviours occurred during the **six months** prior to your beginning this programme. Your answers are strictly confidential.

Circle a number from each of the items listed below to show your closest estimate of how often it happened in your relationship with your partner or former partner during the **six months** before you started the programme.

1.	Called you names and/or criticised you	1	2	3	4	5
2.	Tried to keep you from doing something you wanted to do, such as going out with friends or going to meetings	1	2	3	4	5
3.	Gave you angry stares or looks	1	2	3	4	5
4.	Prevented you from having money for your own use	1	2	3	4	5
5.	Ended a discussion with you and made the decision himself	1	2	3	4	5
6.	Threatened to hit or throw something at you	1	2	3	4	5
7.	Pushed, grabbed or shoved you	1	2	3	4	5
8.	Put down your family and friends	1	2	3	4	5
9.	Accused you of paying too much attention to someone or something else	1	2	3	4	5
10.	Put you on an allowance	1	2	3	4	5
11.	Used the children to threaten you, such as told you that you would lose custody or said he would leave town with the children	1	2	3	4	5
12.	Became very upset with you because dinner, housework, or laundry was not ready when he wanted it done or done the way he thought it should be	1	2	3	4	5
13.	Said things to scare you, such as told you something 'bad' would happen, or threatened to commit suicide	1	2	3	4	5
14.	Slapped, hit or punched you	1	2	3	4	5
15.	Made you do something humiliating or degrading, as in making you beg for forgiveness or having to ask his permission to use the car or do something	1	2	3	4	5
16.	Checked up on you, when he listened to your phone calls, checked the mileage on your car or called you repeatedly at work	1	2	3	4	5
17.	Drove recklessly when you were in the car	1	2	3	4	5
18.	Pressured you to have sex in a way that you didn't like or want	1	2	3	4	5
19.	Refused to do housework or childcare	1	2	3	4	5
20.	Threatened you with a knife, gun, or other weapon	1	2	3	4	5
21.	Spanked you	1	2	3	4	5
22.	Told you that you were a bad parent	1	2	3	4	5
23.	Stopped you or tried to stop you from going to work or school	1	2	3	4	5
24.	Threw, hit, kicked, or smashed something	1	2	3	4	5
25.	Kicked you	1	2	3	4	5
26.	Physically forced you to have sex	1	2	3	4	5
27.	Threw you around	1	2	3	4	5
28.	Physically attacked the sexual parts of your body	1	2	3	4	5
29.	Choked or strangled you	1	2	3	4	5
30.	Used a knife, gun, or other weapon against you	1	2	3	4	5

Table 3C   Abusive behaviour inventory – scoring directions

To determine a physical abuse score, total up the ratings for each physical abuse subscale item and divide by 10. This yields a physical abuse score that reflects an average frequency from one (for no physical abuse) to five (for very frequent physical abuse).

Physical abuse subscale items

7, 14, 18, 21, 25, 26, 27, 28, 29, 30

To determine psychological abuse score, total up the ratings for each psychological abuse subscale item and divide by 20. This yields a psychological abuse score that reflects an average frequency from one (for no psychological abuse) to five (for very frequent psychological abuse).

Psychological abuse subscale items

1, 2, 3, 4, 5, 6, 8, 9, 10, 11, 12, 13, 15, 16, 17, 19, 20, 22, 23, 24

References

Anderson, G., Colley, D., Hall, R. and Jenkins, A. (1997) *Competency Standards for Intervention Workers: Working with men Who Perpetrate Domestic Abuse and Violence.* Adelaide: Office For Families and Children.

Arendt, H. (1978) *The Jew as Pariah – Jewish Identity and Politics in the Modern Age.* New York: Grove Press.

Bograd, M. and Mederos, F. (1999) Battering and Couples Therapy: Universal Screening and Selection of Treatment Modality. *Journal of Marital and Family therapy*, 25: 3, 291–312.

Bograd, M. (1984) Family Systems Approaches tTo Wife Battering: A Feminist Critique. *American Journal of Orthopsychiatry*, 54, 558–68.

Braithwaite, J. (1989) *Crime, Shame and Reintegration.* Cambridge: Cambridge University Press.

Braithwaite, J. (2002) *Restorative Justice and Responsive Regulation.* NY: Oxford University Press.

Buchanan, I. (2000) *Deleuzism: A Metacommentary.* Edinburgh: Edinburgh University Press.

Campbell, B. (1993) *Goliath.* London: Methuen.

Chomsky, N. (2002) *Understanding Power.* Carlton North: Scribe.

Colebrook, C. (2002) *Understanding Deleuze.* Crows Nest, NSW: Allen and Unwin.

Colebrook, C. (2002) *Gilles Deleuze.* London: Routledge.

Colebrook, C. (2006) *Deleuze: A Guide for the Perplexed.* London: Continuum.

Conley, V. (2005) In Parr. A. (Ed.) *The Deleuze Dictionary.* Edinburgh: Edinburgh University Press.

Connell, R.W. (1995) *Masculinities.* St. Leonards: Allen and Unwin.

Connell, R.W. (2000) *The Men and The Boys.* St. Leonards: Allen and Unwin.

Conroy, M.A. and Murrie, D.C. (2007) *Forensic Assessment of Violence and Risk.* New Jersey: Wiley.

Daly, K. and Curtis-Fawley, S. (2005) Gendered Violence and Restorative Justice: The Views of Victim Advocates. *Violence Against Women*, 11: 5, 603–38.

Daly, K. (2003) Mind The Gap: Restorative Justice in Theory and Practice. In Von Hirsch et al. (Eds.) *Restorative Justice and Criminal Justice: Competing or Reconcilable Paradigms?* Oxford: Hart.

Daly, K. (2006) Restorative Justice and Sexual Assault: An Archival Study of Court and Conference Cases. *British Journal of Criminology*, 46: 2, 334–56.

Deleuze, G. and Guattari, F. (1983) *Anti-Oedipus: Capitalism and Schizophrenia.* vol.1, trans. Hurley, R., Seem, M. and Lane, H., Minneapolis: University of Minnesota Press.

Deleuze, G. and Guattari, F. (1987) *A Thousand Plateaus: Capitalism and Schizophrenia.* trans. Massumi, B., Minneapolis: University of Minnesota Press.

Deleuze, G. (1981) *Nietsche and Philosophy.* New York: Columbia University Press.

Deleuze, G. (1997) He Stuttered. In *Essays Critical and Clinical*, trans. Smith, D.W. and Greco, M.A. Minneapolis: University of Minnesota Press.

Derrida, J. (1992) Force of Law: The Mystical Foundation of Authority. In Cornell, D., Rosenfeld, M. and Carlson, D.G. (Eds.) *Deconstruction and The Possibility of Justice.* NY: Routledge.

Derrida, J. (1994) *Spectres of Marx.* NY: Routledge.

Derrida, J. and Dufourmantelle, A. (2000) *Of Hospitality.* Stanford: Stanford University Press.

Derrida, J. (2001) *On Cosmopolitanism and Forgiveness.* London: Routledge.

Diprose, R. (2002) *Corporeal Generosity.* NY: State University of New York Press.

Due, R. (2007) *Deleuze.* Cambridge: Polity Press.

Edley, N. and Wetherell, M. (1995) Jockeying for Position: The Construction of Masculine Identities. *Discourse and Society*, 8: 2.

Edley, N. and Wetherell, M. (1997) *Men In Perspective – Practice, Power and Identity.* NY: Prentice Hall.

Edwards, T. (2006) *Cultures of Masculinity.* NY: Routledge.

Epston, D. (1993) Internalised Other Questioning with Couples: The New Zealand Version. In Gilligan, S.G. and Price, R. (Eds.) *Therapeutic Conversations.* NY: Norton.

Fossum, M.A. and Mason, M.J. (1986) *Facing Shame: Families In Recovery.* NY: Norton.

Foucault, M. (1971) *The Order of Things.* NY: Pantheon.

Foucault, M. (1972) *The Archeology of Knowledge.* trans. Sheridan Smith, A.M. NY: Pantheon.

Freedman, J. and Coombs,G. (2004) *Relational Identity and Narrative Work with Couples.* Workshop presented at Therapeutic Conversations Conference, Toronto.

Gaita, R. (1991) *Good and Evil.* London: Routledge.

Gaita, R. (2004) Breach of Trust: Truth, Morality and Politics. *Quarterly Essay*, 16.

Gilligan, J. (2000) *Violence: Reflections on our Deadliest Epidemic.* London: Jessica Kingsley.

Goldner, V. (1992) Making Room for Both/And. *Family Therapy Networker*, 16, 54–62.

Goldner, V. (1998) The Treatment of Violence and Victimisation in Intimate Relationships. *Family Process*, 37: 3, 263–86.

Goldner, V. (1999) Morality and Multiplicity: Perspectives on the Treatment of Violence in Intimate Life. *Journal of Marital and Family Therapy*, 25: 3, 325–36.

Gondolf, E. (2001) *Batterer Intervention Systems: Issues, Outcomes and Recommendations.* Thousand Oaks: Sage Publications.

Hall, R. (1994) Partnership Accountability. In McLean, C., Carey, M. and White, C. (Eds) *Mens Ways of Being.* Boulder, CO: Westview Press.

Hansen, M. (1993) Feminism and Family Therapy: A Review of Feminist Critiques of Approaches to Family Violence. In Hansen, M. and Harway, M. *Battering and Family Therapy: A Feminist Perspective.* Newbury Park: Sage.

Hardt, M. and Negri, A. (2004) *Multitude: War and Democracy in the Age of Empire.* NY: Penguin.

Hooks, B. (2004) *We Real Cool: Black Men and Masculinity.* NY: Routledge.

Irigaray, L. (2002) *The Way of Love.* London: Continuum.

Jenkins, A. (1990) *Invitations to Responsibility: The Therapeutic Engagement of Men who are Violent and Abusive.* Adelaide: Dulwich.

Jenkins, A. (1991) Intervention with Violence and Abuse in Families: The Inadvertent Perpetuation of Irresponsible Behaviour. *ANZ Journal of Family Therapy*, 12: 4, 186–95.

Jenkins, A. (1994) Power and Politics in Practice. *Dulwich Centre Newsletter*, 1: 1119.

Jenkins, A. (1996) Moving Towards Respect: A Quest for Balance. In McLean, C. et al. (Eds.) *Men's Ways of Being: New Directions in Theory and Practice.* Colorado: Westview Press.

Jenkins, A. (1999) Invitations to Responsibility: Engaging Adolescents and Young Men who have Sexually Abused. In Marshall, W. (Ed.) *Sourcebook of Treatment Programs for Sexual Offenders.* NY: Plenum.

Jenkins, A. (2005) Making it Fair: Respectful and Just Intervention with Disadvantaged Young People who have Abused. In Calder, M.C. (Ed.) *Children and Young People Who Sexually Abuse: New Theory, Research and Practice Developments.* Lyme Regis: Russell House Publishing.

Jenkins, A. (2005) Knocking on Shame's Door: Facing Shame Without Shaming Disadvantaged Young People Who Have Abused. In Calder, M.C. (Ed.) *Children and Young People Who Sexually Abuse; New Theory, Research and Practice Developments.* Lyme Regis: Russell House Publishing.

Jenkins, A. (2006) Shame, Realisation and Restitution: The Ethics of Restorative Practice. *ANZ Journal of Family Therapy*, 27: 3, 153–62.

Jenkins, A. (2006a) The Politics of Intervention: Fairness and Ethics. In Longo, R.E. and Prescott, D.S. (Eds.) *Current Perspectives: Working with Sexually Aggressive Youth and Youth with Sexual Behaviour Problems.* Holyoke: NEARI Press.

Jenkins, A. (2006b) Discovering Integrity: Working With Shame Without Shaming Young People Who Have Abused. In Longo, R.E. and Prescott, D.S. (Eds.) *Current Perspectives: Working with Sexually Aggressive Youth and Youth with Sexual Behaviour Problems.* Holyoke: NEARI Press.

Jenkins, A. (2007) Becoming Respectful: Approaches to Relationship Counselling in Situations of Domestic Violence and Abuse. In Shaw, E. and Crawley, J. *Couple Therapy in Australia: Issues Emerging From Practice.* Kew: PsychOz Publications.

Jenkins, A., Hall, R. and Joy, M. (2002) Forgiveness in Child Sexual Abuse: A Matrix of Meanings. *International Journal of Narrative Therapy and Community Work*, 1: 35–51.

Jory, B. and Anderson, D. (1999) Intimate Justice: Fostering Mutuality, Reciprocity and Accommodation in Therapy for Psychological Abuse. *Journal of Marital and Family Therapy*, 23: 3, 349–64.

Jory, B. and Anderson, D. (2000) Intimate Justice: Healing the Anguish of Abuse and Embracing the Anguish of Accountability. *Journal of Marital and Family Therapy*, 26: 3, 329–40.

Jory, B., Anderson, D. and Greer, C. (1997) Intimate Justice: Confronting Issues of Accountability, Respect and Freedom in Treatment for Abuse and Violence. *Journal of Marital and Family Therapy*, 23: 4, 399–419.

Larner, G. (1999) Derrida and The Deconstruction of Power as Context and Topic in Therapy. In Parker, I. (Ed.) *Deconstructing Psychotherapy*. London: Sage.

Lear, E. (1912) *The Complete Nonsense Book*. NY: Dodd, Mead and Co.

Marks, J. (2005) Ethics. In Parr. A. (Ed.) *The Deleuze Dictionary*. Edinburgh: Edinburgh University Press.

May, T. (2005) *Gilles Deleuze: An Introduction*. Cambridge: Cambridge University Press.

McMaster, K. and Bakker, L. (2006) *Will They do it Again: Assessing and Managing Risk*. Lyttleton: Hall McMaster.

Messerschmidt, J.W. (1993) *Masculinities and Crime: Critique and Reconceptualisation of Theory*. Maryland: Rowman and Littlefield.

Morton, T. (1997) *Altered Mates: The Man Question*. St. Leonards: Allen and Unwin.

Murdoch, I. (1970) *The Sovereignty of Good*. London: Routledge.

Nietzsche, F. (1967). *The Will to Power*. Trans. Kaufman, W. and Hollingdale, R. NY: Random House.

Nietzsche, F. (1990) *Beyond Good and Evil*. London: Penguin.

Nyland, D. and Corsiglia, V. (with commentary by Jenkins, A.) (1998) In Hoyt, M. (Ed.) *The Handbook of Constructive Therapies*. San Francisco: Jossey-Bass.

Pence, E. and Paymar, M. (1993) *Education Groups for Men who Batter: The Duluth Model*. NY: Springer.

Protevi, J. (2003) Love. In Patton, P. and Protevi, J. (Eds.) *Between Deleuze and Derrida*. London: Continuum.

Ransom, J. S. (1997) *Foucault's Discipline*. Durham: Duke University Press.

Reynolds, J. and Roffe, J. (2004) *Understanding Derrida*. London: Continuum.

Roughan, P. and Jenkins, A. (1990) A Systems-Developmental Approach to Counselling Couples with Sexual Problems, Part I. *ANZ Journal of Family Therapy*, 11: 3, 193–201.

Schneider, C. D. (1992) *Shame, Exposure and Privacy*. NY: Norton.

Shepard, M.F. and Campbell, J.A. (1992) The Abusive Behaviour Inventory. *Journal of Interpersonal Violence*, 7: 3.

Singer, P. (1993) *Practical Ethics*. Cambridge: Cambridge University Press.

Smith, D.W. (1997) Introduction: A Life of Pure Immanence. In Deleuze, G. *Essays Critical and Clinical*. Minneapolis: University of Minnesota Press.

Smith, D.W. (2003) Deleuze and Derrida, Immanence and Transcendence: Two Directions in Recent French Thought. In Patton, P. and Protevi, J. (Eds.) *Between Deleuze and Derrida*. London: Continuum.

Tamasese, K. and Waldegrave, C. (1993) Cultural and Gender Accountability in the 'Just Therapy' Approach. *Journal of Feminist Family Therapy*, 5: 2, 29–45.

Wexler, P. (1992) *Becoming Somebody: Toward a Social Psychology of School*. Bristol: Falmer Press.

White, M. (2008) *Maps of Narrative Practice*. NY: Norton.

Zizek, S. (2008) *Violence*. London: Profile Books.

Children and young people who sexually abuse

New theory, research and practice developments

Edited by Martin C. Calder

Includes:

Making it Fair, Respectful and Just: Interventions With Young People Who Have Abused

By Alan Jenkins

'This book is well written and a good buy for anyone who might be working with children or young people who sexually offend.

Discusses ways to engage with such young people, using fairness in interactions whilst still encouraging them to take responsibility for their actions . . .'

Seen & Heard

ISBN 978-1-903855-50-8

Substance misuse and child care

How to understand, assist and intervene when drugs affect parenting

Edited by Fiona Harbin and Michael Murphy

'Topical, informative and thought-provoking.'

The Drug & Alcohol Professional

'Much information is given in a clear, straightforward manner.'

Community Care

ISBN 978-1-898924-48-7

Children living with domestic violence

Towards a framework for assessment and intervention

By Martin C. Calder

'Useful for clinical practitioners, social workers and other professionals.'

Child Abuse Review

'Busy practitioners will welcome the practical assessment checklist and bullet point practice guidance.'

Community Care

'A mass of research findings along with indicators of domestic violence, a screening assessment and principles and engagement issues for working separately with perpetrators, mothers and children. There are questions and indicators for establishing the level of risk or lethality, differential approaches for dealing with contact disputes that do or do not involve allegations of abuse, plus a schedule for ongoing work with the child or young person and methods for assessing the process of change.'

Young People Now

ISBN 978-1-903855-45-4

Parents' anger management

The PAMP programme

By Gerry Heery

Acknowledging that almost all parents have at least some difficulties with anger, PAMP is suitable for social work, counselling, mental health, justice and community work.

It provides guidance on:

- conducting sessions;
- the values and knowledge base;
- the support, quality assurance, monitoring and evaluation;

that are essential to PAMP's positive, ethical and effective use.

Eight two-hour sessions, deliverable individually or in groups, help parents:

- Think about why they are doing the programme and their motivation to change.
- Assess their own anger; how it relates to their thinking, emotions and actions; what they need to do to manage it.
- Reflect on their thinking, beliefs and mindset.
- Manage their emotional lives.
- Look at how mismanaged parental anger and parenting styles impact on children and their development; and how children learn to manage their own anger.
- Reflect on links between gender and anger; and the impact of past traumatic experiences.
- Learn safer ways of handling conflict, and gain confidence in their management of conflict and provocation.
- Sustain their learning and plan future progress.

ISBN 978-1-905541-04-1

Empathy for the devil

How to help people overcome drugs and alcohol problems

By Phil Harris

For counselors and therapists, substance misuse teams, police officers, probation officers, prison officers, housing workers, social workers, youth workers, teachers.

'Discusses the complexity of drug and alcohol problems with more references to cultural and social aspects than previous work that I have read in this area . . . The focus is explicitly and empathically on helping clients to establish and achieve their own goals to overcome their addiction . . . Harris does not treat people as living in a vacuum, But as living within and being part of an extremely influential cultural context. I particularly enjoyed Harris's astute reflections upon the therapeutic relationship, something not always talked about, and found the chapter on solution-focused therapy so inspiring that I wanted to rush out and try it . . . I thoroughly enjoyed this book, it is a great read.'

The Psychologist

Includes case studies, exercises and tools.

'Book of the month . . . his bibliography makes for extensive further reading.'

Drugscope Members Briefing

ISBN 978-1-903855-54-6

The carrot or the stick?

Towards effective practice with involuntary clients in safeguarding children work

Edited by Martin C. Calder

In child protection, family support, domestic violence, youth justice . . . many practitioners and managers struggle to engage clients who resist involvement with services that are needed or offered, often with wearying and dispiriting effect on everyone.

For work with children and young people, men and women, fathers and mothers in all relevant circumstances.

'The carefully selected chapters in this book offer systematic and evidence-based approaches.'

ChildRIGHT

They are 'no-nonsense' approaches that will fit with practice wisdom and practice realities of work. They address:

- Making and maintaining working relationships with clients.
- Concepts of consent and coercion.
- Frameworks for understanding and working with motivation, resistance and change.
- Links with risk assessment, including risks to staff.
- Innovative ways of enhancing their clients' motivation and helping them to change.
- Helping anyone in training to enter the workplace with a sense that they can succeed.
- Rekindling confidence and enthusiasm amongst more experienced staff.

ISBN 978-1-905541-22-5

Contemporary risk assessment in safeguarding children

Edited by Martin C. Calder

For anyone involved in the protection and safeguarding of children and young people, at any level, risk and risk assessment are key concerns and preoccupations. This book's varied and illuminating perspectives help refine the exercise of professional judgement in estimating and managing uncertainties prospectively, rather than being judged retrospectively.

'The authors call for an evidence-based, comprehensive and equitable approach to risk assessment and teach the reader to produce risk management strategies where levels of intrusion are commensurate with levels of risk.'

ChildRIGHT

'Provides a lot of information . . . the topics are well presented and can be read in chapters or as a whole . . . a useful training resource . . . I found myself reading parts of the book and stopping to reflect on how it related to my own practice and the systems in which I work . . . I've already used some of the material in day-to-day practice.'

Rostrum

'An absorbing and exciting read . . . A broad perspective of thinking about risk and the challenge of interpreting information gathered from and about children's lives . . . a good reference guide . . . extremely useful.'

Children & Young People Now

'Gems that will be a real boon to practice . . . tablets of wisdom set as a feast before you.'

PSW

ISBN 978-1-905541-20-1

Sexual abuse assessments

Using and developing frameworks for practice

Edited by Martin C. Calder

This significant new book addresses the contemporary challenges of practice by building on and replacing Calder's *Complete Guide to Sexual Abuse Assessments* (RHP 2000) which was hailed as:

'A onestop guide to risk assessment . . . comprehensive and well-informed.'
Community Care

'. . . will be plundered for ideas by practitioners and trainers alike.'
Clinical Child Psychology & Psychiatry

With all the original material fully reworked and expanded, this new book updates assessment frameworks, incorporating latest research and practice wisdom and adds several new frameworks, including those concerning rape, learning disability, the internet.

Offering help undertaking or commissioning the most appropriate assessments, supporting reflective practice, and for anyone involved in child protection, safeguarding children or community safety, this essential guide is for practitioners, trainers and managers who want to keep up, but are starved of the time and resources needed to read everything. Providing carefully selected and critical access to what is known, distilled in ways that are readily useful, it will also inform the work of academics, students and researchers.

CONTENTS:
Introduction. Victims of child sexual abuse: frameworks for understanding impact. Assessing children and young people's sexual behaviour in a changing social context. Assessing children with sexual behaviour problems. SHARP practice. The core assessment of young females who sexually abuse. The assessment of young people with learning disabilities who sexually harm others. Core assessment of adult male offenders. Assessment of women who sexually abuse children. Core assessment of adult sex offenders with a learning disability. Assessment of internet sexual abuse. Rape assessment. Mothers of sexually abused children. Body safety skills. Contact considerations where sexual abuse and domestic violence feature: adopting an evidence-based approach. Safe care.

ISBN 978-1-905541-28-7